ADVENTURES
IN BIRDING

ADVENTURES
IN BIRDING

Confessions of a Lister

JEAN PIATT

 Alfred A. Knopf · New York · 1973

THIS IS A BORZOI BOOK

PUBLISHED BY ALFRED A. KNOPF, INC.

———————————

Library of Congress Cataloging in Publication Data

Piatt, Jean.   Adventures in birding.

1. Bird watching—North America. I. Title.
QL677.5.P48   1973   598.2′073′097   72–11048
ISBN 0–394–48442–8

Manufactured in the United States of America
First Edition

———————————

Grateful acknowledgment is made for permission to reprint the following:

"A New North American Bird Record" by G. Stuart Keith, from
Audubon, the magazine of the National Audubon Society, Vol. 63, No. 5, 1961.
Copyright © 1961 by National Audubon Society.

"Message from the President" by G. Stuart Keith, from *Birding*,
Vol. 2, No. 2, 1970.

Excerpt from *Principles of Systematic Zoology* by Ernst Mayer.
Copyright © 1969 by McGraw-Hill, Inc. Used with permission
of McGraw-Hill Book Company.

Excerpt from *A Guide to Bird Finding East of the Mississippi*
by Olin S. Pettingill, Jr. Used by permission of Oxford University Press.

In memoriam:

RAPHUS CUCULLATUS 1681

PINGUINUS IMPENNIS 1844
CAMPTORHYNCHUS LABRADORIUM 1878
ECTOPISTES MIGRATORIUS 1914
CONUROPSIS CAROLINENSIS 1914

HOMO SAPIENS ????

Sons of the city! ye whom crowds and noise
Bereave of peace and Nature's rural joys,
And ye who love through woods and wilds to range,
Who see new charms in each successive change;
Come roam with me Columbia's forests through,
Where scenes sublime shall meet your wandering view:

—ALEXANDER WILSON
from *The Foresters*

Contents

Proepilogue

Cold Bay was certainly living up to its name. Not only was it cold and windy on this ninth day of August 1967, but out here on the western end of the Alaska peninsula there was a steady, intermittent, subdued, torrential drizzle. At least that was how it was variously described by the members of our party. Marybelle and I had joined the Crowder Nature Tour on its pioneer trip through Alaska. Our earnest but futile efforts to arrange our own itinerary through the Big Land had convinced us that joining a tour was the only practical way to do the "Outposts" of Alaska for the first time. In 1970 we did go it alone, but more of that much later. Needless to say, birds were our prime objective on the trip, as they had been on other peregrinations through North America. It was not just birds at this point, though, but *the* bird. We were en route to the Pribilof Islands for our six hundredth North American bird! If only the weather would behave!

I quit the stuffy little waiting room for the nth time to see how the refueling of the plane was progressing and to scan the sullen sky for anything that might possibly be a Gyrfalcon. This, the largest of the falcons and the Royal Bird of the kings of yore, is reported occasionally from the Alaska peninsula, although the Seward peninsula and other more inland areas of Alaska probably offer more suitable habitat for this species. At any rate, Pete Isleib of Cordova had told us to watch for Gyrfalcons at Cold Bay. Because of the rain, binoculars were almost useless, but it would have made little difference what the weather was because nary a speck in the sky did I see. Ravens were plentiful, however, and perhaps they were more in keeping with the spirit of the day and place. The fuel truck had by this time pulled into a nearby shed so I returned indoors sans Gyr-falcon but with distinctly damp raiment. The pilot was no longer swilling coffee and this was a good augury for our immi-nent departure. We trooped out to the waiting plane and were soon airborne on the final leg of our journey across the Bering Sea to St. Paul Island, the only one of the Pribilofs with an airstrip. It would have been difficult to say if more gasoline than coffee had come aboard at Cold Bay, but this was hardly a profitable speculation one way or the other.

The heavy overcast prevented us from seeing the ocean once we were up a few hundred feet, so I spent the time checking over our Alaska bird list. Besides, as far as I have ever been able to make out, oceans from planes are traditionally said to "crawl" and nothing more. Actually, in my own limited experience of seeing oceans from planes, they have never crawled. Just exactly what it is they do, I have never quite been able to determine. It is just barely possible that they may "gyre and gimble in the wabe." The more I think of it the more firmly I am convinced that this is the correct view. The little girl sitting across the aisle from me was a startling replica of Tenniel's Alice and I should very much have liked to ask her opinion on the matter. The forbidding mien of her mother, though, effectively squelched this quixotic impulse. Nevertheless, I feel quite certain that oceans, as seen from ten thousand feet, can only be described in Jabberwockyesque. This being the case, they could not possibly be said to crawl. And now perhaps we had better get back through the Looking Glass before something really serious happens and examine that bird list. Oceanography has always affected me queerly.

On the previous day between Anchorage and Palmer we had seen our 595th and 596th North American bird, respectively—Harlan's Hawk. This bird, alas, will probably be relegated to subspecific limbo once the sixth edition of the American Ornithologists' Union Check-list is finished. I shall dwell on the "lumpers" and "splitters," the bane of every loyal bird lister, in another part of this book but, for the present, hiss the "lumpers" and applaud the "splitters" as all good listers do. Marybelle's count was the lower by one because a bad chest cold, rain, and a sizable hill had all conspired to deny her the Wheatear at McKinley National Park. If at St. Paul Marybelle could see five new species, in the argot of the Brotherhood called lifers, she would be eligible for membership in that most exclusive of all clubs, the 600 Club. My magic number, of course, was four. The 600 Club is a more or less official assemblage of all those birders throughout the land who have seen and identified six hundred or more full species of bird north of Mexico. The 600 Club is the leitmotif of this book, and its legends and traditions will be discussed more fully later.

As the plane droned steadily along on its northwest course, the paramount question in our minds was whether our respective desiderata of five and four life birds could be met. Would we see them? The chances were excellent from all the information we had been able to glean about those species that inhabit the Pribilofs in summer. To a birding fanatic, though, hell hath no torment like the anguish of mind that invariably precedes the actual achievement of his hopes. So it was with us as we neared the end of our journey. Miraculously, the clouds began to thin away and we glimpsed patches of sea and, yes, land too. The Great Spirit in those faraway isles was in a beneficent mood and, for the present at least, there would be no pea soup fog as we had feared. There was actually a hint of blue in the sky and, almost, there were shadows.

The airline had furnished the party with a bus and driver to take us over the island to the bird cliffs and the fur seal rookeries. There is a small lake near the hotel and we all piled out of the bus to scan the shore birds that littered its muddy edge. Red and Northern Phalaropes were there in fair numbers, the females conspicuous with their more colorful plumage. I have often wondered why Women's Lib does not adopt the Phalarope as its votive emblem. The female does the courting and lays the eggs; her stint for the year is over. The more somber-garbed male, still very striking, builds the nest, incubates the eggs, and cares for the young. Uxoriousness can be carried no further. The females of the three species of Phalarope that inhabit this planet, all of which can be seen in North America, bear the unmistakable imprint of genetically determined "liberation" in their double helix macromolecules or, as we used to say in the good old days, in their genes. Compared to the Phalarope, Women's Lib with its contrived "equality" is "as moonlight unto sunlight and as water unto wine." But enough of Phalaropes and Libs. The important thing at this juncture is the fact that beyond the Phalaropes was a very large flock of Rock Sandpipers, hundreds at least. The Rock Sandpiper is a bird that superficially resembles the Dunlin in summer plumage but is actually more akin to the Purple Sandpiper, a bird of the northeastern shores and rock jetties in winter. We had failed to find this bird along the California coast the preceding winter and loud and bitter had been my lamentations. Now we had them at our mercy, for the Rock Sandpiper is a common breeding bird in the Pribilofs. The count was now four and three for the two of us.

Standing on the cliff overlooking the seal rookery, I saw two specks out over the sea growing larger every half second until, in the proverbial wink of the eye, they shot past us like cannon balls at no more than fifty feet. Yes, their underparts were all white; we had seen our first Horned Puffins. Puffins, of which there are three species in North America, have a fabulous bill capable of catching and holding fish at one and the same time. We had seen the other two species some years earlier. Now we had seen them all and, the next morning, through a 30x telescope at extreme near focus, the erectile horns over the eyes stood up like small, decapitated mushrooms. There were Fulmars, Pelagic Cormorants, Harlequin Ducks, Tufted Puffins, Common Murres, and several other feathered specialties. We reveled in them all, especially the Fulmars that tilted by on stiff wings almost brushing our faces with their wing tips. But we had seen all these birds before. Our lifer luck was temporarily in abeyance, so we needed to visit the bird cliffs of the northeast part of the island to climax our day.

When we reached the northeast end, things began to happen. It all took about a minute and a half once we were established on the edge of the cliff. Never again, North of the Border, will it be possible for us to see five life birds in so incredibly short a time. The Red-faced Cormorant was the six hundredth bird for me, but the Thick-billed Murre had preceded him by so few ticks of the second hand that it was a near tie. The Red-legged Kittiwake was next. Crested and Parakeet Auklets were festooned over every crevice of the rocks and so many were continually coming and going that the wonder is we saw any on land at all. Orville Crowder was leading the tour, as he usually does on pioneer trips, and during the frenzy of the moment I heard him cry out that he too had seen his six hundredth North American bird. Orville has a tremendous world list, probably one of the biggest, but that day, at least, he, Marybelle and I were all warriors of the same stripe. We had fought the good fight and won. For the Piatts it was a consummation of birding efforts that had extended over forty-nine states and all but two provinces of Canada.

That evening found us down along the shore where the big,

smooth boulders lay piled on top of one another. It was the nesting retreat of the Least Auklet, a little stubby-headed alcid with a white throat patch and red bill—in summer, that is. We had been told by a knowledgeable native, who had been with us in the afternoon, that this bird was more or less crepuscular in its habits. Therefore, we had waited till then to look for this species, the last of the lifers we would probably be able to see in the Pribilofs at that time of year. It was getting darker and at last the fog was beginning to drift in from the sea. In a very few more minutes visibility would be seriously impaired. Our internal gloom occasioned by that of the external world was suddenly dissipated by a whirr of wings as a living projectile shot away from us out to sea from almost under our feet. Another followed the first farther along the boulder heaps and then another. There was just light enough for us to observe all the necessary field marks; it was the Least Auklet. Marybelle was now 603 and I one more. We congratulated ourselves on a near miss, for we were scheduled to leave St. Paul the next day and there would have been no more evenings in the Pribilofs for us. Actually, we saw several small flotillas of these little Auklets in broad daylight the next morning close in toward shore. It was one more example of the old adage among the birding tribe that once you see a lifer, after years of waiting, the bird will roost by the dozens on the foot of your bed from then on. And, with the perversity of human nature, we were mildly chagrined that our darkling vigil of the previous evening had not, in fact, constituted our last chance to see this bird. We felt in some unaccountable way that we had been betrayed by that evening of suspense, mystery, and adventure among the fog-girt boulders along the misty sea Vitus Bering had sailed so many years ago. Besides, I was coming down with a first-class wretched cold.

Thus ended our birding experience on the misty isles. We had yet to spend three days on Umnak in the Aleutian chain, where, as it happened, perpetual fog and drizzle were our lot. No plane could reach us until late on the third day. That first night in Umnak, Whitney and Karen Eastman, both charter members of the 600 Club, toasted the three new members of the Club and all was as merry as could be inside the airline "hotel." But fate denied us the Rock Ptarmigan while we were on the despoiled tundra of Umnak and hollow, hollow all delight.

Thus ends the prolegomena of this little saga anent lifers and listers. Then come away with me, dear reader—that is the time-honored phraseology, is it not—to the inception of all this delicious nonsense. Go back with me some ten years or so to the beginning of the end.

ADVENTURES
IN BIRDING

I

The Spark

Birders are wont to say it was this bird or that which first aroused their interest and set their feet along the glory trail toward the big list or, perhaps, simply dancing along some mysterious path of their own choosing in unpurposed fulfillment—there are many kinds of birders. Marybelle and I are no exception to this shibboleth, and since we "officially" began birding at the same place and only one day apart, we often speak of the Rufous-sided Towhee as the spark that ignited the flame. I wonder, though, if we are not deluded in this cherished conceit, all of us. The miserable human creature clings so stubbornly to his self-deceptions. God knows he has need to upon occasion. But in the nonvital matter of "spark birds" surely we can afford to be honest with ourselves. It is my belief that time, place, and mood are all important in starting one on a birding pilgrimage; the particular species is an accidental irrelevance. Of course, now, if my first bird had been the Quetzal . . .! But you shall judge for yourself.

I grew up, so help me, in Indianapolis. If any Hoosier reading this begins to splutter, let him look into the inner recesses of his being and ask himself whether he would have chosen Indianapolis, Indiana, rather than Parnassus as his place of rearing. On second thought, though, I'm afraid he would. Marybelle's mother was exactly the type. She could have sailed the Aegean Sea, skirted the coast of British Columbia, scaled the Alps, or roamed the streets of Paris, and they would all have suffered by comparison with the sunsets over Sugar Plain at Thorntown, Indiana. She could have been right but I take everlasting leave to doubt it. Anyway, when I was a boy I used to tramp out to the banks of White River and its shady woods with an ax on my shoulder just to be alone. I have always liked to use an ax and many a fallen tree I left with deep gashes in its sturdy trunk. Even in those faraway times when timber was more plentiful, I would never have touched a living tree. I learned to know the Indigo Bunting, Downy Woodpecker, White-breasted Nuthatch, and the Towhee. There must have been dozens of others there too but for some inexplicable reason I can recall only those four. The Towhee moved me no more than the others and, naturally, the Bunting was by long odds the most exotic of the four to me. No spark was kindled. Why? I felt a sublime communion with all living and nonliving things about me but none awakened special interest. Perhaps when we are very young we possess an innate sensibility of the wholeness of creation and fail to discriminate. I had visions, though; or did I dream dreams? ". . . your old men shall dream dreams, your young men shall see visions." Yes, they were probably visions but, after all, a vision is only a waking dream. Whichever, I should eagerly exchange my entire list of North American birds for the fulfillment of just one of those radiant fancies.

In my late teens and early twenties I became deeply involved with herpetology, even took an M.A. in this fascinating scientific discipline under the direction of Professor Emmett Reid Dunn at Haverford College. I collected snakes and lizards in Sonora, Mexico, and Abe (Morrow) Allen and I discovered a new subspecies of lizard; *Dipsosaurus dorsalis sonoriensis* is its name, I believe. Why I left herpetology or, rather, why it left me is of no consequence here. What matters is that in collecting snakes and salamanders one of my frequent companions on these jaunts was Frederick Baumgartner, who subsequently took a Ph.D. in ornithology at Cornell under Professor A. A. Allen and is, of course, now a professional ornithologist. Fred was eternally scanning the treetops when he wasn't looking for ducks on the river, and I was just as doggedly turning over stones and logs with my eyes glued to the ground. We often saw the Towhee and I even learned to know a few birds I'd missed back there on the banks of White River. One memorable day, notable for birds, not snakes, we saw a Wood Stork, then called Wood Ibis, in the company of seven Great Blue Herons and any number of egrets only about twenty miles south of Indianapolis. Fred was so excited that he was somewhat incoherent for several days. But me? I appreciated the magnificent tableau of these stately birds, especially the Stork, but I remained perfectly calm and lucid. The same fate overtook the Red-breasted Nuthatch at Indian Gap in the Great Smoky Mountains in April 1930. Fred was ecstatic but I paid the bird no mind, even though Fred insisted I use his glasses. I had just found my first *Plethodon jordani* in an icy mountain stream and my state of entrancement would brook no hiatus. *P. jordani* is a handsome salamander with dark body and strikingly contrasting red cheeks. It was described by a famous coleopterist, Willis Stanley Blatchely, and named after the dean of American ichthyology, David Starr Jordan. It is only too apparent that Jordan's salamander had nothing in common with ornithology that day.

Some years later, when I was a National Research Council Fellow at Columbia University, Marybelle and I used to spend weekends with our good friends the Camerons, Angus and

Sheila, at Walker Valley near the Catskills. It distresses me intensely to blurt out the truth in this fashion, but I have no other recourse under the circumstances: Angus has always been a murderer of God's living creatures—euphemistically known as a hunter. What transpired on those weekends or what potent spell the magic of those autumnal days with their scarlet and gold foliage instilled into me, I cannot say. The deplorable fact remains that I occasionally found myself in the possession of a fowling piece, borrowed, of course, and more than likely forced into my unwilling hands, treading the forest paths in search of game. Fortunately, the hunting was poor and I am a miserable shot; unfortunately, Angus is not. In ROTC in my freshman year at college I unerringly put three shots into my neighbor's target. Note: I refused to continue in ROTC in that year 1927 and stuck to my guns—the figurative kind, the only kind I could tolerate. Again, lest my garrulity tire you, let us come to the birding point. In one of these senseless forays upon living creatures I became separated from Angus and was sitting quietly on a stump watching a deer approach. It was not deer season and even had it been I should not have shot and even if I had shot I should have missed by the proverbial mile. I'm sure you grasp the essential point; the deer wore the Tarnhelm. Over the racket the deer was making—I had first fancied it was a cow from the noise—I heard close by a scuttering of the leaves. It was my friend the Towhee going about his business of kicking the leaves with both feet at once to secure his food. As so many times before, I was struck by his handsome attire and vastly admired his scuttering of the leaves, but no tocsin sounded, no inner voice was heard. Surely, in my receptive mood, with the nostalgic odors of the woods all about, odors redolent of things past and things to come, there should have been at least a portent of the future madness, some stirring. There was nothing. I continued to sit as one bemused till roused by the return of my companion, Angus the hunter. A limp Red Squirrel was draped over one of his fingers. That squirrel made mighty good eating, but it was uncommonly small.

There did come, however, a time, a place, and a mood. The time was a February afternoon in 1957. The place was Furness's Upper Bank Nursery near Media, Pennsylvania. The mood? Well, the mood does not lend itself so readily to bald description. I do not know exactly what kind of a mood it was unless, perhaps, it was the right one. Marybelle and I had toyed with birding the last year or two in Maine where, in a delightful retreat on Upper Wilson Pond near Moosehead Lake, we had spent a number of summer vacations. We did not have a field guide but this did not deter us from naming the dickey birds ourselves; most of the bigger birds we knew. I shall never forget the first time we heard the loon, the Common Loon. It was on East Pond in the Belgrade Chain in 1951, late at night, and it was the "wolf call." I may as well out with it: I thought it was a wolf. I had never heard a loon before, to say nothing of a wolf. I can never hear that shamanic witchery of sound or even conjure it up without a shiver passing over me. I say the trite, of course; who is there that doesn't venerate the loon? Well, anyway, we called the Phoebe the "Round Head," the Redstart "that pretty little bird," and so forth. We even bought a pair of 7 x 35 binoculars.

That February afternoon was golden. It was a day lifted right out of Indian summer but with a more bracing tang in the air. One does not usually associate such days with dour February. However, in eastern Pennsylvania they occur more often than one might expect. (When we lived in an apartment in the city, we used to call them "zoo days." We had no car or any ready access to the country then. So on such days we invariably shut up the lab and spent the day at the Philadelphia zoo.) I took our pair of binoculars and walked down the road a hundred feet or so to where a loop of the "old road" entered Furness's Nursery. In the five years we had lived in Upper Providence Township the traffic had measurably increased and I was glad to leave the swish of passing cars and enter the sequestered "old road," long since barred to traffic. I did not linger in the formal gardens of the Nursery but sought the woods high up on the hill in back.

I'd split wood most of the morning and was tired, tired with that restful tranquillity of body and spirit which comes after hard, physical labor well done. At least I had the feeling it had been well done and that is all that matters. I sat on an old beech log with my back to the low sun; the trunks of the big beeches were refulgent with the nearly horizontal rays. Let things come my way. I was ready.

This wood lot of some fifteen acres or so was the property of a Miss Hanna, whom I had only seen once and who was never referred to by any other appellation, so far as I know. To be more accurate, the lot used to belong to Miss Hanna. It was now owned by the Township, for Miss Hanna had been forced to sell and had moved to parts unknown. A new high school occupied the far side of the adjacent field and the woods were soon to suffer the desecration of more suburban ticky-tacky. Most of the big timber, red oak and tulip trees, had been felled to help assuage the ravenous appetite of the saw mills. Only the beeches and smaller trees were left standing. I had come here often during the past five years to walk beside still waters and restore my soul. Both Marybelle and I loved its cool solitude in summer and the dark, naked branches etched against the sky in winter. We were to find out later that it had been an excellent warbler place during spring migration because of the many big oaks, which always attract these treetop sprites. I was not thinking of warblers that February afternoon, however, and would scarcely have known the names of any had I been so disposed. I was conscious only of the many vacant places against the sky and the despoliation all about me. Few warblers would come to this bereft spot next spring. And it had all happened so fast, four or five weeks at the most. The snarl of the chain saw and the everlasting moan of the logging cat still vibrated in the stillness about me.

I silently cursed them all. Do not importune with that old bromide about more lumber for more houses for more people. In plain truth, what we need, man and beast, is less lumber for less houses for less people. There is no problem of major proportion today that is not compounded tenfold by population pressure. *Homo sapiens* today is living on borrowed time, time borrowed from the future. And no debt goes unpaid, really. Personally, I want no part of a society that cheers the birth of its two hundred millionth citizen at a time when the earth is overrun by pullulating humanity. What a travesty! That moment should have been the occasion for intense mourning; death, not birth, was acclaimed that day. The death of man's environment and, perhaps, the eventual death of man himself—his psyche if not his germ plasm. Egocentric, belligerent, arrogant man, the only voyager in the Ark educated beyond his intelligence. The Greeks had a word for it; they usually do, as we all know; they called it hubris, excessive pride. It did not please their gods.

A few yards off to the right of where I sat glooming on my log was a tangle of fallen branches and the shattered trunk of a big tulip tree. Just two days before, Marybelle and I had watched a fox stumble around over the same impediment. Yes, this fox stumbled. He was the clumsiest fox I have ever seen and a disgrace to the sixth and seventh generation of his fox brethren. He never saw us, or smelled us, and we out of sympathy for his maladroit maneuvers pretended we did not see him either. He passed within thirty feet of us and continued on his way. In the midst of this tangle I gradually became aware of a commotion on the ground. Leaves were being tossed about and there was a poignantly familiar sound. Yes, it was a scuttering sound. My old friend the Towhee was scuttering leaves with each backward kick of his feet, just as he had done that day at Walker Valley. Through the glasses his contrasting black, white, and rufous plumage was like a portrait at such close range. It was at that moment I decided to start a bird list. Why this particular Towhee should have pressed the button, I cannot say. But with all the solemnity of the Count of Monte Cristo I figuratively raised one finger and spoke the sibylline words, "Number one!" Like any other acolyte, I felt immediately invested with all the mysteries and responsibilities of the Order. This, then, was the spark. But was it the Towhee?

As I rose to leave, a Red-bellied Woodpecker lit on the trunk of a beech and the bright rays of the setting sun shone full upon him. This was number two, and before I reached home the Tufted Titmouse, Cardinal, White-breasted Nuthatch, and Common Crow were in the bag. Why these particular birds and not any of the other equally common winter birds is one of those inconsequential arcana of the day-old birder. All that can be said is that Marybelle began the next day to count her birds. The Towhee was her first bird, too, but whether this was genuine or contrived I do not know. There was no official 600 Club in that auspicious year, 1957, but had there been, we would have been none the wiser. I was blissfully unaware of such fabulous numbers and could not know that I had seen just one percent of all those birds I would yearn for in the years to come. But we were launched on the birding trail and I was content with my six lifers. There would be many others in the days to come.

II

The Flame

Because our quest for life birds had its genesis in Miss Hanna's erstwhile wood lot, it was only natural that Fairman Furness's Upper Bank Nursery would be the scene of our early triumphs and travails. The Nursery, simply Furness's to us, adjoined Miss Hanna's old place and included within its extensive acres woods, fields, and a bewildering variety of both indigenous and exotic shrubs and trees. Best of all, Ridley Creek flowed for almost a quarter of a mile along one side of the grounds. It was only a stone's throw from our house and afforded an excellent habitat for birds of the woods, such as the Kentucky Warbler and Red-eyed Vireo, and birds of the field, such as the Meadow Lark, Sparrow Hawk, etc. It is to this day one of our favorite birding sites, especially in winter, when the deciduous woods alone harbor so few birds. But here, too, the chain saw and logging cat have ravaged the wooded areas in recent years; assuredly, our birding incunabula is doomed. For about two years our activities were confined almost entirely to Furness's. Why forsake our birthplace for strange lands when we were only learning to walk? I used to call the arched tunnel of hemlocks that lined the old road the "gateway to the unknown." It was for us a fitting portal of mystery into an unexplored country. If we did not always rise early before the dawn, still we faithfully followed the latter half of Thoreau's injunction, for we sought adventure, always. Discovery is always a potent elixir and for the birding neophyte Media, Pennsylvania, can be as alluring as Zanzibar or the Galapagos Islands are for the hierophant—and, we had scarcely set foot within the temple door. True, we each now had a pair of binoculars but they only exemplified our verdancy; we were acutely embarrassed at such open extravagance. Marybelle usually concealed her pair when we passed by the few houses between ours and Furness's.

We had no guidance during our first year or so of birding, either from tyro or expert. It is probably true that most birders begin by joining a bird club or at the instigation of some more or less experienced person. At least this has been the case with almost all the first-class birders I have known. I do not mean to imply that we were unique in going it alone; undoubtedly, others have had the same experience. I emphasize this early aspect of our birding because it explains to a great extent our relative slowness in the acquisition of lifers, just 124 our first year, and the often egregious mistakes and fumblings that beset us at the beginning. For instance, that first spring during the height of the Ruby-crowned Kinglet migration we reported, to ourselves only, of course, an unconscionable number of "Least Flycatchers." On one glorious occasion we spied at least four in one medium-sized Norway spruce! All eye rings, wing bars, and small birds were much the same to us at the start. Any birder out of his swaddling clothes could have pointed out to us the difference in bills, behavior, size, or voice but there was none such

around. Again, late one evening about the middle of May, I saw
a "warbler" high in a walnut tree near the bridge over the creek.
I failed to identify the bird and took so long in the vain attempt
that had not merciful darkness descended on that small walnut
grove I might have ended up with a dislocated neck. The next
day I found this bird in a more favorable location but it still
puzzled me. I concluded that it must be a Tennessee Warbler
but my "identification" lacked that indefinable ring of inner
conviction. It was not till the monotonous, repetitious song
penetrated my consciousness that something clicked. I remembered that Peterson had said the Red-eyed Vireo's song went on
forever and reminded one of a Robin. It was my first indication
that a bird's voice is frequently its best means of identification. I
never hear the Red-eye's song without recalling my infancy and
neck strain.

My worst blunder, though, is to this day an acute source of
embarrassment to me. It is one of those birding fiascos no sane
birder would ever admit. In the words of Huck Finn, good
honest sin is just old pie alongside of it. Worst of all, I may be
accused of gross misrepresentation, an apocryphal episode
drummed up for the occasion. So be it, true or false, I shall reap
well-deserved opprobrium. It does not take long in the telling.
This smallish bird with streaked underparts had been flying up
and down the creek almost every day since early May. It
bobbed and teetered whenever it lit on a rock or walked along
the shore. That cinched it for me. I had a vivid recollection of a
bird I had seen under just such conditions and displaying just
such behavior on White River in the old days. Fred Baumgartner had told me it was a Spotted Sandpiper. When we
returned from Maine the latter part of August, the bird was still
in residence. I had had time to learn more about the warblers and
had read about the waterthrushes and their habits. I rechecked
my bird, crossed off Spotted Sandpiper, and put down Louisiana
Waterthrush. To me, warblers had always been associated with
tall trees or thickets of one sort or another, not walking and
bobbing along stream margins. I can only hope that some high

Mogul in the Brotherhood reading this does not, in his own mind, strike all my birds off the list. I earnestly hope in all events that he will allow me to retain the Louisiana Waterthrush. In these parts the Louisiana arrives in early April and his sweet, wild song heard in some wooded ravine is one of the earliest and most gladsome harbingers of spring. I'm going to keep him anyway, no matter what.

Then there was the lamentable incident of our first duck. I think by that time we knew the Mallard and I suppose he is technically number one duck, but this was our first real test. It was one of those rare occasions when we ventured beyond the familiar terrain of Furness's—we were parked along Springton Reservoir, a sizable body of water. Far out but well within glass range were about a dozen small ducks, some with lots of white and others mostly dark. The proper clues were all there but we failed to profit by them. When one has only been birding a few weeks, ducks in different plumages signify different species, not different sexes. Well, to make things brief, it took us about fifteen minutes or more to realize it was the same species, male and female, and what the species was. We were inordinately proud of ourselves. But before we had the opportunity to actually make a formal pronouncement, I heard a quiet, feminine voice asking, "Have you seen anything besides Buffleheads today?" It was petite Polly Crawford, a former medical student of mine. She must have spied our intensive and prolonged investigation from afar and decided that something unusual was out there beyond the Buffleheads. Well, it confirmed our identification but I felt like the charlatan I was when I glibly replied, "No, nothing but Buffleheads." A male Bufflehead is a duck that is all field mark and any birder strong enough to carry a Peterson guide in his hip pocket can tell one almost as far as the eye can see. The Bufflehead has always been my favorite duck—our first loves are the ones that last.

It was not all humiliation and corrigenda, though. We steadily increased our list by careful observation and correct identification. Also, we were catching on to a few simple tricks well known to the birding fraternity. Namely, unless you are exceedingly tall, shorten the binocular straps for ease of carrying and maneuverability. In dense foliage, don't attempt to locate the bird with the glasses until you have taken an additional fraction of a second beforehand to also locate some peculiar configuration of leaves, branches, or other conspicuous object near the bird for a reference point. He who raises his glasses instantaneously to a flitting warbler in the top of a huge oak may discover he is looking at nothing but a tangle of leaves and branches.

We were such empty vessels in those days and there was so much to pour into us that each weekend found us exhausted. It became an old joke with us that Mondays we could go back to the lab and rest. That April thirtieth, for instance. I was alone all day at Furness's because Marybelle had a bad cyst on her knee and was in the city having it attended to. I saw six life birds that day, two of them being the Blue-winged and Golden-winged Warblers. I was on the lookout the rest of the spring for their nest. Naturally I had decided that they would surely mate and nest in the vicinity and I could observe at my leisure the resulting Brewster's hybrid and, maybe, the coveted Lawrence's Warbler. Needless to say, I did not find their nest and it was ten years before I saw my first Brewster's Warbler and twelve years before my first and only Lawrence's. But the excitement of that day is as fresh in my memory as though it were this morning. It was not just those six new birds, although the Blue- and Golden-winged, Hooded and Chestnut-sided Warblers would add luster to any list; it was the whole endearin' flock. Those I had seen but yesterday were also there to glorify the day. Even now I still go forth every April 30 expectantly, but somewhat tempered by experience, to recapture the long glories of that April day in 1957. There has never been a repeat. The migration was very early that year and, also, I had beginner's luck. When Marybelle came home that evening, I was able to produce every blessed one of those little varmints for her own list. It was a painful procedure for her, what with the stiff knee, but it was well worth it. That Hooded Warbler jumped straight up from a thicket, perched for a full two seconds or so, and then dropped back into the dense cover. As I'm writing, there are three pairs of Hoodeds nesting at Gradyville, and only last Sunday I tried patiently to see at least one of them. It was no go; despite their singing, I could never find the little devils. Hooded Warblers are not what they used to be.

All in all we saw eighty-two lifers at Furness's those first two years. We have added six more since. At this writing, the total number of birds we have seen at Furness's stands at 137 and includes such goodies as the Pileated Woodpecker, Barred Owl, and White-winged Crossbill. The last bird reminds me of a promise I gave Marybelle. She has been whimpering ever since I began "making with book words" (Gypsy Rose Lee's pungent expression) that I have designedly employed the ruse of inter-jecting her various physical debilitations to allow me to hero it alone. You will recall she missed the Wheatear because of a bad cold and my April thirtieth just described. And, she lamented only today, "You're going to tell them about my broken ribs too, I suppose." I intend to do just that. But, right now, let me hasten to affirm that she has seen many a bird before I have and is frequently in the field by herself. One Saturday morning in December 1963 to be specific, I had just stepped into my lab for a moment's respite from the rigors of the Gross Anatomy Laboratory when the phone rang. Marybelle had just returned from Furness's where she had been watching a White-winged Crossbill for half an hour or so, a lifer for her and, of course, a lifer for me too. Only, I hadn't seen it yet! I couldn't stand it. I drove straight to Furness's and saw that bird; it was still there. Medical education has some fragile claim to importance, I sup-pose, but that Crossbill could not possibly have done without me and I knew the Gross class could. The White-winged Crossbill is the last lifer, to date, that we have seen at Furness's.

By 1959 we were beginning to meet other birders, and be-tween that year and the summer of 1961 we broadened our horizons considerably. We began to make trips to the Jersey shore, "discovered" Brigantine and Bombay Hook National Wildlife Refuges, and learned of Hawk Mountain in the Kittatinny Ridge of Pennsylvania. Everyone, of course, has heard of Hawk Mountain. The wonder is that we were so slow in tapping the birding grapevine. Our first pilgrimage to this famous sanctuary was a memorable one, for it produced our first Golden Eagle, real beginner's luck. I'll never forget the authentic ring of urgency in Maurice Broun's voice as he directed our attention to the rapidly enlarging speck over "number three" that morning. Before the bird vanished from our sight to the southwest, Broun had given us all an eloquent and moving prediction as to the fate of this magnificent raptor. The presentiment that this might be my last Golden Eagle was far more impressive than the accidental fact that it was also my first.

Maurice Broun has shown us many a hawk, all unbeknownst to himself. What I mean is, Maurice does not know us personally. We were just two of many perched on the lichen-covered rocks of the Lookout who have profited by his vast knowledge of the Falconiformes. Hawks and their ilk present formidable difficulties in field identification, not only to the beginner but to the average birder as well. Many species have different color phases and immatures often differ in their plumage from adults. Size, shape, wingbeat, and other flight peculiarities are often of great diagnostic value; a perching hawk is not easy to identify. The Falconiformes is one group of birds that the novice should treat warily unless he is fortunate enough to have the guidance of some expert to teach him the ropes. It gave us no small pleasure and thrill, therefore, to be able to point out the Curlew Sandpiper to Maurice Broun and his gang of birders at Brigantine just three weeks ago. I do not know if it was a lifer for him and I did not ask. Somehow, when a man knows as much about birds as Maurice Broun does, he instinctively shies away from trivia. Don't misunderstand me. Broun was almost dancing with excitement, as we had done earlier that day. Real birders are no stuffed-shirt dummies; they get at least as much kick out of a new bird as hangers-on like myself. But still, I did not ask him. We know it was a lifer for us but neither you nor I shall ever know if it was for Maurice Broun.

Our best and most practicable find was Tinicum Wildlife Refuge. Tinicum is about 140 acres occupying, of all things, the extreme southwest part of the city of Philadelphia. It is marshy ground with a shallow, central lake. We have seen as many as fifteen species of duck there in one day and probably Jim Carroll, the refuge manager, has seen more than that. In the years we have frequented Tinicum, Avocets, Red-necked Grebes, Northern and Wilson's Phalaropes, Buff-breasted Sandpipers, Ruffs, Hudsonian Godwits, European Widgeons, Common (European) Teals are among the more outstanding species that have been reported. For the past few years both Iceland and Glaucous Gulls have been seen there off and on through the winter. It is because Tinicum Marsh and its environs are included in the area of the Glenolden, Pennsylvania, Christmas Bird Count that we have led the state for some years in the number of species recorded. Tinicum serves a further function for local birders besides being a convenient place to observe ducks, shore birds, and waders; namely, it is a clearing house for exchange of up to the minute information on birds in the area and affords an opportunity to check the doings of other members of the Brotherhood. Marybelle and I have acquired a number of lifers by listening to the latest reports or just to the gossip in general. We all stand around and brag about our latest rarity or the number of warblers we have seen that morning and, in the long run, much benefit accrues from this rodomontade. We have picked up fifty-two lifers at Tinicum, all but four of these during our first three years of birding. Also, we met the kids there.

The kids, as we so unceremoniously dubbed them, were a group of six or seven boys from south Philadelphia in the first year of high school. Their science teacher, an ardent birder himself, put a real bee in their skulls about birding and listing. Being with them on a birding expedition was like holding a live wire in one hand while trying to fend off an aggressive rattlesnake with the other. The direct and indirect ways they helped us in birding and, incidentally, in understanding young people, are legion. The real eager beaver of the bunch was George Spitalny. As I write this, he is now a graduate student at New York University in, of all things, parasitology. During the height of his onslaught upon the bird world George did not know a tapeworm from *Plasmodium vivax*, but he knew his birds. He literally slavered for lifers. I recall the day he and several other kids had been with us in the morning birding at Gradyville, a place I'll introduce before long. We had some hamburgers at home and then set out to spend the afternoon at Tinicum. As we reached the intersection that could lead us to either Tinicum or Brigantine, George uttered a heart-rending cry as we turned onto the Tinicum route. His words were, "I want a lifer," but it was the wailing desperation of the utterance that shook me. That unmute appeal rose from his very toes and seemed to exhale all the accumulated frustration of the ages. The prolonged, quavering wail of the word "lifer" haunts me yet. You see, it was this way. George had hoped we would drive over to the Jersey shore, where the seaside locality and much more extensive terrain of Brigantine Wildlife Refuge would have offered plausible chances for a lifer. Marybelle and I just didn't want to drive the 120 miles round trip to Brigantine that late in the day, to say nothing of the torture of keeping those kids in tow once we were there. So George had to content himself with Tinicum, a place where he already knew every stick, stone, blade of grass, and bird. It was only a few days later he told us that when he was eighteen he was going to get a 1960 Corvette and spend all his time taking bird trips. George was fourteen then and the year was 1960, so I expect he did not actually plan four years in advance to buy a four-year-old car. In the unaffected imagery of youth current models never grow old, be they cars or loves. And the sequel? When George did get his car, a 1965 Mustang borrowed from his older sister, he used it for dates just like any other young idiot! George's birds began to suffer when the Mustang was available.

One further and final episode about the kids, chiefly to illustrate a universal frailty of mankind in general and inexperienced birders in particular. We were still spending our summer vacations in Maine during our early birding years and, needless to say, the fishing gradually declined to near zero as the birding virus waxed more virulent. In the Moosehead Lake region we were on the breeding grounds of the Yellow-bellied Flycatcher and learned to know the bird and its call fairly well. It does not nest as far south as eastern Pennsylvania, a fact to bear in mind. The Yellow-bellied Flycatcher is one of the smaller members of the Flycatcher family, *Tyrannidae,* and belongs to the confusing and controversial genus *Empidonax,* whose numerous species look so much alike that in the field they are usually distinguished from one another by voice alone. Most of them do have an eye ring and rather prominent wing bars, though, which serve to separate them from other small Flycatchers and birds of the same size. In addition, the Yellow-bellied Flycatcher can usually be recognized in the eastern states by the distinctly yellowish tinge of its underparts, as its name implies. Some of this is necessary background for what follows but I need not have been quite so verbose. Give a birder even the most transparent excuse and invariably he piles it on. At all events, it will give nonbirders an evanescent glimpse into the complexities of field identification and afford birders an opportunity to feel superior, because, undoubtedly, I must have got something or other wrong. And now, back to the kids.

East of the Appalachian Mountains at least, the Yellow-bellied Flycatcher is not often seen in migration; it seldom calls and is shy and retiring. One morning in May 1960, however, Marybelle and I spotted this bird near Springton Reservoir; it was an undoubted Yellow-bellied Flycatcher. The bird gave every indication that it was in no hurry to leave the small spruce grove and when we told George and Mark about it that noon, they cajoled us into taking them back out to the Reservoir. It would be a lifer for both of them. Despite his tender years, George was beginning to acquire a well-deserved reputation as a sharp birder among the local Brotherhood. Mark was still just so-so. We were, therefore, somewhat flattered that we would be able to show George a bird we "knew so well" and he had never seen. Well, we waited and wandered and wandered and waited, still no Yellow-bellied Flycatcher. After almost an hour, George began to manifest unmistakable signs of acute impatience. The rock he was perched on was one of the very hard kind. In his present mood he gave eloquent testimony to the fact that bird watching and birding are connotatively poles apart. We, on our part, were vexed and embarrassed because we could not "produce" the bird. All at once a small, yellowish bird flew from the spruce grove out over a small pond. "There, you see it, George," we yelled. Marybelle even called his attention to the wing bars and I, dupe that I was, followed through with, "Look at that eye ring!" The bird flew unerringly to our side of the pond and plummeted into its nest in a small viburnum bush. The Piatts exchanged one covert, sheepish glance and looked at George; George looked at neither. He got up from his rock with measured deliberation, dusted off his behind with first one hand and then the other, and walked straight over to the car and climbed in. Mark followed suit. Not one word did any of us speak. That wretched bit of yellow fluff was a female Yellow-throat, probably the most common nesting warbler in these parts. Incidentally, she has no wing bars and no eye ring to speak of. We had fallen into that most familiar of all birding traps—seeing what we wanted to see rather than what the fates presented. We had not actually even raised our glasses until we saw the bird enter the nest. It is an extremely minuscule segment of one of mankind's besetting sins, namely, heedless distortion of reality. George never committed the unpardonable affront of challenging our identification of that morning but I know damn well what he thought. It just so happens that our bird of the morning was a Yellow-bellied Flycatcher, but Marybelle and I learned our lesson from that immense moment of mortification. We recall the transmogrification of that afternoon—and the big word helps us remember.

A record of our early birding years would not be complete without some mention of Maine summer vacations at Muzzy's Upper Camp on Upper Wilson Pond near Moosehead Lake. The Upper Camp, as its name implies, was situated farther up on the sloping, wooded bank of the lake and offered a much better view of the water and Elephant Mountain than did the Lower Camp. Besides, the Upper Camp had character. The Lower was simply a frame house built to house hordes of obstreperous fishermen and their screen-banging kids. The lower campers lived in their boats from dawn to dusk. If it had not been for the incontestable evidence of the automobiles and outboard motors, we would have deemed them the descendants of some autochthonous, piscatorial tribe that had fished these waters in the high and far-off times. This fanciful little conceit of ours, however, was invariably shattered by the banging of more screen doors or the receding whine of the outboards.

The Upper Camp, so the tale runs, was built for a railroad president in 1923 before a road was made, and everything had to be ferried across the lake from Lower Wilson through the "narrows" between the two. It had a magnificent fireplace and a spacious screened porch facing the east, the lake, and Elephant Mountain. When those nor'easters came with their attendant three days of rain or drisk, it was cozy and delightful to live in front of the blazing fire and read aloud, play chess, or just dream away the time. On the good days the porch was our haven, with all the wilderness spread before us—forest, lake, and mountains. No other camp was visible, although there were seven altogether on the lake; it was Thoreau's Maine Woods that encompassed us. Many a wild thing have we seen and heard from that porch. A sunrise over Elephant Mountain with its wisps of saffron and green clouds was a sight for the gods. And the long, dark shadows of the birches stole ever farther and farther out over the lake in the evening hush. But the kitchen, with its big wood-burning range, was the focus of all delight. There must be wood-burning ranges in heaven or I don't want to go there. And that smell of burning birch in the still morning air! There may be celestial glories to equal it, but I have my doubts. Yes, that railroad president did a good job. The Muzzys, Ed and Elaine, from whom we rented the Camp, were wonderful people and it was a toss-up who loved the place better, they or we. We returned to the Upper Camp for eleven gloriously happy days in 1966, after being away for five years. It was precisely as we had remembered it. Nothing had changed! In this terrifying and apocalyptic period of man's existence with its idiotic, ceaseless change and insane turmoil, what words could be more hallowed. We felt as though we were on our second honeymoon although, of course, we had shaken the last grain of rice from our clothes long before those earlier Maine summers. There were no human voices but our own, and from afar over the still waters of the lake came the lusty, throaty hooting of the Barred Owl. It was dusk, and he was calling from the fastness of Baker Mountain. We wished him good hunting. We, too, rejoiced that there are owls.

Somewhere I must have a list of the birds we saw at Upper Wilson Pond and the adjoining country but I cannot find it. It would not have been large, however, because, with one or two doubtful exceptions, only the resident breeding birds were there in the summer and habitats were largely restricted to lakes and coniferous and mixed forests. We did, however, see our first Pileated Woodpeckers there. They were all around the Camp and it was a rare day that one was neither seen nor heard. I recall vividly our first pair of Pileateds and the amusing denouement of this incident is one that surely a number of birders have experienced in similar circumstances. They were magnificent, of course. Whose first Pileated is not! They were very close and completely oblivious of our gaping presence. The thing is that apparently they had made up their minds to work over every cubic inch of that old hemlock. We looked and we looked and we looked. After fully twenty minutes of this sort of thing an unaccountable surfeit overwhelmed me. A White-throated Sparrow was singing nearby and I turned from Woodpeckers to Sparrow. And aren't birders odd? I experienced a palpable sense of guilt in forsaking this splendid lifer for a view of a bird that abounds in every heath, hollow, and homestead for seven months out of every year in southern Pennsylvania. But I just got tired of looking at those damned Woodpeckers. They didn't play the game according to the rules. They should have stayed for a decent interval of time, enough to give us good looks, and then with loud cackles flown away to parts unknown. We could then have lamented their early departure with the customary exclamations of regret. As it was, they stayed on and on and I, perforce, had to leave them. It was like the host going off to bed before his guests depart.

There was a small number of species, such as the Gray Jay and Spruce Grouse, of special interest to us because they are seldom if ever seen as far south as eastern Pennsylvania. Also, we could renew our romance with the loon. Several pairs nested on the two Wilson Ponds and it was a never-ending source of delight to listen to their eerie calls. Best of all, on the far shore of Upper Wilson there was a steep wooded hill, the haunt of that elusive nymph, Echo. The loons knew exactly the most advantageous range from shore to captivate this particular echo. They seemed to derive intense pleasure in listening to their own yodeling cries resounding from the hillside. They were like young children with a cherished toy. For us, it was two loons for one, always an unexpected bargain.

From a birding point of view, the greatest advantage of those summers in Maine was the opportunity to observe a number of species, known to us only in winter or migration, on their breeding grounds. We could study their nests and watch the rearing and feeding of the young. Our first year at Upper Wilson, for instance, a pair of Juncos had made their nest almost under the porch of the Camp before we arrived. It was well concealed in the side of a small hummock overhung by long grass. Had we come earlier, I'm sure they would never have built so close to the disturbing influence of the man animal. As it was, they had made their bed, so to speak, and had to lie in it. It was the only Junco nest we ever saw in Maine; they are not easy to find. Most of all, we learned to know the warblers. About seventeen species nested around Upper Wilson or within a few miles of the Camp. We could see Mourning Warblers every day and could watch that jet of flame, the Blackburnian, feeding its young. The Parulidae, the New World family of Warblers, is our favorite "tribe" of birds. It was our daily and intimate contact with these colorful sylphids that aroused the special interest we now feel for the warblers. Our shore birds are always neglected. Every spring and fall we make the most solemn vows that next season we'll spend more time at the shore, but when the months roll around we are always in the woods and fields of Gradyville looking for warblers. To paraphrase Faust outrageously, what doth my shore bird list profit me if it stand between me and the thing that I love?

One final incident and we can have done with the salad days of our birding. It happened at Tinicum, not Maine, and marks in a true sense the symbolic ending of an era for us. Late in the afternoon of October 29, 1960, we were walking the east dike of Tinicum Refuge. We saw this bird. It displayed the character-istic behavior of a flycatcher, had a bluish head, bright yellow belly, and its outer tail feathers were edged with white. The sun was beginning to set and long shadows were stealing over the marsh but we saw all these markings distinctly. Unlike our Maine Pileateds, the bird did not tarry long and the light was fast fading in any event. We had left our Peterson in the car and had only our mental notes to help us identify the species. We knew we had never seen it before but that was the extent of our knowledge. We rushed back to the marsh house and babbled out our tale to Joe Devlin. Joe Devlin in those days and for some years later represented the Father of American Ornithology to us. There was some vague talk in inner circles about an Alex-ander Wilson but we gave no credence to such canards. Joe sat like the proverbial graven image until we wound down. "What about the Western Kingbird?" he asked. "But that wouldn't be in Peterson," I replied. I meant, of course, the eastern field guide; we owned no western guide at that time. Joe said it would be in the book and he was right. We had seen our first "accidental" and our first truly western bird. It was a first record for Tinicum and we had done it all by ourselves—well, Joe may have helped a little but it was we who found it.

This little adventure evoked a disturbing and inchoate restlessness within us. Maybe it was the faraway magic of the word "western" that did it. From that moment on we began to long for distant places and strange birds. There was a ferment we had not known before.

III

The Conflagration

PART 1

The days that succeeded our sighting of the Western Kingbird at Tinicum led inevitably into winter, as November and December are apt to do. Neoteric man builds without windows but, thank God, the seasons still come and go outside his unfenestrated monstrosities. We recorded only four lifers that winter of 1960–1. Among these was the Common Teal, seen twice at Tinicum and once at Brigantine. In the event some unwary nonbirder may have become enmeshed in the snare of this birding chronicle, I should point out that the Common Teal is common only in the Old World; it is a rare visitant to North America. During the early spring of 1961 we added five more lifers, among which was the Prothonotary Warbler. Any normal person with a true set of values would be content merely to survive for an indefinite stretch of time after seeing a Prothonotary Warbler; it is a gorgeous hunk of bluish and gold. But, fortunately or unfortunately, listers are not normal people in the conventional sense of the word. They resemble more that Corinthian king, Sisyphus, condemned for all eternity to push his heavy stone uphill. The lister can never sink back in restful, contemplative bliss but is ordained forever to wander homeless over the face of the earth in pursuit: unremitting, soul-searing, mindless pursuit. Had I only the prescience to have looked more closely at my "gateway to the unknown" at Furness's in those early days, I should have seen, blazoned in letters of fire above that innocent-looking portal, the Dantean inscription: "Through me the way among the people lost. Abandon hope all ye who enter here!" If, perhaps, but only perhaps, this dreadful decree appears a mite too extreme, as applied to sinless but lost listers, certainly those nostalgic lines of Keats, so dear to tremulous, impressionable youth, are not. You will recall that in the frieze of Keats' Grecian Urn a youth pursues a maiden forevermore, in unrequited love: ". . . though thou hast not thy bliss, for ever wilt thou love and she be fair." The unhappy fate of the lister probably lies somewhere between hell and that luckless youth of the Grecian Urn. At all odds, I trust I have "established" one point and adumbrated another by these sledgehammer blows, oblique though they may be. First, that the author is a jolly old gentleman steeped in classical lore; his age alone could be calculated roughly by that Tarkingtonian phrase, "tremulous, impressionable youth." Second, that Marybelle and I were tired of the town and wanting the sea. To put it in brutally plain words: we wanted lifers. Not just "a" lifer, as did modest George Spitalny, but dozens of lifers, lots of lifers, millions of lifers! We were goners.

So we planned our first birding trip—to Florida, of course. Where else do all east coast birders eventually gravitate to? I sometimes think that come the Götterdämmerung of the birding world, the heroes of the Brotherhood, in North America at least, will choose to remain in either Florida or California. To them Valhalla is only a name and the Valkyrie, it is well known, are not birds. In preparation we did no real planning or letter writing for we knew no one in Florida or en route. We did have Pettingill's *A Guide to Bird Finding East of the Mississippi* and Peterson's *A Field Guide to the Birds* and a Lark station wagon. We also had a good deal of enthusiasm, and although this commodity is absolutely essential to a successful birding trip, contact with local birders would have been more practical in the end. In retrospect, however, I like it just the way we did it. We were again on our own. Besides, it is much more fun to discover your own birds than to have some expert lead you by the nose; albeit, we have blessed these experts many a time on later trips. If the ungarnished truth be told, lifers were chiefly a means to an end on this first trip of ours. The end was birding adventures amidst new scenes and climes. I am even proud of the snail-like pace we set those first few days after leaving home. We explored the land, took time to see beyond the roadside. We left Philadelphia with our list of 252 birds early on the morning of June 6, 1961, and the day's end found us no farther than Pocomoke City, Maryland. We birded the lower Pocomoke Swamp all the next day. Consequently, it took us three days to reach Virginia. When we did leave Maryland, though, we had drunk three toasts in rum to our three new birds and, thereby, established a ritual to which we have ever since rigidly adhered. A new bird is not an official lifer to us until its entry has been consecrated by a toast, preferably in rum. Lest an eyebrow or two be elevated at this plebeian ceremony of ours, allow me to state that lifers have never been so plentiful within the space of a single day as to leave us "stoned." As a matter of fact, there has been many a day that I have longed for besottedness. No, our intoxication was of a different kind.

It is not my intention to give a blow by blow account of this first birding trip or systematically record in chronological sequence our acquisition of new birds. Each lifer was a thrilling experience to us, naturally, but thrills of this sort do not lend themselves to summation. An accomplished, sophisticated writer wouldn't even attempt it and certainly I won't. Frankly, I should probably become surfeited before the reader. So let us leave that exquisite palette of color, the Painted Bunting, flitting about the storied plantations of Wilmington, North Carolina, and proceed forthwith to the Seewee Supply Co., situated on Route 17 some thirty miles or so above Charleston, South Carolina.

Bachman's Warbler was our major goal on this first trip as it has been for countless others before and after us. It is the rarest passerine nesting bird in North America and its summer home is limited to deep forests and impassable cypress swamps in the South. Furthermore, its song somewhat resembles that of the Parula Warbler, which also shares these forbidding regions; vocally, the two are easily confused by the uninitiated. Long before leaving home I had read page 502 of Pettingill's eastern book so often that I knew it by heart. It states that the Fairlawn Plantation, owned by one Hugh Belser, is the one place in South Carolina where Bachman's Warbler may be found. You have only to inquire at the Seewee Supply Co., ask for Mr. Belser, and the keys of the place are yours. Pettingill brings coals to Newcastle by adding, "Listen for it, and look for it just inside the locked gate . . ." The shivers that went over me every time I read that line, sitting snugly at home that winter of 1961! Well, we located the Seewee Supply Co. right enough, a despairingly dingy shack with a few melted, flyspecked candy bars arranged in an untidy heap in an antiquated glass showcase. Although out of their bailiwick, I halfway expected to see Ruthy and Winfield Joad straining with flattened noses against the glass case. There were a few rows of canned goods on the shelves and a well-worn ice chest for soft drinks. What else the place supplied I never found out. All this was of supreme unimportance, however. The anemic-looking young man behind the counter was the object of my undivided attention. He would be the first link in the concatenation of events that would lead us unerringly to Bachman's Warbler. Oh blissful ignorance!

A detailed account of our Bachman's Warbler fiasco would make dreary reading and only harrow my own soul needlessly. If we had only arrived earlier or had had a local birding contact! So let us creep through the pathetic affair with the minimum of wailing. The net result of my frequently interrupted parleys with the young man behind the counter was to learn that the elder Hugh Belser was dead and that one of his sons must be contacted for permission to enter the plantation. Where were the sons and how could I reach them? It took two full days for that energetic youth to find out absolutely and literally nothing! And all the time the chiggers and mosquitoes were exacting a frightful toll as we foraged the area between conferences. On the third day I discovered, inadvertently, that one of Hugh Belser's sons was a physician in Charleston but, needless to say, it was not that human dynamo at the Seewee Supply Co. that volunteered this information. Dr. Ritchie Belser was most co-operative and, indeed, actually offered me the keys to that same arcanal gate. A round trip to Charleston would have taken too much time, however, so we declined the offer and proceeded on foot to the heart of the plantation. We lingered a whole day on the hallowed ground but Bachman's was either gone or had stopped singing, probably both. The writing on the wall was only too plain. There was not even the titillation of a singing Parula to quicken our pulse. We had had it by this time and even climbing and reclimbing the gate no longer held any allure for me; it was just the same on one side as the other. We had spent almost three days waiting and one day searching and the bird was not there.

The following day we left the Seewee Supply Co. and the Fairlawn Plantation for good. However, before heading south for Charleston, we turned off on the dirt road that ends at Moore's Landing, hoping to see a Red-cockaded Woodpecker. This small detour proved to be the anticlimax of our shattering failure. On one of the utility poles along this road we spied a sign, manifestly homemade. Scrawled on this miserable piece of cardboard were these fateful words: Bachman's Warbler seen here May 16. What did we do? What else could we do with those mocking words searing our fretting souls deeper and deeper—we patrolled the area the better part of the day. The day was June 12 and we had no real hope of seeing the bird, but we were trapped like moths at a light. It could have been a hoax, but subsequent correspondence with Mr. Ellison A. Williams, a local authority on the birds of the Charleston area, inclines me to believe the notice was genuine. It also may have spelled doom for the bird—professional collectors are a ruthless lot with no more scruples than a CIA official. As we made our final exit amid the jeers and hoots of the Furies, I bethought myself of that statement in Bent's *Life Histories of the Warblers* to the effect that a pair of Bachman's Warblers was present all during the breeding season one year at Indianapolis. The elusive pair that haunted my boyhood home so long ago seemed no more remote to me at this time than did the bird of May 16, 1961. I recalled the story of the Blue Flower—perhaps I should never have left home.

Our ignominious retreat from Charleston would have warmed Jeff Davis's heart but we had learned one thing. Namely, do not attempt to see rare species without local, on-the-spot assistance if it is available. Find out in advance, if possible, who knows about the bird and also the best time of year to look for it. George Spitalny had preceded us to Florida by one year, not in his own car, to be sure, but with an older friend. Although George was certainly no authority on Florida birds, his experiences and suggestions were a great help to us on our trip. For instance, while at Clewiston, Florida, on the south shore of Lake Okeechobee, we hunted in vain for the Smooth-billed Ani, a "frumious" bird that always looks as though its tail was stuck on with glue. A much folded and worn scrap of dirty paper I carried in my wallet contained random notes given to me by George. Sure enough, there it was: Ani—see George Espenlaub. We located Mr. Espenlaub in his big shed where he kept his swamp buggy and accumulated junk. I had scarcely explained our mission when he stepped to the big open door and pointed up to a tree.

Three Smooth-billed Anis were perched there as big as life. Spitalny had also told us, "See Uncle Joe at his fish camp for the Everglade Kite." Uncle Joe, it turned out, was an expert on the whereabouts of this rare Kite, although I should never have thought of hiring a fishing guide to see a bird. Uncle Joe showed us five Everglade Kites and we must have watched them for fully an hour extracting snails from their shells. At that time, it was estimated that only about eight of these birds were extant in Florida. It was a day of excitement for us and I only wished once more that Marybelle and I had been able to produce that Yellow-bellied Flycatcher for George. Five Everglade Kites to no Yellow-bellied Flycatcher was a grossly disproportionate score.

In the adventure of the Spot-breasted Oriole, though, we took George's notes too literally. This bird, a native of Central America, had been introduced into the Miami area some years previous to our Florida trip. At the present date it is widely spread throughout much of Dade County and the last time we were in Miami we saw a number at several places. In 1961, however, the bird was confined to a few parks and especially, according to George, the grounds surrounding the main public library. The library is pretty much in the center of town, as I recall, and we had some difficulty finding a suitable parking place for the car. We had to walk a block or two through busy thoroughfares to reach the library. In those days, our shabby field clothes and binoculars made us rather conspicuous objects. Our every movement seemed to arouse further suspicion from the hordes of people sitting on benches or just walking through the grounds. By this time we had begun to place so much reliance upon George's infallibility that we were reduced to compliant vassals accepting without demur his slightest admonition. If George said the Spot-breasted Oriole was to be found on the south side of the library, that was unquestionably the locale. After minutes of perambulating back and forth on the south grounds, I began, nevertheless, to feel some misgivings. Just suppose that in some wild frenzy of abandon or some caprice of unknown origin those orioles had decided to migrate north to the other side! As I was mulling over this daring speculation, I noticed an old gentleman sitting on one of the benches reach over and pluck at his neighbor's sleeve. The man lowered his newspaper and both of them were staring at us. That settled it. I would put my migration hypothesis to the test, George or no George. I cannot rightfully say we slunk away, our movement was too swift; it might best be described as an expeditious shamble. And when we reached the north side of the library, we didn't have long to wait—the orioles were there. It was most gratifying to see one's bold theory vindicated in so short a time. We very prudently left by the north side, but not before I had looked behind to see if someone in uniform was following us.

From Miami we explored the Keys all the way to Key West. We were particularly hoping to see that glamour bird, the Roseate Spoonbill, a large wader with bright pinkish wings and underparts and an incredible bill. We had almost given up when, on our return journey north from Key West, we spotted two of these birds on Bahia Honda Key. I drank an extra big toast to them that evening. We saw most of the regular summer residents of south Florida and the Keys: Mangrove Cuckoo, White-crowned Pigeon, Gray Kingbird, Great White Heron, and Black-whiskered Vireo.

After the Keys we spent three days at Everglades National Park. We were so busy scanning the sky and marshes for Sandhill Cranes that most of the other species we "needed" were sadly neglected. We saw no Sandhill Cranes on the trip. In retrospect it was a lesson to us that he who covets one lifer above another may end up with none. A construction crew with pneumatic hammers and countless other tools of the devil were at work on Anhinga Trail and not one Purple Gallinule appeared. It was a bitter blow to us, for this bird, so we had been told, was impossible to miss on Anhinga Trail. For some unaccountable reason I am still at a loss to explain, we never even thought about the Short-tailed Hawk; Everglades Park is the prime spot for this rare bird. The three Flamingos, reported there the year before, had been routed by a hurricane that fall and were gone. All and all, our first trip to Everglades Park was a resounding bust. Incredible as it may seem to an experienced birder, not one single lifer did we garner in the Everglades. Besides, it was murderously hot and the "air conditioner" we had in our motel at Homestead would not have lowered the temperature of one cubic millimeter of air more than half a degree at the most. The Everglades is a superb wildlife sanctuary and if the Army Corps of Engineers would only disband and drown itself to the last man in one of its ten thousand canals, it just possibly might last a few years longer. But, somehow, the Everglades and we did not hit it off that summer of 1961. My last attempt to pluck a lifer from this desiccated inferno of grass and sun was a masterpiece of futility. As we headed west along the Tamiami Trail I would stop every five miles or so, get out of the car, and walk up and down the road scanning the endless expanse of grass to the south for the Cape Sable Sparrow. It was early afternoon and must have been 110° in the shade. Need I go on?

Corkscrew Sanctuary and Sanibel Island were havens of delight after the Everglades. Corkscrew was extremely dry that summer, though, and some of the nesting species were very scarce, at least along the boardwalk trail. My old acquaintance of bygone days, the Wood Stork, was there in fair numbers, however. He looked much more at home in Corkscrew Sanctuary than he did in central Indiana. He was not now a lifer, however, for we had first spotted a group of these big characters south of Orlando on the way down. Our single lifer at Corkscrew was a very old friend indeed, none other than the Barred Owl. As you will recall, we had seen the Barred Owl several times and heard him many times in Maine even before we began birding. Furthermore, every fall and spring for a number of years there was a Barred Owl at Furness's and we often heard his roisterous hooting from our house, but we had never seen him sitting in broad daylight at close range. At Corkscrew he sat regarding us with those big brown eyes, looking for all the world like a wizened old woman wearing a gray shawl. We really should have counted this bird long before but we were trying to play the game according to the "rules," i.e., all field marks in good light. There is a bit of foolishness, if not downright chicanery, in adhering too rigidly to sight identification rather than sound in counting lifers and I hope to bring this issue more in focus later on.

My most intimate contact with this feathered hobgoblin, the Barred Owl, occurred one night at the Upper Camp in Maine. I had not been in bed long before I heard a Barred Owl calling from the "lagoon," a small pond near the Camp. I padded out on bare feet to the back steps and gave my best imitation, none too good, of the Barred Owl call. I repeated this several times and the owl returned my challenge with a right good will. We continued this antiphonic nonsense for some minutes when, suddenly, the real owl stopped calling. All I could hear was the just perceptible rustling of the leaves in the big yellow birch immediately overhead. "I sure hooted him down," I thought. "The coward!" Just then, not ten feet above my head, that owl let me have it! I froze a fraction of a second and then fell backwards up the steps. Again he sounded off. I was too astonished to be terrified and too terrified to be astonished. I was simply fluid jelly. Once more! I felt, as someone has so aptly described it, like a mouse inside a very active fiddle. He left then, and I could see his great bulk as he rose against the sky, so close. He had blasted the pusillanimous man thing with just those first eight hoots. Why tarry? That is when I should have counted the Barred Owl. But, on the other hand, I was more his lifer than he mine. Perhaps that is why I waited till that moment in Corkscrew Sanctuary. Daylight had given me courage.

We continued our trek up the west coast of Florida picking up a lifer now and then. We particularly enjoyed St. Marks National Wildlife Refuge on the Gulf, where we finally saw our first Purple Gallinule, with two Red-cockaded Woodpeckers thrown in as a bonus. We had decided by this time to go as far as Rockport, Texas, a famous birding area, and to try to see in the nearby Aransas Wildlife Refuge the three immature Whooping Cranes that had, so we were told, not flown north with the others.

A few miles below Houston en route to the Rockport area, I spied on one of the roadside power lines a bird with long, trailing tail feathers. It just couldn't be, but it was! The car came to a screeching, crazy halt and I was out on the road frantically fumbling with my glasses before the wheels had literally stopped. The car behind me—I had not bothered to look in the mirror—also came to a skidding stop within three feet of our bumper. I heard the driver yelling something at me but I was too engrossed in yelling myself and gesticulating toward the bird to be more than half conscious of what particular, nasty insults were being hurled at me. When the instant of madness passed, I hastily turned to make my profoundest apologies to the car in back, and very nearly crashed into its occupant. He was a giant of a man wearing the inevitable ten-gallon hat. "Look, sonny," he said—he was at least twenty years younger than I—"The next time you want to look at them little wire birds, just put your flipper out and let other people know what you're aimin' to do!" I stammered out some words of hearty agreement to this flawless bit of advice but he was already getting into his car. As he pulled alongside he leaned over and said, "Remember what I told you, now. People down here figure they might as well keep on livin'." We always think of the Scissor-tailed Flycatcher as the "wire bird" and I've liked Texans ever since.

There were no Whooping Cranes at Aransas. Those immatures that had refused to leave with the others had been flown by plane within a few hundred miles of their northern breeding ground, Buffalo Wood Park. Let us hope they did not hijack the plane to foreign parts. We were bitterly disappointed; the Whoopers would have made our three hundredth lifer, a good round figure for this magnificent creature now tottering on the brink of extinction. The Long-billed Curlew proved to be our three hundredth bird, a satisfactory enough stand-in. Anyway, four years later on Christmas Eve day at Aransas we saw thirty-three Whooping Cranes out of the total, estimated population of forty-four birds. A Christmas gift indeed.

I called on Connie Hager to pay my respects and to find out where the birds were. Connie is a little slip of a woman who has made herself famous among the Brotherhood. She is Mrs. Birder on the coastal stretch of Texas. She met me at the door bare-footed and with a scimitar-like butcher knife in one hand. I must have started, for she said mildly enough, "I won't hurt you." And she didn't. Instead, she set us onto several excellent birds. One of them was the Least Grebe, a Mexican species that is now regularly reported along coastal Texas and also inland to some extent. And now, I think it's about time we hit the long trail home. The first trip had added fifty-nine new birds to our total North American list, making the total 311 lifers. We were now over halfway along the "Excelsior" road to the 600 Club, albeit there still was no actual Club as of that date. Besides, Texas is the birding empire of North America and we shall return many times to the Lone Star State as the years hurry each other along.

PART 2

After returning home that year of 1961, we recorded ten more life birds and in the spring another seven. The Little Gull, a straggler from Europe and a rare visitor in North America, was the most notable of the lot. A male Lark Bunting, a bird of the western Great Plains, was another unusual find for the east coast Brotherhood. It stayed all winter at a feeder near Valley Forge but we saw it in late April, when its contrasting plumage of black and white was beginning to show at the prenuptial molt. Before that time no one had any clear idea what the little drab, sparrow-like bird was. If it had been a female, it might still be a mystery bird, for it departed almost before its molt was completed. Despite the comparative rarity of the gull and the un-usual occurrence of the Lark Bunting, the prize bird to us was the Worm-eating Warbler. It is by no means an uncommon bird and nests in southeastern Pennsylvania, but up to the summer of 1961 we had missed it. Our first Worm-eating Warbler was perched on, of all things, a barbed-wire fence at Gradyville. I had fully expected that only by braving dense thickets of greenbrier would I ever see this bird. To celebrate the event we bought a box of candy to hand around to the other idlers at Tinicum marsh house that afternoon. I handed it to George to do the honors and, let it be stated here in all fairness, he scrupulously executed the commission. After that first round, though, both George and candy disappeared and when next I saw the box in the walled off partition behind, there was little but the familiar crumple of paper cups to mark our commemorative gesture in honor of the Worm-eating Warbler. If the good Dr. Watson had been the scrivener upon this occasion, he would have called it the "adventure of the candy-eating boy" rather than the adventure of the Worm-eating Warbler. Whatever the title, it was hardly a case that would have taxed the analytical genius of his famous friend.

But all at once it was May again, late May, and all but a few tardy migrants had passed on to the Pennsylvania mountains or the north country. The spring honking of the northbound geese had already stirred us with a nameless longing, an ache that could not be assuaged. Besides, we had seen but seventeen lifers in almost eleven months and we recalled the yet vivid experience of almost sixty new birds in a single month of that preceding summer. Some way, I was always humming to myself those words that had been part of a popular tune in the late forties, "faraway places with strange-sounding names." I had taken a sabbatical at the University of Michigan in 1949 and Marybelle and I had taken two weeks vacation in the Upper Peninsula, our first real vacation alone since we had been married. As we had rolled through the countryside north of Ann Arbor we both had sung these very same words out of pure lightness of heart and the incomparable feeling of freedom that a first vacation instills. Now, like the migrating birds, we were filled with the wanderlust again. As we used to say when I worked on the railroad and bummed rides on freight trains, there was gravel in our shoes. And so, our second birding trip.

This was to be a big one. We would go north through Michigan and "collect" Kirtland's Warbler; then west and south through the prairie states to the Edwards Plateau of Texas, where another warbler, the Golden-cheeked, would be waiting for us; on to the Rio Grande delta area for the fabulous Mexican species of that most southern point in the United States and then along the border to west Texas, the Davis Mountains, and Big Bend National Park, where the famous Colima Warbler would be ours. Silver City, New Mexico, would be next and then on to the Safford Mountains of Arizona and, if time was on our side, out to southern California and the west coast. I give this outline of our intended itinerary in advance so that our general route and main objectives will be clear. In the course of the narrative I shall omit many in-between places, and without this general plan of travel the reader might become as lost as we did on several occasions. Unless the writer is exceptionally gifted, I detest travelogue sequences and have sworn a solemn oath to eschew as much of that sort of aridity as the circumstances permit. But bear in mind, oh best beloved, that after all, in the cant of Gertrude Stein, trip is a trip is a trip . . .

We left home on May 27, 1962, and on the second day were in Kirtland's Warbler territory. An Upland Plover, perched on a fence post as Peterson had said it would be, was our first lifer of the trip, number 329. Much has been written on the vagaries, habits, and history of Kirtland's Warbler and those who are interested should consult Harold Mayfield's monograph on this species, published by the Cranbrook Institute in 1960. The bird's entire breeding area is confined to six or eight counties in the north-central portion of lower Michigan and its winter range is restricted to the Bahamas. Its summer breeding ground was not discovered until 1903, twenty-four years after its winter range had been established. The first specimen of this species was collected in the Bahamas in 1841 and the first specimen from the North American mainland was collected ten years later in spring migration near Cleveland, Ohio. It is rarely reported, however, in migration, chiefly because the total population in recent times has probably never exceeded fifteen hundred birds. Its numbers have declined precipitously during the last ten years, primarily because of increased parasitism by the Brown-headed Cowbird. The year before we made our first trip to Michigan 502 singing males were recorded, indicating a total adult population of just over a thousand birds. In 1971 only 201 singing males were recorded, a decrease of sixty percent in ten short years. Kirtland's Warbler is fast approaching that perilous limbo already inhabited by the Whooping Crane and California Condor.

Our first encounter with Kirtland's Warbler was uneventful but extremely rewarding. We did experience some difficulty, though, in seeing the bird well at first. The preferred habitat of Kirtland's Warbler is extensive stands of young jack pine with dense undercover. Oddly enough, the bird shuns those areas in which pines have grown to fifteen or more feet even though it actually builds its nest on the ground. Unless one is almost directly underneath the particular pine that harbors a singing male, the foliage is usually so thick that it blocks the view; yet always as one approaches, the bird retreats ever farther and farther away. We finally saw at least five singing males and could have seen more had we not felt the relentless hand of time pushing, forever pushing. We had scarcely been on the road three days and already I was breathing in prospect the crisp, rarified air of early morning on some high mountain peak in Arizona and could hear the pounding of the surf along the rocky coast of California. I'm the type that revels in the quiet, unhurried travels of a David Grayson but I am constitutionally unable to follow my own precepts when it is I who travel the "Friendly Road." But it was good to have at last seen this famous little bird of north central Michigan. I recalled only too well that day at Gradyville when my birding friends the Rigbys had laughed and reminisced over their trip to see Kirtland's Warbler. I felt as though I had been left behind to tend my sheep on some forgotten hillside while others journeyed to the

Holy Land. But now the good, brown needles of the jack pine were under our feet and above was the singing bird. Seney National Wildlife Refuge in the Upper Peninsula of Michigan was our next stop and the sun was already high in the east.

We reached Seney Refuge about noon on Memorial Day. I regret to say that I cannot recall the Manager's name, for he deserves every recognition. He was one of those rare individuals who wish to share the treasures of wilderness with other responsible people, instead of locking them up for a privileged few or a gang of gun-toting hunters in winter. He was leaving for the weekend, but took time from his packing to explain the Refuge to us and point out the most likely places for the birds we wanted to see. Seney Refuge has always been famous for its Yellow Rails and, of course, this was one of the birds we wanted to see. The other was the Sandhill Crane, which we had missed in Florida the year before. Before he left the Manager took a ring of keys from a desk drawer and dropped them into my eager hands. No gate was barred to us and, as Marybelle put it, we had been presented with the "keys to the wilderness." There was not another soul but ourselves that day or the next in all that vast expanse of forest, marsh, and field. The informality of it all was especially pleasing. When we were "tired of the place" we had only to drop the keys in the Refuge mailbox at the main entrance off the highway.

I hope we had the courtesy to thank that Manager properly but I've always had an unpleasant feeling that we did not. Oh, I'm sure we thanked him, of course, but we were so delirious over the prospects of exploring what lay beyond that first gate that our expressions of appreciation must have been, under the circumstances, rather perfunctory. The days were long at this time of year and we stayed on the Refuge until well after dark that first day, listening and looking for Yellow Rails. The Manager had thought it might be too early for Yellow Rails, for he had not heard any yet that year, and he was probably right. We neither heard nor saw the Yellow Rail during our stay at Seney; I clicked pebbles together until I was sick of the sound but, apparently, so were the Rails, for there was never an answering rally. I did not know it then, but for six more weary years I was doomed to wander over the length and breadth of the land clicking pebbles, forever and ever clicking pebbles. It was like Hercules calling for Hylas, only my quest was not for a youth but a diminutive yellow bird.

The Sandhill Cranes were much more cooperative. We saw ten or more of these big, red-topped birds in a grassy glade near a woods and large field. The place was called, of all unapt names, Chicago Farms! One does not associate farms with Chicago nor Chicago with a north Michigan wilderness. Nor could one associate Chicago with that evening! It was our mood, of course, in part, and the Arcadian setting, but Marybelle and I look back upon that time and place with a nostalgia that still aches and hurts. Only those who ken of Eden will understand. Being a modern ignoramus, I learned ever so long ago that God is dead. But that evening, in the solitude and mystery of the nonhuman world, with the shadows lengthening over the field, my faith was shaken, slightly. It came to me, I know not why, those piquant little lines of Thomas Edward Brown, so dear to the Veders and David Grayson. "Not God! in Gardens! when the eve is cool? Nay, but I have a sign: 'Tis very sure God walks in mine." I had a sign that evening—almost. Twentieth-century man, who prefaces every prayer with: "Oh, God, if there be a God . . . !" How much more exciting the universe would be if God, in truth, had never died. The mandates of science are a sorry substitute. Perhaps after man is gone, perhaps . . .

We spent the entire next day at Seney but added only three more lifers to our list. One of them was that evasive little wretch, Le Conte's Sparrow. There was so much to hear and see! Often that day we were guilty of the most irremissible of all sins—forgetting about the list. The next day we repented but it was too late. We deposited our "keys to the wilderness" in the Refuge box and headed west across the Upper Peninsula. Two years later we came to Seney again. I wish we had not. In these two brief years the Refuge had undergone "improvements" and the clarion cry was now "recreation." There was a different manager, a busy staff with all the appurtenances, and, worst of all, much of the Refuge was now barred to the public. And, I might add, there was plenty of "public" milling about. I had to "give reasons" for wanting the keys to the more secluded areas and when they were reluctantly given to me, I was told to be sure and return them before the office closed at five. We had lost our "keys to the wilderness." It was a minuscule intimation of our present predicament: mob activity in the parks. We enjoyed our second visit, naturally, but the magic was gone. It was more a social visit than otherwise. We had no sign.

Our next major objective was the Edwards Plateau of south-central Texas, the breeding home of the Golden-cheeked Warbler. The Golden-cheeked, like Kirtland's, is another one of those Warblers with a relatively small, circumscribed breeding range in North America. When we started on this trip, I swore a solemn oath that whatever else the gods presented us in the way of lifers, the three warblers—Kirtland's, Golden-cheeked, and Colima—must fall to our lances. It is quite a journey from northern Michigan to extreme southwestern Texas, but this was the irreducible core of the trip. The Golden-cheeked would be number two. Between Seney and Kerrville, Texas, the latter town being the operational center for our escalading of the Plateau, we saw ten more lifers. They were marvelous, but this is a story, not a list and so we shall on, on. I just can't ignore the Yellow-headed Blackbird, though. We saw our first one calmly standing on the edge of the pavement as we were about to enter Dawson, Minnesota. To an easterner who habitually thinks of blackbirds as black birds, a first view of the Yellow-headed is incredible. I just couldn't believe my eyes! Yes, I know it's a hackneyed expression, but just try and find me a better one. And, as if that yellow head isn't enough, the male has startling spots of white on the wings in flight! Yellow-headed Blackbirds are reported as vagrants from time to time in the east, but our blackbird luck has never been good.

We rolled into Kerrville on the fifth of June and ensconced

ourselves at a cozy motel with kitchenette. That afternoon I went into action. Not birding, you understand, but the necessary preliminaries. Pettingill speaks of both a Bell and a Davis Ranch as good localities for the Golden-cheeked. For no good reason at all we picked the Davis Ranch. Concerning the Davis Ranch, Pettingill states: "Permission to enter this property must be obtained from its owner, who manages the Louise Dress Shop, Water Street, Kerrville." It sounded like Bachman's and the Seewee Supply Co. all over again but amidst more pleasant surroundings. When I pushed open the tinkling door of the Louise Dress Shop the surroundings were, indeed, most charming. Two very pretty girls were engaged in adorning themselves with new finery and one of them was pirouetting in a new frock with a grace and allurement my masculine sensibilities told me at once the anemic youth at the Seewee Supply Co. would have been totally incapable of. Things looked most propitious. Besides, the two salesgirls were not bad at all, not bad at all! Even should the Golden-cheeked Warbler elude me, I thought, my efforts this time would not have been wholly wasted. Such is the male creature, even an old one.

One of the salesgirls detached herself from the little group and eyeing me with only the barest hint of disapproval—my field clothes were, I suppose, just a trifle incompatible with the decor of the place—asked the inevitable, "What can I do for you?" I explained the situation and asked for Mr. Davis. Mr. Davis, it seems, had sold his ranch and quit the dress shop. Did she know who owned the ranch now? No, she didn't. Did the other salesgirl? No, the other salesgirl did not but she thought Elsie might. Elsie would be back at four o'clock. (I don't really remember that third girl's name but Elsie is a good, sensible name and will do well enough.) Apparently, we had reached a temporary impasse and already my jaunty feeling of confidence had appreciably diminished. Marybelle and I had several hours to kill before Elsie would return to the shop, so we decided to try to locate the Bell Ranch and have a go at it. And would you believe it, I left this oasis of the beau monde in the heart of

Texas without one backward glance at those two pretty girls. Admittedly, I was shaken. It was this accursed Seewee hex still dogging our steps! Why did every plantation or ranch owner from South Carolina to Texas have to up and die or move away just before we put in an appearance? As I got back in the car, I was grumbling fretfully about outdated guides to bird finding and the instability of ranch owners.

Somehow, we never did find the Bell Ranch. It was not only the conspiracy of silence we met on every hand but also our own ineptitude. At the most likely place, although the name Williams was on the mailbox, I started to climb the locked gate but two man-eating dogs, each bigger than a pony, descended on me. I dropped back on my side of the gate and let them bark and moan for fully five minutes. Surely this racket should attract the attention of someone in the house. It didn't. To this day I am convinced that the occupants were waiting for me to brave those dogs in the gruesome expectation of enjoying their own private Roman carnival. There was nothing to do but return to the dress shop. Elsie was there—beautiful, wonderful Elsie! She was not pretty in that fatuous worldly sense that had captivated my cruder sensibilities only a few hours before. She had a beauty transcending the things of the flesh—she knew all about the old Davis Ranch. People named Evans now owned it and Mr. Evans owned a supermarket in Kerrville. She thought it likely Mr. Evans would be home at this hour and told us just how to get to the ranch. A veritable dream girl was Elsie.

Mr. Evans, as it turned out, was not home but his wife was. I asked permission to look for birds on their ranch the next day, and though Mrs. Evans consented reluctantly, she did consent. The next day we had the run of that whole beautiful place. Before we started out on the ranch, Mr. Evans cautioned us at such length about rattlesnakes and pantomimed so vividly several of his own narrow escapes that I began to suspect he was using this ploy to discourage us. He did not know my appetitive craving for the Golden-cheeked Warbler or he might have saved his breath. Besides, his wife had given her promise. Thus we entered the lair of vipers. Actually, we were extremely careful, for there is no nonsense about a rattler. An old friend of mine had nearly died from a rattlesnake bite in this very same Texas years ago. But not one snake of any kind did we see that entire day.

The ranch had several good-sized juniper-clad hills, the favorite habitat of the Golden-cheeked. Almost before we were well into the ranch we heard a male singing but could never locate the bird. Our first Golden-cheeked proved to be a female stuffing food down the throat of a fledgling Brown-headed Cowbird. We could only hope that there were young warblers, too, receiving like attention. We soon became familiar with the Golden-cheeked's song and eventually saw at least four males. Before the day was over we also added the following lifers: Black-tailed Gnatcatcher, Rock and Canyon Wrens, Rufous-crowned Sparrow, and, best of all, the Black-capped Vireo. This Vireo in the United States breeds only in cedar-oak thickets in central and western Texas and is a difficult bird to find. We were fortunate in seeing two of these birds at very close range. I wanted very much to hear their song but they were most unobliging in this respect. The ranch had small herds of several species of African antelopes but they were extremely wary and seldom did we catch more than a glimpse of them far up on the hills. Peacocks abounded also and were continually startling us with their weird cries. We ate our sandwiches by the side of a small pool in the shade of an oak and enjoyed ourselves thoroughly that day. I had now seen two of my three coveted warblers. If only the Colima would behave, the trip would be eminently successful so far as I was concerned.

We have been back to the Edwards Plateau and Kerrville twice since that June 6, 1962, but never again on the Evans Ranch. I wrote to the Evanses upon our return home, thanking them for their kindness. Before other birding trips to Kerrville, I also wrote letters asking for permission to bird their ranch again. I received no replies. The last time we were in Kerrville they still owned the ranch and the supermarket still bore their name. But what could be gained by personal confrontation after those silent rebuffs? In my heart, I do not blame them; I also should be loath to let strangers have the run of my own ranch. There are just too many irresponsible fools abroad today seeking what and whom they may devour. But it does hurt a little and angers utterly that trust is so often withheld in our present-day society because of the marauding few. Or is it a few? Personally, I'm getting damn sick and tired of rampant evasion of responsibility, both between nations and between individuals. Of course, such ranting is platitudinous, but think it over nevertheless. Just being alive is not ipso facto guarantee of a place in the sun. The average man today never blames himself. There is always a transference to mask his guilt, be it race, age, sex, background, or just society at large. Our mechanistic eighteenth-century heritage and today's scientific determinism have warped our judgment. God's death is no excuse for personal immorality—if we are to continue to be men in the animistic sense of the term. Yes, I know, in a few inapposite sentences the birding trail has been left far behind. This book apparently is fated to alternate between moods of light-hearted persiflage and "thus sayeth the preacher" fulminations. In the despair born of concurrent love and hate there seems to be no other recourse. Man has always wept a little and laughed a little, else he would have destroyed himself long ago.

There are two famous National Wildlife Refuges in the lower Rio Grande Valley of south Texas, Laguna Atascosa and Santa Ana. Laguna is large and part of it borders the Gulf; Santa Ana is much smaller and is bound on one side by the Rio Grande itself. Laguna has rattlesnakes; Santa Ana, apparently, does not. The two Refuges share many birds in common; each, especially Santa Ana, has a few species of its own. There is no lister of note who has not birded both these Refuges at least once. The birds are characteristically Mexican and certain species are found nowhere else north of the border, except, of course, occasionally in nearby areas like Bentsen State Park. There is so much excitement and novelty in birding these Refuges for the first time and so many lifers gleaned that I really cannot do justice to either place, let alone both, by describing in detail our first visit. One is torn between the twin rocks of dispassionately recording a list or describing each momentous experience in detail. Neither suits the design of this book. We have birded both places several times since the 1962 trip and perhaps our last trip, in the winter of 1971, will be the most opportune occasion to describe the bird life of these Refuges more fully. Suffice it to say now that we saw thirteen new birds at Laguna Atascosa and eight at Santa Ana on the 1962 trip. At Santa Ana we were unable to cover the area adequately because the Manager was away; the entrance gate was locked and all birding had to be done on shanks' mare. The last afternoon at Santa Ana we walked a total of five hours and saw only one new bird, the White-collared Seed Eater. I've seldom been so hot and exhausted! Marybelle and I call this sort of birding "bogging it"—bullheaded, unrewarding, obstinate perseverance.

Before leaving the lower Rio Grande Valley, we stopped at Bentsen State Park because we had heard that a pair of Rose-throated Becards was nesting there. The Becard, sometimes pronounced Bécard, sometimes Becárd, is the only representative of its family that, occasionally, breeds north of the border; it is quite a plum in the birder's pie. Besides, its nest is a fantastic affair, a big pendant sack, well worth seeing in itself. As we approached the superintendent's house, there were a number of small doves flying in and out of the shrubbery. These proved to be Inca Doves, a lifer for us, and I rejoiced because I had not expected to find this dove of the arid southwest so far "east." We had yet to learn of the Inca curse! The superintendent and his wife, both expert birders of the area, gave us directions for finding the Becard's nest but added the chilling comment that the birds had not been seen for a week or so and, maybe, had left the nest. As we stood talking on the wide veranda of the house, the dolorous coo-coo, coo-coo of the Inca Dove slowly but inexorably began to intrude itself into our talk. The superintendent must have noticed my flagging attention because he abruptly said, "You know the old legend of the Inca Dove, don't you?" I didn't, and I had a vaguely uneasy premonition that I did not want to, either. The legend, such as it is, is simply that the call of the Inca Dove has always been translated by desert folk as "No hope—No hope—No hope." The "No hope" of the Inca, supposedly, is the last sound the thirst-crazed wanderer ever hears in the trackless wastes of the burning desert. With that blithesome little knell ringing in our ears, we set out for the Becard's nest. We sat on the ground and watched that nest all morning but to no avail. Nothing remotely resembling our picture of the Becard ever came near the nest. And all the time, like the beating of a tom-tom, the incessant calling of the Inca Dove, "No hope—No hope—No hope!" It was more like a wake than a watch. For the record, however, I wish to state that since that day at Bentsen we have heard the Inca Dove a number of times—and the Inca curse *can* be broken. But that is another story.

Marybelle and I fell in love with the Davis Mountains of Texas and the town of Alpine at their southern extremity. Six years later we found the mountains much the same but Alpine was in the process of "expanding." Better the town than the mountains, of course, but inevitably the Davis Mountains will suffer too. So often in our more recent birding trips we have returned to memory-sanctified spots only to find "expansion," "improvements," "recreation areas," or the "Abominable Snowman"—snowmobiles, that spawn of the devil. Why is it that so many obnoxious contrivances make noise? Is it cause or effect? Anyway, I'm not at all sure that I would relish a third visit to the Davis Mountains; it might be sad beyond endurance.

We had come the first time to Alpine because it is one of the two jumping-off places for Big Bend and, to us, the Colima Warbler. We birded the relatively cool Davis Mountains for two days before descending into the west Texas inferno that lies between Alpine and the Chisos Mountains. We added fourteen lifers from the Davis Mountains, among which were such prizes as Vermillion Flycatcher, Pyrrhuloxia, Violet-green Swallow,

Hepatic Tanager, and Black-headed Grosbeak. At dawn on the third day we started off on the eighty-odd miles across the desert to Big Bend. Southwest Texas is an awesome land in summer with its scorching desert floor and jagged islands of mountain peaks. We had no "adventure" on the way and I, for one, was glad. I was born a redhead, alas, and the sun and I are ancient foes. For all that, I love the desert and its stark, overpowering desolation. There is no nonsense about the desert. If only I had feathers or fur or a decent skin.

That evening at Big Bend we walked down to the corral to make arrangements for a guide and horses to take us up to Boot Spring the next day, the prime breeding ground of the Colima Warbler. On the way over we were fortunate in obtaining a very close view of the Black-chinned Sparrow, an uncommon Junco-like sparrow of the southwest. I have known birders who went to Big Bend and saw the Colima but missed the Black-chinned Sparrow. At least if we missed the warbler, we should have the sparrow as a consolation prize. There was no difficulty in getting a guide and horses, and we were told to be there at dawn. Marybelle had had a few youthful experiences with horses in Colorado, but my sole acquaintance with this long-headed, mile-high quadruped was a single turn around a small track at a slow, sedate walk. I laid great stress on our ignorance of horses and riding but the owner of the concession made light of all such protestations and assured me we would be as safe on his horses as in my rocking chair back home. I have no rocking chair either at home or elsewhere but I was in no mood to take umbrage at so oblique and casual a reference to my creaking joints. We had several big Texas hamburgers for supper, and although I suppose I should have dreamed of huge flocks of Colimas eating bread crumbs out of my hand, I didn't dream at all. That allusion to my rocking chair, however, still rankled a wee bit.

We were at the corral in that mysterious moment between dawn and sunrise. Lynn, our young guide, met us, looking very sleepy indeed. While he was saddling the horses, it was growing lighter and from above suddenly came a shrill series of swallow-like twitterings. They were not swallows, however, but a small flock of White-throated Swifts. It was a lifer for us and most startling to eastern birders familiar only with the all-dark Chimney Swift. What is more to the point, it was our four hundredth bird! I had imagined the night before that the Colima would be our four hundredth bird but neither of us voiced protest over this alteration in the tally.

I got on my horse some way and I saw Marybelle was on hers. Lynn had positioned my horse, Brownie, with his starboard flank near a wall, undoubtedly in the dread expectation that I should attempt to mount on the wrong, right, side. Marybelle's horse was a trim-looking animal compared to Brownie and Lynn told her it was a quarter horse. And now you know more about Star than I do, except Lynn did mention that Star was more of a thoroughbred, or words to that effect. As things turned out, we could have wished that Star had been only a plodding nag. I shall say little of our ascent, for nothing remarkable happened, unless the mere fact that I kept my seat be considered in itself momentous. It is a six-mile trail up to Boot Spring, situated on the east side of Emory Mountain, and Lynn stopped the procession at Laguna, a mountain meadow, for a rest. This diversion was also uneventful, except that when Marybelle and I dismounted our limbs were so stiff that our movements for a few seconds resembled those of a quaint Pawnee Indian dance I had once seen in a movie. From Laguna to Boot Spring, Marybelle experienced no little difficulty in keeping Star on the go. He stopped every half minute to nibble stuff as though he were in the last stages of starvation. Lynn was not the man to be put off by Star's vagaries, though, and he quickened the beast in some unobtrusive but effective way that kept Star right at Brownie's heels for the rest of the trip. When we finally reached Boot Spring, Lynn told us where the Colima was usually seen and how to get there. He did not go with us but stayed behind to look after the horses and, we discovered later, to get some shut eye. Lynn was a likable young fellow, a superb horseman and good guide, so we did not begrudge him his siesta. It was more fun to bird by ourselves anyway.

The Colima Warbler derives its name from the locality where it was first discovered—Colima, Mexico—in 1889. The first North American record of this warbler was in 1928, the twelfth all told at that date, at this very same Boot Spring in the Chisos Mountains. It is not a colorful bird, as many North American warblers are, and is actually one of the more drab members of the family. The two obvious things that endear it to all birders, both pros and listers, are the remoteness of its North American breeding range in the Chisos Mountains and the limited area involved. As we stood in the narrow little canyon Lynn had pointed out to us and looked back over the long journey from Philadelphia to Seney to the Edwards Plateau to the lower Rio Grande Valley to Big Bend, we felt literally out of this world and its times. Those who stand on the summit of Mt. McKinley can boast a greater distance and a whole gamut of canonical adventures we shall never experience—but adventure is an attitude. It's an abstraction and, therefore, a peculiarly human attribute. Animals, other than man, probably do not have adventures. Adventure has its raison d'être in the temper of the man, not in the deed. Irrespective of one's definition of adventure, however, remoteness lends enchantment to any endeavor. And thus it was with two effete easterners in the high and far-off Chisos that day.

We spent almost three hours in and around Boot Spring before we saw our first Colima Warblers. We had not yet begun to despair but we did experience a growing concern. It is one thing to miss the Mourning Warbler in spring migration on your own home grounds; it is quite another to miss a real quest bird at the "ends of the earth." There is a finality about the latter eventuality that weakens and destroys. We kept listening for the song of the Colima but the birds were not singing. It was the middle of June and, probably, singing was only done in the early morning hours if at all. We were finally alerted to their presence by the call notes, which are rather distinctive once heard. It was a bit ironic that we should have risen before dawn to see our first Colima exactly at high noon. Our total was only three but I was rapturously content. We should have been there in late April or May, of course. I also experienced my first "buck fever." When we did locate our first Colima, my glasses were shaking so badly that, like the novice hunter, I was forced to lower them until I regained control of my adrenalin output. Fortunately, the Colima is a rather leisurely little bird in its activities and this one did not fly away.

The Colima Warbler was our 404th bird. At Boot Spring we also saw our first Acorn Woodpecker, Blue-throated Humming-bird, Black-eared Bushtit, and Hutton's Vireo. We had lunch in a secluded spot and foraged about afterward for an hour or so but did not see any more warblers. All in all, we were elated at the success of our safari, but tired, too, from the strain of watching and waiting. Lynn thought it about time to start back and we offered no protest.

The trail down from Boot Spring is a long series of mountain-side switchbacks. Before beginning the actual descent, Lynn got off his lead horse to tighten and inspect the saddle girths. Down we went, Lynn first, I next, and Marybelle and Star last. Brownie was most deliberate on the hairpin turns and would frequently pause and shuffle his forefeet around to make sure no loose stone was underfoot. Star, on the other hand, sensed the return trail home and the good, green hay; he repeatedly tried to push past Brownie at every turn. It was a bit harrowing for Marybelle and me but Lynn made nothing of it, so we gradually gained confidence in the brutes. I have really never liked horses and neither Brownie nor Star did anything that day to dispel this prejudice of mine. Star, on the contrary, exerted himself at every opportunity to intensify my disaffection.

We had reached comparatively level ground and had stopped to have a last look at our route of descent. And then it happened! I heard a terrifying thud and a dreadful groan, the memory of which was to haunt me for days. Marybelle was flat on her back and, obviously, in great pain and shock. Neither

Lynn nor I had seen it happen but from the sound of the fall it could be nothing trivial. Apparently Marybelle, in a transport of pure joy and abandonment at the success of the day, had thrown out her arms to utter some words of delight, and the gesture had startled the horse. When breath returned and all of us were more composed, Marybelle found that she could stand and walk, very painfully, but still walk. She could not ride, for the pain was too great, so all of us walked back that last two miles or so in the blazing heat of the afternoon sun. I didn't feel like riding and Lynn, who was almost as distraught as I, would not ride if we were to walk. Lynn as our guide was technically responsible for mishaps of this sort, I suppose, but, of course, there was nothing he could have done and I felt sorry for his very evident distress. I said nothing at all about the accident when I paid the bill at the corral. That triumphant day of fun and exultation had suddenly become a nightmare; the closest physician was ninety miles away at Alpine.

Neither of us slept much that night, and I had the car packed well before dawn. It was a shame that we couldn't enjoy that ride across the desert in the early cool of the morning. I do recall, however, the mile-long shadows of the mountains reaching out over the still, ghostly land and there were several big rattlesnakes to guide the car around. You can imagine my relief when the doctor at Alpine pronounced no broken bones or internal injuries, only bad bruises and minor lacerations. Relief was short-lived, however, for by the time we got to Silver City, New Mexico, two days later Marybelle was becoming very short of breath at the slightest exertion. I rushed her to a private clinic there in Silver City, jumping several curbs in my frantic attempt to find the entrance drive, and by the time the doctor got to her she was markedly cyanotic. The final diagnosis was three ribs broken and one pleural cavity punctured—hence the shortness of breath. At the altitude of Silver City, there is approximately a twenty-five percent oxygen deficit. This was the extent of the damage; there were no visceral injuries. Our real worries were over but it was a dreary prospect for Marybelle—four days in the hospital at Silver City and several weeks before the ribs and bruises stopped hurting. The Colima Warbler had been our most nerve-wracking and expensive lifer to date. But, as Marybelle said, it could have been worse. Suppose we had not even seen it!

I had four days to "hero" it alone at Silver City while Marybelle was in the hospital—Cherry Creek Canyon in the Pinos Altos Mountains, Signal Peak, Gila River bottoms, Little Walnut Ranger Station, the whole works. By the fifth day, when Marybelle was discharged from the hospital, I had specific locations for most of the lifers and consequently was able to show her all but a few. The latter desiderata she has picked up readily enough on subsequent western trips. Marybelle's doctor wished her to remain for check-ups several days more, so we spent a total of nine days in Silver City. We have been back twice since our first hectic introduction and I know of no better place for a birder to have been "stuck" than that marvelous birding area. I had with me Dale Zimmerman's article in *Audubon* Magazine about bird finding around Silver City and it was an invaluable aid. Dr. Dale A. Zimmerman is a professor at New Mexico Western College, Silver City, and the outstanding bird authority of the region. I should have called him for on the spot briefing, but even in 1962 I was still laboring under the misapprehension that crack birders would not be interested in comparative neophytes. What a lamentable misconception! In all of our wanderings and in all my erratic but voluminous correspondence with birders of every shade, I have suffered only two rebuffs. One individual discouraged us from "tagging along" on the Monterey Peninsula Christmas Bird Count because he would be too busy; another did not answer either of my two letters asking for information on the Ringed Kingfisher in Texas—I had enclosed a stamped, self-addressed envelope both times. Before our second birding trip to Silver City, I received a cordial, helpful letter from Dr. Zimmerman but, unfortunately, he was going to be in Africa when we arrived.

The first day alone I birded Cherry Creek Canyon, then an

unpaved road but not bad as such roads go. It was a day crammed with excitement. I list the eight lifers of that day because each one, especially two of them, is a jewel beyond price to anyone who has never birded west of the one hundredth meridian. They were as follows: Pygmy Nuthatch; Gray-headed Junco; Mexican Chickadee; Western Tanager; Black-throated Gray, Virginia, Painted Redstart, and Red-faced Warblers. The Painted Redstart was incredibly beautiful. I watched the adults feeding brownish-black fledglings not long out of the nest. On our homeward route over the mountains east of Silver City we also saw the juveniles in their plain but strikingly black and white plumage; the adults have scarlet breasts and bellies as well as the contrasting black and white. I can well understand why the inexplicable occurrence of a Painted Red-start in the fall of 1947 at Marblehead, Massachusetts, caused an unprecedented commotion among the east coast Brotherhood of that region. But the Red-faced Warbler was the pièce de résis-tance! Found only in the southern and central mountains of Arizona and southwestern New Mexico in North America, usually at higher elevations, this striking red, black, white, and gray warbler is a veritable treasure among North American birds. It is rather deliberate in its movements and has a sweet but rather subdued song. At Cherry Creek Campground it often forages close to the ground. I had my second attack of "buck fever" when I spied my first Red-faced Warbler and continued to shake so badly that I never did get a satisfactory look. It all seems extremely silly in retrospect but it happened, nonetheless, just as I have stated it. Since that day, I have several times had both the Painted Redstart and the Red-faced Warbler in the glasses at once, and every time my frontal lobes refuse credence to what the occipital lobes tell me is there. This sort of neural block poses an intriguing topic for debate among the sophists of the Brotherhood. When does one record a lifer: when it is optically apparent, or only after the association centers are convinced? Birding is like the game of golf in many respects. In the abstract, the principal objective of each is singularly uncomplicated but the pragmatic implementation is fraught with innumerable casuistic rules and petty regulations.

The second day I birded along the Gila River at several places. Again, each lifer was an easterner's vision of the promised land: Western Bluebird; Black Phoebe; Gila Woodpecker; Lucy's Warbler; Phainopepla; Black Hawk. The Black Hawk, of course, was the best find of the day. This hawk of Mexico and Central America is uncommon in North America and its occurrence sporadic. My amateur birding soul, never finely attuned to axiological judgments, derived the most kick out of the Phainopepla, though. Like the Rose-throated Becard, this species is the only representative of its family found north of the border. The male is glossy black with broad patches of white in the primaries of its wings and it has a perky black crest. It has no close affinities with the Cardinal but many of the Brotherhood, including your scrivener, think Black Cardinal would be most appropriate. After all, a Night Hawk is not a hawk, a Waterthrush is not a thrush, and a Meadow Lark is not a lark. The Phainopepla, however, still labors under the handicap of its ugly generic name, just as does our esteemed friend the hippopotamus. The etymological interpretation of the Greek name is rather pleasing, though—"shining robe." It would be an interesting diversion for someone to determine why certain species of animals and plants were never awarded common names.

The third day the list began to taper off, only three lifers and all in the mountains: Western Flycatcher; Mountain Chickadee; Grace's Warbler. It is interesting that on each of my first three days at Silver City, one of the "three sisters" was first seen. The name "three sisters" is my own colloquialism for the three western warblers named after women. Lucy was the daughter of the famous naturalist Baird; Grace was the sister of another old-timer, Coues; Virginia was the wife of the man who collected the first Virginia Warbler. Wife, sister, daughter—as you perceive, no genetic relationship is implied. From the purely birding aspect, it is also of interest that we have found a Virginia Warbler at precisely the same location in Cherry Creek Canyon each of three summers. The fourth day, and the last solo flight for me, there were Bridled and Plain Titmice (I have been told it should be "Titmouses" but I can't abide such a flagrant solecism), Gambel's Quail, and Broad-tailed Hummingbird—all strictly western species. Finally, on the ninth and last day at Silver City we saw Steller's Jay, Olivaceous Flycatcher, and Zone-tailed Hawk. The Zone-tailed Hawk was the prize, naturally; it is of erratic occurrence in the southwest and relatively rare. With regard to Steller's Jay, I never see or hear this noisy bird without thinking of the ill-fated naturalist, Georg Wilhelm Steller, who sailed with Vitus Jonassen Bering in 1741 to Alaska. Steller, as you may recall, spent ten years in preparation for his biological survey of northwestern America and was permitted just ten hours of exploration on the mainland by his preposterous captain.

We left Silver City on the tenth day after our inauspicious debut with 431 lifers, twenty-four of them seen at Silver City. It was a real treat for me to have spent nine days in one region. I had gotten the feel of the place and, to a much lesser but satisfying extent, the birds. I apologize for listing all the lifers we saw at Silver City but every one is so entirely western and so seductive to an easterner that I can only hope some birder who has yet to journey west will get a vicarious thrill out of conning over the names. I did before I saw them. Marybelle was recuperating rapidly now that the pleural cavity was healed, but I had to do most of the driving from then on; the broken ribs were still painful.

One foolish lacuna of mine and we are off toward home. At the summit of the mountains just east of Silver City I saw perched on a rock by the side of the road an undoubted Townsend's Solitaire. I have never seen this bird better than I did that day; no one could. But, a very decided "but," it was the occipital lobes that registered, not the frontal—I just couldn't ken that bird, preposterous as this will seem to any normal birder. I simply told Marybelle—she had remained in the car at this relatively high altitude—that I had seen a pinkish-brown bird with an eye ring and white outer tail feathers. It was not until we reached home that the frontal lobes, or whatever, woke up. What a disgrace! I felt like such an idiot I didn't count that bird. I had to wait another year before "officially" recording Townsend's Solitaire. It was a concrete example of seeing but not comprehending. The discerning birder will at once perceive that the hypothetical problem I tossed out to the sophists a few lines ago, with tongue in cheek I confess, has now assumed the prosaic status of a real problem and must needs be adjudicated. Looking back on the episode, I think my decision not to count the bird was eminently quixotic—it smacked more of the mad Don than his practical-minded squire.

Arizona and California were not in the cards that trip; the nine days spent at Silver City had consumed most of our allotted vacation time. As a compensation for this disappointment, we spent a day of birding in Cimmaron Canyon in northern New Mexico. Like so many other western retreats, Cimmaron Canyon and the adjoining areas of Eagle Nest and Red River Gap are fantastic birding treats to the eastern birder. We acquired two more warblers, Audubon's and MacGillivray's, and saw a Dipper feeding young. The electric blue of the Mountain Bluebird is unforgettable and a pink woodpecker, Lewis's, hardly credible. One year later at the same Red River Gap, up and beyond Cimmaron Canyon at about nine thousand feet, we saw our first "official" Townsend's Solitaire but, appropriately enough, nòne deigned to appear in that year 1962. After all, no bird with a shred of self-respect wishes to court insult twice within so short a span of time. We totaled seven lifers that day in and about Cimmaron Canyon and picked up one more, Sharp-tailed Grouse, east of Raton, New Mexico—extreme southeastern range.

At last we were home from the hills with the most lifers, 111, we have ever seen on a single birding trip through North America and, obviously, the most we shall ever see. Our total North American list now stood at 439 birds. The hard core of the trip had been the Kirtland's, Golden-cheeked, and Colima

Warblers. We had also seen eight other warblers, eleven in all. When we had been on our way to Seney, I had not dared dream of so many new warblers, always my favorite birds. Several days after our return, I ran into Paul DeAoun at Tinicum and was describing our trip. Paul is a good birding friend of ours, despite the incident I am about to relate, and has aided us often, directly and indirectly, in seeing lifers about Philadelphia. Paul was obviously not impressed, or perhaps depressed, and with painstaking thoroughness registered his silent antipathy. He stretched, fiddled with his camera, examined with elaborate care every moldy Coot and Gallinule in the near vicinity and, finally, in an irritable outburst he savaged me, "Jean, why don't you go to hell!" Your typical birder will descant for hours about birds and places shared in common, but at the barely perceptible reference to a place or a bird he himself has not experienced, boredom, ennui, inattention, and other equally ungentlemanly manifestations of displeasure rise swiftly to the surface. I just *had* to tell Paul about the eleven new warblers, though, no matter what the cost to his nervous system. "But, Paul," I pleaded, "just think of it, eleven new warblers!" DeAoun got up from the big plank he had been sitting on and without one word or glance at his tormentor climbed into his car and simply drove away in a cloud of good old Tinicum dust. I thought of that venerable adjuration: "May the dust of your carriage blind the eyes of your enemies." To put it succinctly, what was incomparable adventure and achievement to me was just plain stuff to Paul DeAoun.

PART 3

After the backlash I received from my worthy friend Paul DeAoun that summer of 1962, I kept my mouth buttoned up and talked over our exploits with only Marybelle and Louis, our Siamese cat. Indeed, during the next ten months there was precious little to boast about in the way of lifers. We visited the

Jersey shore frequently and were out in the woods, fields, and marshes of the Philadelphia area at every available opportunity, but our total acquisition of lifers was five birds only. We realized, of course, that any one area can hold only so many birds, be they residents, migrants, accidentals, or what not. Those halcyon days of lifers without blood, sweat, and tears were fast coming to an end. However, both Common and King Eiders in the same day—DeAoun's phone call gave us the tip—is always an accomplishment, particularly when each is a lifer. Furthermore, one doesn't see the Iceland Gull every day in southeastern Pennsylvania. But that month of the Diaspora, May, came at last and we left for Arizona and California on our third birding trip. No broken ribs should deter us this time from our appointed rounds.

We always refer to the 1963 trip as the California trip although we have birded several times since then in this over-populated but still awe-inspiring state. It is also probably our longest by car, 11,064 miles from door to door. The first three or four days were prosaic enough, for we headed straight for St. Louis and its one bird of note, the introduced Tree Sparrow from Europe. We drove the entire width of Indianapolis in a pouring rain—a fitting reception for the return of the traitorous native son. We saw several European Tree Sparrows at Grand Marias Park in East St. Louis. It is a comely little bird, con-generic with its ubiquitous forerunner the House Sparrow. These two immigrants from Europe are not true sparrows but belong to the Weaver Finch family. I recall that when Mary-belle and I saw this bird in England in 1967, we involun-tarily called it the "European" Tree Sparrow, such is American provincialism. Since its successful debut in 1870, it has been confined entirely to the St. Louis area but, as I write this, the European Tree Sparrow is extending its range eastward and north into Illinois. (So much here for my meager ornithological lore; Archilochos of Paros, I believe, is credited with the apho-rism: The fox knows many things but the hedgehog one big thing. I am the hedgehog—my one big and only thing is North American lifers.)

We picked up six more lifers between St. Louis and Cave Creek Canyon, Arizona; one of these was the aforementioned Townsend's Solitaire near Eagle Nest, New Mexico. When we left Eagle Nest on June 2 there was new snow on the ground, and south of Santa Fe and east of Albuquerque it alternately snowed and hailed for an hour or so. By the time we had reached the Rio Grande Valley south of Socorro, it was so hot that the insulating tar of the car battery boiled out and we had to buy a new battery. Such is New Mexican weather at high and low altitudes in early June. We reached Cave Creek Canyon in the Chiricahua Mountains of southeastern Arizona on June 3, a long, long way from the City of Brotherly Love.

The Chiricahua Mountains rise straight up from the floor of the surrounding desert, a magnificent spectacle to the traveler coming down from the north, a true sky island. Weldon F. Heald's book *Sky Island* should be read for an entertaining and intimate account of the geology, biota, history, and legends of these mountains. Cave Creek is one of the major canyons of this isolated mountain range and a birder's land of milk and honey. We spent only three days at Cave Creek on this first visit, but we returned for eight days in 1965 and yet another ten days in 1968, three weeks in all. Like Madera Canyon near Tucson, it is a Mecca of the North American bird world. We have met scores of eager birders at Stewart Camp Ground, Rustler's Gap, Cave Creek Ranch, and the Research Station near the head of the Canyon. Furthermore, it has trees and lots of shade and the altitude is high enough to afford cool nights. It is a veritable oasis. And the birds!

There is no official list of birds for the Chiricahuas and adjacent desert areas, so far as I am aware. Our own list of 102 birds is very incomplete. Also, it should be borne in mind that this list was compiled during a total of only twenty-one days and covers only late spring or early summer, May 18 to June 6.

Therefore, we have failed to see a great many species, particularly spring and fall transients. Finally, I should wish to point out that we have birded only a small fraction of the total Chiricahua area: Cave Creek Canyon, Pinery Canyon, Rustler's Gap, and the desert near Portal. The true Chiricahua Wilderness Area we have scarcely touched, except on the trail to Snowshed Peak. It is not so much the number of species, though, that endears Cave Creek Canyon to the eastern birder but the "specialties" found either in the Canyon itself or on the road to Rustler's Gap. The glamour bird, of course, is the Coppery-tailed Trogon, which nests there in the summer. This Trogon is a member of the same family as the famous Quetzal of Central America and the only species of its kind that nests north of Mexico. The Sulphur-bellied Flycatcher is another southwestern species that never fails to quicken the pulse of the eastern birder. The Mexican Chickadee and Mexican Junco are both restricted to the southern mountains of Arizona and New Mexico in the United States. The Painted Redstart is always to be found in Cave Creek Canyon, especially South Fork, and Red-faced and Olive Warblers nest at Rustler's Gap. It is a prime area to see the Arizona Woodpecker; and Acorn Woodpeckers are as thick as fleas. If one is lucky, as we were, that rare, diminutive bird, the Beardless Flycatcher, may be found in the dense desert scrub near the village of Portal. At the feeders maintained by the staff of the Southwestern Research Station, we have seen four species of hummingbird, and two or three additional species are seen almost every year. There are Elf, Whiskered, and Spotted Owls, among others; Hooded, Scott's, and Bullock's Orioles; Western, Hepatic, and Summer Tanagers; Black-headed and Blue Grosbeaks. But why continue! Marybelle and I shall probably not return to Cave Creek Canyon for at least two years and I only torture the reader and myself needlessly. But before we leave to meet Bill Harrison, Warren Winslow, and our first Rose-throated Becard, come with us for a brief early-morning trip up to Rustler's Gap.

The canyon road as far as the Research Station is paved but

from there up to Rustler's Gap Campground it is unpaved. It is actually a good road, as mountain roads go, but when I drove it that first time in a relatively low-slung station wagon, it was fraught with peril at every turn. We had no mishap of any kind, however, and the peril was all of my own making. Still, a mountain road is not a suburban loop and I was greatly relieved that no other car was descending as we crept around each sharp turn near the summit. At several places there are spectacular views, with the desert laid out below for countless miles until lost in the shimmering haze to the east. Marybelle, who wasn't driving, saw much more scenery than I did. It was still early morning when we reached Rustler's Park; the air was crystalline and it was very cold. I could not stop shivering for some time but I'm sure some of this was accentuated by my taut nerves at the end of that drive. Rustler's Gap is only eighty-four hundred feet high but it was sufficient elevation to quell any notions we may have had of scampering here and there or climbing rapidly. I shall not dwell on the Olive Warbler, a lifer for us, or the other "summit" birds of that incomparable spot. I've mentioned some of them in the preceding account. Now that we are safely on top, I can tell you why we are here—the three of us. It is to hear the Meistersinger of these mountain solitudes. Yes, look if you must—but listen, listen!

It is Coues's Flycatcher singing. The thin, clear notes made me catch my breath that first time at Rustler's Gap. The sound seems to come from everywhere and nowhere. We have heard Coues's a number of times since and in other places, and the bird's song always affects me deeply. It is the mountain setting and clear, bracing air partly; but it is the sound above all else. It sings "Ave Maria," or José Maria as some would have it, with a rising inflection on the second syllable of "Maria." Coues's Flycatcher is no virtuoso like the Hermit or Swainson's Thrush, but its simple, ethereal song of adoration is the articulate soul of these austere, timeless mountains. It is a prayer, a hope, and other things I am powerless to word. He is the wandering minstrel of the high mountains and neither would be whole without the other. The bird is named after Elliott Coues, a famous naturalist of the nineteenth century. Coues is pronounced "cows," not coo-ees, a bitter blow to me when some know-it-all corrected me. It is a remarkably drab bird, much like the Olive-sided Flycatcher of more extensive range. It is found only in the southwestern mountains in the United States, usually at altitudes above seven thousand feet, and normally retreats south of the border in winter. But I entreat you, forget these barren commonplaces. Remember only the voice, the invocation. That is the mountain's way.

We set out for Nogales the next morning with our ten Chiricahua lifers to speed us on our way. We were fortunate, indeed, to have Bill Harrison and Warren Winslow join us on our first afternoon of birding at Patagonia, Arizona. Both of these men are crack birders, especially Bill, who is known to scores of North American birders he has helped in southern Arizona. Patagonia is as famous among birders as Cave Creek and the prime area borders Sonoita Creek, a portion of which has now been made into a wildlife sanctuary by Nature Conservancy. We added four more lifers that afternoon and the next morning along Sonoita Creek. The Thick-billed Kingbird and Gray Hawk were prize acquisitions, but the Rose-throated Becards and their nest, this time not deserted, were the apéritif to us. We waited a long time close to the nest and finally the female of the pair appeared. The next morning, after only a ten-minute wait, we saw the more colorful male. There were no Inca Doves calling this time and we could now regard our former failure at Bentsen State Park with equanimity. But, I hasten to add, this was not yet the true extirpation of the Inca curse.

The last time we were in the Patagonia area, in 1968, we watched a pair of Becards building their nest in a big sycamore tree at a roadside rest area off route 82 south of Patagonia. This particular rest area is a favorite and convenient birding spot well known to the Brotherhood and carefully monitored by Bill Harrison and other local birders. Harrison and I have maintained a rather erratic but continuous correspondence over the intervening years but, as you may surmise, Bill has given me far more information than I have ever given him. I may be all wet, but it has always seemed rather odd to me that hordes of eastern birders regularly invade the west every year and receive help from field experts all the way from the Black Hills of South Dakota to the Pacific shore. Western birders, on the other hand, never seem to come east, or if they do, it is so unobtrusively done that no one is aware of them. This, obviously, is not strictly true; many western birders come east. The fact remains, however, that from the Black Hills to Cape Flattery one can always find eastern birders gawking at western birds while, on the other hand, I've run across comparatively few western birders on the Atlantic coast. Florida birders, undoubtedly, would have a different tale to tell.

In the Tucson area and the Santa Catalina Mountains we added five more new birds. The prize bird, from our standpoint, was the Rufous-winged Sparrow. This sparrow has a very limited range in the United States, a small area of south-central Arizona, and is most readily seen about Tucson, since its yearly whereabouts are continually checked by the Tucson Brotherhood. I had written to Florence Thornburg and she received us in her trailer home on the outskirts of Tucson upon our arrival. She told us of two places to look for the Rufous-winged and we chose the more southern locality because it was more conveniently reached from our motel. We were up early, if not bright, the next morning, but our search was in vain. I knew we had the correct locale but, as it turned out, I did not appreciate the truly monastic habits of this singular bird. That evening I called Dr. Joe Marshall and poured forth my tale of woe. Joe T. Marshall in 1963 was a professor at the University of Arizona and is a co-author of *The Birds of Arizona*. Marshall's single query was, "On which side of the road did you look?" I told him the north side, where Mrs. Thornburg had said they would be. "Try the south side," was Dr. Marshall's laconic enjoiner. It sounded just plain silly to me. Why in the name of all the slaughtered Dodos would a small, passerine bird refuse to cross a

narrow dirt road? But the next morning bore out the good
doctor's prediction, weird as it had appeared to me at first—Dr.
Marshall hat immer recht; the sparrows were restricted entirely
to the south of the roadside fence. We must have seen ten or
more sparrows and a small rattlesnake into the bargain. I almost
stepped on the snake and both Marybelle and I agreed that
stumbling upon a rattlesnake while looking for birds was a
serendipity we could well have done without. You will perceive
the corrosive effects of time and birding upon my earlier herpetological predilections. Two years later we climbed that same
fence, sans rattlesnake, and the sparrows were still on the south
side of the road. Would that all birds were so permanently
fixed! But, of course, I don't really mean this; birding would
degenerate into a sightseeing tour if it were so. On our way back
to the motel and well within the city limits of Tucson, a coyote
ran across the road. The coyote is a great favorite of ours. If
every town had more coyotes and less people, the world would
be a much safer place in which to live. You will understand that
my aversion to the human species is not so much that I dislike
people as that I can't stand them.

In order to avoid the heat of the southern Arizona and California deserts we left Gila Bend at two A.M. bound for Yuma
and San Diego. The sunrise shortly before we entered Yuma was
spectacular and we stopped the car several times to watch the
flaming majesty of sky and desert. It was very cold through the
hills east of San Diego and we wondered whether we had made a
mistake leaving Gila Bend so early. But, had we not done so, we
would probably have missed that sunrise. By the time we
reached San Diego and had our first glimpse of the Pacific,
everything was as it should have been. East of San Diego and
along the shore of the bay we added six lifers that day and on
the way north to Los Angeles we saw one White-tailed Kite. At
the present writing, this Kite is presumably making a decided
comeback. We found a place to stay somewhere in that sprawl-
ing wilderness of brick and mortar, familiarly known to natives
of the area as Los Angeles. A sign told us we were only three

minutes from Disneyland but our Pettingill told us we were only about thirty minutes from the Dorothy Tucker Sanctuary in the Santa Ana Mountains. Our inclination was for humming-birds that afternoon, not animated rodents. The Tucker Sanc-tuary specializes in hummingbirds and all one has to do is sit on a deliciously shaded veranda and watch them by the dozens fly in and out to the feeders. The Sanctuary's sugar bill must be enormous. As I have mentioned before, the west is blessed with about fourteen species of hummers and it is always a novelty to an eastern birder to see more than one kind. We saw three different species that day, two of them lifers, Anna's and Costa's. Back at our motel, we planned our campaign for seeing the two Los Angeles specialties, the Spotted and Ringed Turtle Doves. Both of these species have been introduced into the United States and now breed in the wild state. As of this writing, the Spotted Dove is limited to the Los Angeles region and south to San Diego; the Ringed Turtle Dove is found only in central, downtown Los Angeles and Tampa and Miami, Florida.

We saw the Spotted Dove in Griffith Park without undue trouble and the next day found us in quest of the Ringed Turtle Dove. The year before, a birding acquaintance of ours, I cannot recall his name to this day, had repeatedly emphasized that this dove was not at MacArthur Park as Pettingill states, but was only to be seen in Olivera Street in central Los Angeles. Whether he was correct in his defamation of Pettingill I cannot say, for we never went to MacArthur Park. What I do know, though, is that before we were through with that day's search, I was heaping the foulest imprecations on the head of that name-less birding friend. Our difficulty was exasperatingly uncompli-cated—we simply couldn't find Olivera Street. We had groped our way into central Los Angeles fearing the worst in traffic jams. Judging from the crazed bedlam of the outskirts, we had assumed that our lives were forfeit once we entered the vortex of this modern Babylon. But, *mirabile dictu*, there was scarcely any traffic at all. Some streets reminded me of Wall Street on Sunday mornings, no autos, and only a few pedestrians and cyclists. No, it was not traffic that balked us, but Olivera Street might as well have been in Baghdad for all we could glean from the denizens of central city Los Angeles. That day I was the Ancient Mariner, querying one of three.

All farces must terminate sooner or later and, though ours was decidedly later, we did find Olivera Street. It was not, however, until we had been directed twice to the same place that it dawned on us that a street may still be called a street even though it has no traffic and is, in fact, only an outdoor bazaar. I left Marybelle in the car and with binoculars prominently hanging from my neck set out to ascertain for certain that this conglomeration of vendors' stands and booths was, indeed, Olivera Street. It was, but the narrow, cramped little alleyway appeared so unlikely to harbor exotic doves that my patrol up one side and down the other was to me a mere tour de force. I was wrong, of course. As I turned to leave, cursing that nameless, idiot "friend" almost audibly, I happened to raise my eyes to an awning over one of the booths. Blinking and peering over the edge were four grimy-looking "pigeons" that proved to be Ringed Turtle Doves. I summoned Marybelle and we both stood there like dopes peering at those doves with our glasses. Using glasses at all was the crowning fiasco of that unbirding day. Everyone deemed us crazy for staring at tame birds with glasses when we could almost have put out our hands and caught a few—and they were absolutely right. I think we toasted the Ringed Turtle Dove that evening, number 487, but it was not an especially hilarious occasion.

To the northwest of Los Angeles lies the last retreat of the California Condor, Los Padres Forest and the Sespe Sanctuary. Like the Whooping Crane, this magnificent glider over dizzy mountain peaks is nearing extinction and its numbers at present are not much greater than those of the Whooper. It cannot abide man's encroachment on the wilderness and in this respect, consequently, manifests considerably more acumen than many of our public "servants." Arnold Small, one of the outstanding birders of the country, had kindly written me directions and suggestions, together with map, for seeing the Condor. From Fillmore we were to go north on "A" Street for three or four miles to an unpaved road that after eight miles or so would lead us to the high country of Dough Flat and beyond—the choice place to watch for Condors. Our station wagon was crammed and there were no more than seven or eight inches of road clearance. I walked up that road a short piece and stood for some time in "uffish" thought—and then I chickened out. Perhaps if I had had another man with me, I might have attempted it, but I doubt it. Besides, that battered sign at the first turn of the road chilled me. Very dangerous road, it said, proceed at your own risk, or words to that effect. So we opened Mr. Small's letter again and reviewed his directions for second choice, Mt. Pinos near Gorman off U.S. 99 through Frazier Park. Mr. Small was most emphatic that we should go to the very top of Mt. Pinos and added that if we were prepared to spend a minimum of three days, we should not fail to see the bird. He knew his stuff, did Arnold Small, because that's exactly the time it took us to see the Condor.

We were not camping then but had a motel in Gorman. Each of those three days we drove the round trip up Mt. Pinos. What we lacked in courage we made up for in perseverance. The actual summit, which provided a grand view of the surrounding country, was reached by a dirt road about a half mile long that led up from the parking area. We could have driven that road, especially with most of the load back at the motel, but it was interesting birding and we chose to walk it each time. We saw three new birds this way—Oregon Junco, Clark's Nutcracker, and Mountain Quail; moreover, we needed the exercise. Clark's Nutcracker is named after William Clark of Lewis and Clark fame and the Mountain Quail has a call with rising inflection that sounds as if it were asking a question. So we amused ourselves well enough coming and going but it was a weary vigil at the summit scanning the horizon and scrutinizing every speck with my 12 x 50 glasses for Condor signs. I must have read the altitude, 8,831 ft., on the brass geodetic survey plate at least a hundred times. Very near the actual summit, Green-tailed Towhees and Rock Wrens were in residence—at least both of these birds were there on each of the three days we were—and we beguiled the time by trying to find out as much about these two species as the birds saw prudent to reveal. I can't recall that we really learned much, except by noon of the third day I was becoming fairly familiar with the Rock Wren's bewildering repertoire of trills and squeaks. If it had not been for those two White-headed Woodpeckers on the second day, however, our firm resolve to see the Condor might have been sickened over with the pale cast of despondency. Two of those woodpeckers put in an appearance in the late afternoon of the second day and foraged around the stubby trees farther down the slope for some time. To one who grew up with Red-headed Woodpeckers in Indiana, a White-headed Woodpecker is a refreshing novelty. I had coveted this bird ever since I first learned that there was such a species. They renewed our lagging spirits and the next morning saw us once more mounting vigil near that brass plate on our 8,831-foot lookout.

We saw them in the early afternoon, probably about two o'clock. Every now and then for the past two days, hawks or vultures would appear as specks on the horizon and, like ships far out at sea when one watches from the shore, gradually lose themselves in the distant blue haze without revealing much as to their identity. For reasons known only to themselves, only a few hawks and two Golden Eagles ever came near enough for identification. Neither of us is very competent at raptor identification, particularly with western hawks and falcons. The two specks we followed in our glasses that afternoon of June seventeenth, however, were slowly but surely circling ever closer. It still took some minutes before the birds were close enough for us to mark their great wingspread and big heads. In a few more minutes the contrasting white and black pattern of the underwings could be clearly discerned. We felt as did Keats's "Cortez" and his band, silent upon that peak in Darien, and we gazed at each other with a wild surmise—for it was the Cali-

fornia Condor at last! Neither bird came as close as heart could
have desired and in due course they both drifted southward out
of range. A third bird was sighted soaring high and from the
same direction as the two Condors. I feel certain that the third
bird was also a Condor but I could never cinch the underwing
pattern at that distance. Perhaps it was an immature without
white wing linings. If we had seen only the third bird, the situation would have presented a neat problem in birding ethics. I
had that positive, intuitive feeling of certainty that always ac-
companies a correct identification and yet the bird was too
distant to distinguish unequivocally its underwing pattern or
whether it had any at all. Fortunately, the first two were unmistakable and there was no need for soul searching. We bade
farewell to our Towhees and Wrens, companions now, it
seemed to us, of countless days, and went rejoicing down that
upper slope of Mt. Pinos. Near the parking lot a Mountain Quail
queried us again with his old familiar "Whoooo?" "The Condor, you dunderhead," I shouted back at him. My answer must
have satisfied the bird, for he remained silent as we passed on
down the road and out of hearing.

The Condor was number 490 and we rested our aching eyes
that night at Bakersfield. The next morning before it was light
we were on our way to Taft and its adjacent greasewood and
sage desert. Le Conte's Thrasher was our objective. There is no
living creature that would suffer less if consigned to the infernal
regions than this bird of the low, hot deserts of Mexico and the
southwest. I have never been to Death Valley or the Sahara, but
if they are hotter than Taft, California, on June 18, 1963, I
wouldn't visit either for 8,600 lifers—the estimated total of birds
on this our planet earth. By eight that morning we had seen four
Le Conte's Thrashers well, and it was enough for me. I'd like to
take one of those thrashers up to Barrow, Alaska, some winter
and watch its reactions. It would be suitable reprisal for the
torture Le Conte's put us through that day. If the temperature
didn't reach 190° that afternoon, I'll eat my old, frayed straw
hat. Or, in the words of my street urchin days—it must have

been hotter than the hinges of hell. But Marybelle and I didn't linger to find out; we sped straight west for Morro Bay and the cool Pacific.

Birding in and around Morro Bay was a delight after our long watch atop Mt. Pinos and that Gehenna west of Taft. Waiting for Allen's Hummingbird in the garden of a Mrs. Bender, we saw our five hundredth bird, the Lazuli Bunting. Allen's Hummer was also on schedule, five P.M. precisely. About the Bay were Brandt's and Pelagic Cormorants, Heermann's Gull, Common Murre, and Pigeon Guillemot, all lifers. On the way to Pacific Grove at Pt. Lobos Park, we saw the Chestnut-backed Chickadee, several Black Oystercatchers, and our first Red-breasted Sapsucker. At this writing, this last bird is considered only a subspecies of the Yellow-bellied Sapsucker by the camarilla of the Brotherhood, but it is strikingly different in its plumage from the familiar eastern form. There is talk among the Inner Circle that the Red-breasted Sapsucker may be a law unto himself when the chips are finally down and the sixth AOU Check-list goes to press. In the interim of decision, we are on our way to Yosemite National Park and have just seen our first Yellow-billed Magpie—the only California bird strictly indigenous to that state.

At Yosemite we saw our first Crossbill, the Red, and found without anyone's help a pair of Hermit Warblers and their nest. Also we saw a pair of Williamson's Sapsuckers near White Wolf Camp, the sexes so different in appearance that early naturalists, first exploring the far west, thought them different species. We missed the Gray-crowned Rosy Finch at Tioga Pass, shortly to be recounted, and the Great Gray Owl at Peregoy Meadows. We knew from others that the owl was there and a ranger assured me that he had seen one a few days before, but we have yet to see the Great Gray Owl. We should have spent a day or two longer hunting that owl at Peregoy Meadows and, had we done so, I'm sure we would have been victorious. But we gave up too soon. Had I known then that the Great Gray Owl would, seemingly, forever elude us, things might have been different.

We have never returned to Yosemite and surely the reason is not obscure. Even in 1963 the Park was a seething mass of misguided humanity, seeking to subdue the wilderness with blaring radios, destructive brats, and gasoline fumes. They have all but done it by now. I recall the surge of disgust that welled up in me as I watched that milling mob lined up in front of the supermarket near headquarters waiting for room inside, the kids slobbering over ice cream cones and Daddy snapping pictures of everybody and everything except God's superb handiwork. Oh, yes, of course, they snapped the Falls too but only as one might take a picture of a leaky faucet as documentary evidence that water was dripping somewhere. I turned my back on this rabble, of which I myself was a part, and tried valiantly but vainly to concentrate upon the majesty of that ineffable, cascading torrent. It was an empty gesture and, worst of all, I realized it at the time. I was equally guilty of cluttering up the place. Wasn't our car over there somewhere with all the others! My very presence, compounded by ten thousand others, was an insult to this enchanted realm of the past. Gray's *Elegy* is not to be read in the confusion and garish lights of Times Square. At least I cannot do so. And so we left Yosemite on the fourth day without benefit of owl. We headed for the exit at Tioga Pass and one final sortie up the snow-clad slopes for the Gray-crowned Rosy Finch. For many days after quitting Yosemite, we were conscious of a nameless but tangible shame that gave us no peace.

The Gray-crowned Rosy Finch should be the Black Rosy Finch as far as Marybelle is concerned, for to her the former is the original Black Beast. I concur with this sentiment in part, but to me the Pinyon Jay has always been my *bête noire*. But it was the Gray-crowned Rosy Finch that gave us trouble that last day in Yosemite. On either side of Tioga Pass, the exit by which we had chosen to leave the Park, snowfields extend far up the high slopes. These snowfields are the summer home of the Gray-crowned Rosy Finch and by the end of June they were supposedly far up toward the top. We knew we could never reach those summits but we did have hopes of ascending sufficiently to be able to spot and identify the birds with my big glasses. It was a grueling climb for two people with no experience of this sort of thing and none too young to boot. Tioga Pass is 9,941 feet and even ordinary exertion, if prolonged, becomes strenuous. The worst part, naturally, was the deep snow. The alternate thawing and freezing of the surface snow resulted in a hard crust that almost, but never quite, held our weight. Every time our full weight was borne by one foot, the crust suddenly gave way and we would sink in over our knees. Every time I stopped for breath, the intervals more and more frequent, I'd scan the slopes and snowfields beyond for finches. The birds were either not on this particular slope that day or we were too far below them to mark their movements or whereabouts. It was very arduous and unrewarding work, and after an hour or more we were forced to give it up. We made one more futile attempt that day, after leaving the Park, to see the Gray-crowned. After our descent of the east side on the way to Mono Lake, we stopped the car and hiked up a trail for over two miles to the foot of a cirque with a snowfield extending beyond. We were not actually close enough to either cirque or snowfield to spot anything as small as a finch with ordinary glasses but I had hoped our telescope might just do the trick. Even with the 20x telescope, we saw no birds. We admitted defeat for the second time and plodded wearily back the return two miles to the car. I have seldom been so exhausted and discouraged and Marybelle, certainly, was in the same plight. I had developed a bad rash on the back of my legs and also had several blisters from walking all day in wet shoes. At Mono Lake, where we stayed that night, there could have been no more crippled, disconsolate twain than the Gray-crownedless Piatts. I didn't even have the strength of mind to blaspheme those poor, inoffensive little finches in their inaccessible Nephelococcygia of cirque and snow. This, for me, is the pis aller.

Our ultimate encounter with the Gray-crowned Rosy Finch is simply told and perhaps more apropos now than later. The next summer on the east slope of Mt. Rainier we suddenly found ourselves in the midst of a considerable flock of these finches. They were all around us, often so close that our binoculars could not focus. They were probably on their way up to higher altitudes, for this was earlier in June than we had been to Yosemite. A few stunted trees were near and I counted five birds flitting about in just one of these. We could even look down upon a number that were below us! The final expiation of the Gray-crowned Rosy Finch came when we visited the Pribilofs and the Aleutians. The Gray-crowned is a resident of both St. Paul Island and Umnak Island and at both places they are grounded, and as common as House Sparrows on your own courthouse lawn. We almost had to kick them out of our path. Each of these island finches, too, is a different subspecies from those Gray-crowneds we saw on Mt. Rainier, and larger. The Gray-crowned Rosy Finch has long since ceased to be Marybelle's Black Beast and is now a respected member of our avian pantheon. If my memory serves me correctly, Marybelle even stooped to utter a few cooing baby-talk sounds to those finches on Mt. Rainier!

We picked up the Sage Thrasher in the flat lands east of Mono Lake and then headed east and north across Nevada to the Uintah Mountains of northern Utah. The Uintahs are splendid mountains and have a number of peaks well over ten thousand feet, Gilbert Peak rising to 13,422 and Bald Mountain to 11,947. It was toward the summit of the latter that we sought another of the three Rosy Finches of North America, the Black Rosy Finch. Our efforts this time were climaxed by success. After a long but not too strenuous climb up the rocks of Bald Mountain, we came within telescope range of a big cirque topped by a snowfield. There were a dozen or so Black Rosy Finches running about on the lower edge of the snow and several on the rocks below this. It is very simple in the telling but it took a good deal of exertion and patience before we finally could check our identification. And all the time I was looking through that telescope, the mosquitoes fed voraciously.

We looked in at Dinosaur National Monument, hoping to

find that reputedly noisy rascal the Pinyon Jay. We saw no jays and the only trophy we collected there was a bronze replica of Brontosaurus I bought at headquarters. Northern Colorado was a windy furnace and it was a relief when we finally entered the higher ground of Rocky Mountain National Park. On the way up to the summit of the Park we had a real break. A White-tailed Ptarmigan flushed from the side of the road, flew only a few feet, and lit in a tree. We have seen hundreds of Willow Ptarmigans and a Rock Ptarmigan and its nest but thus far that White-tailed Ptarmigan in Rocky Mountain Park is our only record of this species. At the summit, approximately twelve thousand feet, there was a terrific wind. In order to maintain a firm stance to search the adjacent snowfield for the third and final Rosy Finch, the Brown-capped, we took shelter behind one of the buildings nearby. Having done this, there was no problem. Three or four Brown-capped Rosy Finches were within fifty feet of us. Our two lifers at Rocky Mountain Park were the only joyful events in that almost nonstop trip through the Park. Unless one is prepared to take backpack, overnight hikes into the remote portions of our national parks, the population pressure soon dissipates the glories of nature. Unfortunately, too, we hit Rocky Mountain Park during a weekend. Marybelle, who had been there long ago as a child, was aghast at the changes that had taken place. I was aghast at the never-ending crowds of people that wandered aimlessly from view to view, lost souls who did not know they were lost. Our own plight was far worse; we were lost and we knew it. Let's face it—man is the endangered species.

We left Rocky Mountain National Park that same day and headed for Cheyenne. We stopped in Wyoming long enough to add the final lifer, McCowan's Longspur, to our list. We had amassed seventy more lifers on the California trip and our total now stood at 514 North American birds. Thenceforth we were in flight across the land. Scott's Bluff in western Nebraska claimed our attention for a few hours but it was a token sojourn. There were no Pinyon Jays and, somehow, we had known we would find none even before we stopped. It was not apathy nor was it exactly resignation. It was simply the end. We had been engrossed in a thrilling narrative for weeks and now the tale had abruptly ended. There remained only the errand of returning the book to the library.

PART 4

In each of the three summers following the California trip of 1963, we again made extensive birding trips in North America, totaling over twenty-one thousand miles by car. To this exodus by car during the summer must be added several thousand miles by plane to Rockport and Dallas, Texas, in December of 1965 and the Monterey, California, area in December of 1966. For the sake of the reader as well as my own earnest wish to minimize the travelogue consecution inescapable in any bird lister's Odyssey, I shall be guided by the principle of the irreducible minimum in narrating these trips. Once we have caught up with ourselves and are poised for our invasion of Alaska, we can all afford to relax a bit and leave the future sturm and drang of acquiring lifers to the indefinitely definite future. In accordance with the above resolve, let us apply Occam's Razor to the reckoning of the home-front lifers during this three-year period.

It is instructive to witness the steady decline of the home-area lifers succeeding the California trip. We recorded seven lifers between the summer of 1963 and 1964. Noteworthy among these were Baird's Sandpiper at Brigantine, the White-winged Crossbill at Furness's, mentioned earlier, and our first Goshawk at Bake Oven Knob lookout in the Pennsylvania mountains. The number was reduced to five lifers during the next interim of 1964–1965. The Snowy Owl at Philadelphia airport, shown to us by Johnny Miller, and the White-fronted Goose at Bombay Hook in Delaware were outstanding to us. Between 1965 and 1966 the number dwindled precipitously—namely, one bird, Henslow's Sparrow, at Eliot Island, Maryland. During the final interim period before our first trip to Alaska, the number of lifers hit rock bottom, namely, zero birds. Actually, following Henslow's Sparrow it was over two years before we saw another lifer in the entire eastern states area, Cory's Shearwater off Cape May, on July 30, 1968. With only two recent and notable additions, Curlew Sandpiper and Black-tailed Godwit, the above is the up-to-date summary of our home-front efforts since the California trip, sixteen lifers in all. And now we are ready for brief accounts of our 1964, 1965, and 1966 trips.

Northwest Trip, 1964

The first port of call was Waubay National Wildlife Refuge in northeastern South Dakota. We spent several enjoyable days birding this Refuge. There were Upland Plovers on almost every other fence post, a large flock of nesting White Pelicans and, our first lifer of the trip, several Chestnut-collared Longspurs in the vicinity of Enemy Swim Lake. What a name with which to conjecture! Marybelle at last equaled our scores by seeing her first Hudsonian Godwit, side by side with a Marbled Godwit just for ease of comparison. I had seen three of these big waders with the upturned bill at Tinicum way back in 1958 at a time when Marybelle was far away on the banks of the Wabash doing her annual "daughter stint."

From Waubay we drove to the Black Hills, chiefly to see the White-winged Junco and Pinyon Jay. All across the western half of South Dakota Lark Buntings flew up from the roadside fields at every turn of the wheels to remind us of that vagrant lifer we had seen two years before near Valley Forge. It is ever thus in birding, old memories superseded by the new. In the Black Hills, not hills at all but true mountains, the White-winged Juncos were most obliging; the Pinyon Jay was not. We searched the juniper-clad hills assiduously for this Black Beast but we might as well have been on a pelagic trip in the Indian

Ocean for all we saw or heard of this mythical bird. Despite the overwhelming written and verbal evidence thrown at me over the years, I was inexorably coming to the conclusion that the Pinyon Jay must be on the verge of extinction. Worse still, it was disheartening to know that thousands of birders throughout the land were, seemingly, completely unaware of this critical situation. For instance, on the Christmas Bird Count at Silver City, 1964, well over a thousand Pinyon Jays were reported. How could such a flagrant boner slip by the Christmas Count editor of *Audubon Field Notes!* Such laxity was simply appalling. In view of the Pinyon Jay crisis of the early sixties, it gives me intense satisfaction, therefore, to announce that in the summer of 1968 Marybelle and I stumbled upon a small flock of these jays hidden away in some obscure hills in eastern Wyoming. Obviously, this remote colony is the last, pitiful remnant of a once abundant species. I had at first thought to communicate this heartening news to the birding directorate but thought better of it in the end. After all, those bigots had given no cognizance of the disaster from its inception. They would only have mocked me.

On June 3 we stopped overnight at Bozeman, Montana, en route to Red Rock Lakes Migratory Waterfowl Refuge to see the Trumpeter Swans that nest there. We had decided to skip Yellowstone Park because of the crowds. Besides, the road west from the Park to Red Rock Lakes was reputed to be muddy and impassable for ordinary vehicles. Evening Grosbeaks were thick in the shade trees of Bozeman and we had seen two Ferruginous Hawks and several Short-eared Owls just outside the town. Montana State College is situated in Bozeman and I decided to visit the Department of Zoology to get information about the birds of the area. I felt a little self-conscious walking through Lewis Hall in my soiled blue jeans and carrying my dilapidated straw hat, but I had long since become inured to this sort of thing. Too bad it wasn't a few years later; I should have appeared spruce and elegant compared to the present-day students. But Clifford V. Davis couldn't have cared less. We had feathers in common and that was all that mattered. Professor Davis had written the section on bird finding in the Bozeman area, which we had just read in Pettingill, so we were in good hands. At his suggestion, we spent the rest of the afternoon at the fish hatchery looking for the Calliope Hummingbird. We finally saw several of these hummers with the candy-striped gorget and were lucky to witness a display flight of one of the males, a series of swoops with abrupt halts, as though the bird had struck an invisible barrier. Early the next morning we met Professor Davis and he took us to some of his favorite birding spots for a few hours. One of these was a small field that had been used earlier in the year as a display ground for the Sharp-tailed Grouse. It was too late in the season for witnessing the display but several birds were still there and we had good looks at them before they took flight. It was one of the high spots of the trip to have been in the field with an accomplished, professional ornithologist.

At Red Rock Lakes we managed to see at least six Trumpeter Swans, two of them quite well with the telescope. The Trumpeter is larger than the more widely distributed Whistling Swan but resembles the latter closely. The flesh-colored mark at the base of the mandible is a good field mark but difficult to see at a distance and some individuals, apparently, lack this narrow stripe. We could discern this mark on the two we saw up close but the others were too far away. Both the Calliope Hummingbird and Trumpeter Swan were lifers for us and represent almost the extremes in size among North American birds, the smallest hummer and the largest swan.

The dirt road from Monida, a ghost town, to Red Rock Lakes is almost thirty miles and as we drove it both going and coming we kept a sharp lookout for Sage Grouse, the largest of the grouse, but saw none. All through western Montana and its extensive growth of sagebrush we looked for the bird at a dozen or more places but to no avail. In winter it is much easier to see than in summer; in the latter season it tends to move up into the hills—and Montana hills are no joke. We finally saw our first

Sage Grouse about forty miles west of Spokane, near Creston, Washington. Lynn La Fave, a brilliant, young field ornithologist of Opportunity, Washington, directed us to a display ground where he had observed a solitary male still frequenting the area although this spot had been abandoned weeks before by the grouse. Sure enough, in the early morning light, there he was in all his solitary glory of bachelorhood. We saw a few more Sage Grouse on our return home but none we admired quite so much as this loner who had eschewed connubial bliss just to please us.

Our trip through Washington to Cape Flattery and Mt. Rainier was enjoyable but uneventful. We saw our first Varied Thrush at Icicle Creek near Leavenworth, Washington. At Heyburn State Park in northern Idaho we had heard a Varied Thrush but I could never find the bird; it fled ever farther and farther in front of me like the will-o'-the-wisp. Its call is a series of long, minor notes each on a different pitch. It is a sound that eminently belongs to the darksome forests of the fog-shrouded Cascades. On the Pacific coast and along the Strait of Juan de Fuca we picked up Northwestern Crow, Glaucous-winged Gull, three alcids, and an immature Black-legged Kittiwake. Oddly enough, way out on the extreme point of Cape Flattery we saw no alcids or ocean birds of any kind. Our only lifer on this farthest northwest point of conterminous United States was the Rufous Hummingbird, the common breeding hummer of the northwest. Somehow it didn't seem appropriate that this tiny land bird should be dashing out over the mighty Pacific Ocean from such a height. Back along the foot trail leading from the point, there were no hummers at all and we decided that this particular hummer must have had a bit of the sea in its blood.

The day we ascended Mt. Rainier there had been several snowslides the night before and the road had to be cleared. Our upward progress was slow, therefore, but it was so still and beautiful under that canopy of giant trees that we were glad for the delay. We had two lifers that day, the Gray-crowned Rosy Finch, of which you have already heard, and the Northern Three-toed Woodpecker. I almost missed the woodpecker. I had left Marybelle sitting in the car and walked back down the road a short piece to watch a Dipper. It had struck me as odd that a Dipper should be flying up and down a road as though it were a mountain stream, though, as a matter of fact, the melting snow made that road a kind of stream. When I turned and started back to the car, I saw Marybelle frantically motioning me to hurry. Just after I had left, a female Northern Three-toed Woodpecker had alighted on a tree trunk not fifty feet from the car. Marybelle had been afraid to honk or get out of the car for fear the bird would vamoose and had suffered agonies of apprehension that I would be too late. The fates are seldom kind in such matters but this was one of the rare exceptions. I was in ample time to study the bird well before it flew. If I had missed that woodpecker, I should assuredly have gone back and wrung that Dipper's neck. No lister worth his salt could have blamed me.

Heading east from Mt. Rainier on our way back across Washington we picked up one more lifer in that state, the Chukar. This large Eurasian partridge has been introduced successfully in several places throughout the northwest and, like most other members of the quail and pheasant family, is strikingly colorful. We saw the Chukar at Sun Lake State Park as we had planned but not in the way we had anticipated. We stayed at a motel near the park that night and during the late afternoon spent the time picking likely "crowing rocks" in the Park that were to be carefully scanned for Chukars early next morning. We were up and out at the Park by dawn but the Chukars were not so energetic. We neither saw nor heard a single Chukar at any of our chosen sites. The sun rose higher and higher and before we left that Chukarless place it was after ten o'clock. In disgust, we returned to our motel a few miles south of the Park. By the time we were washed, packed, and I had shaved it was near noon. Our departure route, state 17, took us along the edge of Sun Lake Park. There at the side of the main highway at precisely noon were two Chukars! With the exception of that bachelor Sage Grouse and perhaps one or two others, I can't recall ever seeing any lifer at or near dawn, and the Chukar was another glaring example of this false prescription. The dawn patrol, I decided, was one of those inveterate myths that cling to the more gullible of the Brotherhood.

From Sun Lake Park we steered for the extreme northeastern section of Washington, near Lake Thomas. Lynn La Fave had told us this region was his favorite spot for Northern Three-toed Woodpeckers. Our lifer at Mt. Rainer had been a female and we wanted to see a male with his yellow cap. We did not see, or hear, a single woodpecker of any kind that day. As a slight compensation, we did find a nest of the Rufous Hummingbird and shortly thereafter I succeeded in breaking off the door key to the car in the lock. Our second set of keys was in Marybelle's purse locked in the car. We were miles from any human habitation and I had been a stupid ass for locking the car in the first place—just habit, I guess, from long association with the thieving populace of big cities. We spent several tense minutes secretly praying for a miracle or divine intervention, racking our wits for some simple solution to the problem. No genie appeared in a cloud of smoke, and it was all too plain that prosaic Lake Thomas offered no scope for thaumaturgic wand waving. My solution, finally, was unsophisticated in the extreme. I grabbed up a big rock and poised it so as to deliver a shattering blow to the glass of the door. Then sanity struck! Or was it, after all, the genie, invisible and sans smoke? I bethought me just in time that it was a station wagon and the other key to the tail gate was in my pocket still intact. Feeling more than foolish I unlocked the back end, crawled forward, and opened the doors. A man that stupid does not deserve male Northern Three-toed Woodpeckers. Probably not even the female.

Our next birding stop was to be Glacier National Park—only it wasn't. Torrential rains and melting snow combined to wash out most of the roads and practically all the bridges at Glacier that early summer of 1964. For the first time since it had opened, Glacier Park was closed to the public. We lingered in the vicinity of Flat Rock Lake for three days hoping that the Park would open. During this time we explored Nine-Pipe National Wildlife Refuge and the National Bison Range. It was exciting birding but no lifers came our way. Besides, just after Mr. Henry, manager of the Bison Range, gave us the keys to this marvelous place, the car refused to run. We finally got the car moving again but by that time it was almost evening and so we gave it up. The next day in the mountains to the east of Flat Rock Lake on a narrow dirt road at least ten miles from the paved highway, the car went completely dead. Not so much as a whisper of a groan could I get out of the starter. Yesterday it had been the carburetor and this, obviously, was not carburetor trouble. It was past noon so we ate our sandwiches before starting the long trek on foot back to the highway. Even after we reached the highway it would be over forty miles to our motel. And at this crucial point the genie took over again. Working his magic through my frail human form, he invested me with supernatural powers. I slammed down the hood—I had made the customary motorist's gesture—kicked the front end just once but with venomous brutality, got in the car, and pressed the starter. The motor purred and kept purring. The day of miracles was not past! When we finally reached a garage that afternoon, we discovered how the genie had contrived it. The starter wire had come loose and hung just fractions of a millimeter from its proper connection. That superhuman kick had brought the loose ends into temporary contact. The engine would continue to run perfectly without that connection but it wouldn't start. It took a skilled mechanic more than an hour to discover this Achilles' heel, so I didn't feel too woebegone for failing to find it myself. This is a true account in every particular, including the genie. Those who scoff do so at their own peril. It is never wise to offend a genie, either by thought or deed.

Glacier National Park, it seemed, would be closed for some time, so we sped eastward across northern Montana. Just east of a small village, Zurich, on route 2 we saw two Mountain Plovers, a long-sought lifer. I learned from Clifford Davis after reaching home that Elliott Coues on July 23, 1874, reported a pair of breeding Mountain Plovers at exactly this same spot and, of course, other more recent reports have also stated that this species is found along this route clear to the Dakota border.

Our final birding destination on this trip was Kenmare, North Dakota, where we hoped to find both Baird's Sparrow and Sprague's Pipit in that northern prairie country. The first day at Kenmare, we found several Baird's Sparrows on our own but had no luck with the Pipit. That evening, by good fortune, we chanced upon Mr. and Mrs. Charles T. Clark of Illinois at their camping site. Clark also was on the trail of Sprague's Pipit and had contacted Mrs. Gammell of Kenmare, who was to take him next morning to pipit territory. Dr. and Mrs. Robert T. Gammell are both enthusiastic birders and recognized authorities on the birds of the northern prairies. I myself should have known of them beforehand but I didn't, and I hasten to apologize to all concerned. I called Mrs. Gammell that night and she very generously offered to include us in tomorrow's trip.

As it turned out, the Gammells had unexpected guests and so Mrs. Gammell sent her protégé, Russell Rytter, to head the expedition. Russell is one of the sharpest young birders it has ever been my pleasure and wonderment to observe in the field. Whether he would have been so thoroughly the master with our warblers at Gradyville I do not know, but on those Dakota prairies he was superb. Apparently, he possessed preternatural aural endowment, for no slightest squeak or aerial rustle escaped his notice. Russell, Mr. Clark, and a few others led the way in a truck and I had a hard time keeping up with them on the dusty corduroy road. We had no sooner alighted at the spot than Russell heard Sprague's Pipit. He also heard a variety of other birds but for the time, at least, we wished to concentrate on the Pipit. Sprague's Pipit has a peculiar, hissing flight song that it renders high in the air, like the Skylark, only the song of the Pipit is very faint and difficult for a novice to hear. It is even harder to place because of its ventriloquial quality. The most apt description is to liken the sound to the soft, swishing noise made by a length of rope gyrating rapidly in the air. Russell repeatedly called our attention to the song but, for some reason, none of the rest of us were tuned in. It was not a matter of young ears versus old but simply a matter of conscious registry of sound. Russell solved the predicament by placing himself between Mr. Clark and me and grasping an arm of each. When he heard the song he pinched us both as long as the sound continued; when it ceased, he let up on us. That did the trick, and under the stress of this intermittent torture we soon caught on. But my arm was sore for some time thereafter and I heard Clark mumbling something about black and blue spots. Marybelle became attuned without the rigor of physical discipline and Mr. Clark and I bore our battle trauma manfully, so we all rejoiced in the new lifer, for us the last of the 1964 trip. Lest some unduly orthodox member of the Brotherhood misinterpret the Sprague's Pipit affair, let me hasten to add that we saw the bird, or birds, several times on the ground and fence posts with our glasses at lethal range. But it is that eerie, faint aerial song that I remember, not the bird's rather dull exterior.

Thus the 1964 trip to the northwest effectively ended on those ringing plains of windy Dakota, with 24 lifers and a total of 545 North American birds. Late the preceding year, we had read the proclamation in *Audubon* Magazine announcing the birth of the 600 Club. We now knew we had 55 birds yet to see to realize our goal.

Southwest and Mexico, 1965

On this our fifth birding trip, we again journeyed through Texas, New Mexico, and Arizona and dipped into Mexico for eight short days. Of the Mexican trip I shall say nothing; it does not concern the 600 Club nor did we cover ourselves with glory—quite the converse.

We routed our trip through Florida, southern Alabama, Mississippi, and Louisiana, chiefly to see Bachman's Sparrow. This is the same Bachman for whom Audubon named the Bachman's Warbler of ill repute. The Reverend John Bachman of Charleston, South Carolina, was a rare individual and a great naturalist in his own right—but Bachman is not a lucky name for us. Oh, yes, we did finally see the sparrow, but not until we had almost crossed the east Texas border. Our North American lifers for the trip totaled just seven. A lucky number, to be sure, but we should have preferred an "unlucky" higher figure.

There are two episodes of the trip in North America that merit recital—one because of its tragicomic and rather forbidding character, the other because of its humorous aspects. So, of the seven lifers, we'll limit ourselves to the Cave Swallow and the Green Kingfisher.

The Cave Swallow's breeding range in North America is limited to southeastern New Mexico and south-central Texas, in Texas chiefly along the southern extremity of the Edwards Plateau west of Kerrville. The birds are not found north of the border in winter or fall and very little is actually known of their winter range. As its name implies, this swallow nests exclusively in caves or sinkholes and there are a number of such known to harbor this swallow. Mr. Fred S. Webster, Jr., of Austin had sent me explicit directions and suggestions for finding both the Cave Swallow and Green Kingfisher. Once at Kerrville, we decided to try the nearest and most readily accessible of those localities for the Cave Swallow. This was a stock tank right beside highway 39 on a ranch twenty miles or more west of Kerrville. We found the tank with no difficulty and in an hour or less had seen several Cave Swallows hawking for insects around the tank in the company of the much more numerous Cliff Swallow. The Cave closely resembles the Cliff except that it has a lighter throat and a darker forehead. It was instructive to have the two species there together for comparison. Our next spot for Cave Swallows should have been the Devil's Sinkhole farther to the west, the traditional place most people see them. Mr. Webster, however, had also mentioned a closer spot, a cave on the nearby Wilson Ranch. We decided to try it first. Besides, to visit the Devil's Sinkhole one must first obtain permission and keys from the owner in Rocksprings, always a time-consuming project. The road leading to the Wilson Ranch was at that time under repair and was blocked at its northern end. We circled far south and gained the same road from its southern terminus, aiming eventually to reach the Wilson Ranch farther north. We never saw the ranch or the Wilsons.

We drove a little and walked a little along this dirt road. It was good birding and we were in no special hurry to reach the Wilson's place. On one of the walking stints, we passed over a cattle guard beyond which were three horses. After our experience with the temperamental Star at Big Bend, we had a profound regard for equine vagaries and both of us were painstakingly careful not to alarm the three that now stood watching us. We walked slowly, talked quietly, and made no quick movements of any sort. We even stood quietly for a space to let them become accustomed to our presence. The three of them came up to us at this juncture and I, forgetting for the moment that the horse was no favorite of mine, patted one of them on the head. The last view we had as we rounded a bend in the road was of the three standing quietly on the spot where we had left them.

About twenty minutes later, on our way back to the car, we heard two shots. A few more minutes brought us to a pickup truck in a shallow ford across the road. The fellow at the wheel glowered in a surly manner at us and with no introductory remarks of any sort accused us of frightening his horses. One of them, he told us, had charged into a barbed-wire fence and was so badly injured that he had been obliged to shoot the crazed animal. We were, quite understandably, dumfounded and appalled at this baseless accusation. We knew we had frightened no horses; quite the contrary. We gushed out our dismay and indignation and told him every particular of our meeting with the horses. He did not believe us, of course, or feigned disbelief, and sat moodily in his truck saying not a word. When I made yet another attempt to convince him of our innocence and good will, he shut me up short. "There's too many of you damned bird watchers comin' down this road anyway," was his unsavory and unseasonable reply. We tried a few more expostulations, but his only answer was to turn his truck around and drive away. I was outraged by the whole, incredulous mummery, and was also beginning to smell a rat; he had refused to show me where the horse had been hurt.

We continued our alternate walking and driving north on that road. But whenever we were walking, that truck and its jolly occupant were always abreast of us in the adjacent fields. It sounds a bit melodramatic in the telling but we became convinced that the fellow was dogging our route in the expectation that we would sooner or later trespass on his land. Whether he would have shot us out of hand or simply called the sheriff, I cannot say, but his every maneuver plainly indicated it would be one or the other. This was not my idea of joyous birding. We stuck it out for awhile, hating the thought of being intimidated by this oaf. But it was no go. The absurdity of the situation at last disgusted us and we turned the car around and headed away from the Wilson Ranch. For all we knew the fellow might be Mr. Wilson or his brother and if so, a fat chance we should have had of seeing Cave Swallows there. It is within the bounds of possibility, although most improbable, that after we left those three docile animals, something may have startled them—a lizard, a snake, a sound—and the fellow's story be true. I choose to think otherwise. I'll wager a cave full of swallows against one Common Crow that those two shots were fired in the air or into a tree. It was a depressing episode, and we decided to get out of troglodyte country and on to the haunts of the Green Kingfisher.

The Green Kingfisher is preeminently a bird of Mexico, Central America, and much of South America. Its range in the United States is never too far from the Mexican border, in Texas and Arizona. It is much smaller than our common eastern Kingfisher and has a disproportionately large bill. Its colors are striking. All in all, it is a most delectable bird and I coveted it sorely. Through Mr. Webster and other sources, we knew of three or four places in Texas where the bird had been seen or might be seen. The nearest of these sites to the Cave Swallow region is Garner State Park north of Uvalde. We spent the equivalent of an entire day walking up and down the banks of the stream that flows through the Park looking and waiting for the Green Kingfisher, but no luck. The Park was fairly crowded and amplified "music" from the headquarters acted like a coarse file on my nerves. Among the several million idiocies perpetrated by the human animal, amplified, cacophonous noise deluging the countryside is one of the least forgivable. If I attempted to beat my neighbor about the head with a spiked cudgel, I should hardly get in one blow before the local gendarmery had me in a straitjacket. But if I choose to bombard his ears with rock "music" or the aimless never-get-anyplace twanging of an electrically amplified guitar, I can, with utter impunity, drive him stark, raving mad, and all will consider the complaints of the afflicted as an unwarranted constraint upon my "freedom." The aural pollution of this country is at least as serious as air or water pollution. The Green Kingfisher must have had similar notions or sensibilities of a like sort because he remained steadfastly aloof from the Park and its racket. So we left Garner Park and headed for Del Rio on the Rio Grande.

As reported by *Audubon* Magazine in one of Pettingill's bird-finding articles, the golf course and its meandering stream at Del Rio were a cinch for Green Kingfishers. I can recall a letter in a later issue praising the accuracy of Pettingill's article as to the ease of finding the bird—no pun intended—on this same golf course. Furthermore, the Christmas Bird Count for the Del Rio area had listed seven Green Kingfishers, mostly on or about the links. I was more than confident; I was even composed. Our first day on the golf course there was a slight drizzle, just enough to dampen our clothes but not our spirits. The second day our clothes were dry but our spirits were sodden—no Green Kingfisher. One would have reasonably supposed that at least one of those seven Kingfishers would make an appearance, but none did. By the end of that second day, I knew the location and shape of every divot on that course and could have unerringly walked from each tee to green blindfolded. But the Green Kingfisher had undoubtedly gone into aestivation. Too bad we didn't bring our golf clubs, now relegated to forlorn desuetude in the attic. I had once, and only once, shot a seventy-six on a course very much like this one. Maybe if we ignored the bird, it might just possibly show. Foolish reflections like these helped pass time but, obviously, did little else.

On the morning of the third day we set out for the third place where the Green Kingfisher was said to be, Devil's River, a few miles west of Del Rio. We prowled up and down this riverbed, now mostly dry, all morning without success. We gave up shortly after noon and returned to Del Rio. I've always had an unreasoning aversion to telephone prattle but by this time we were sorely in need of advice. Mr. Webster was in Mexico at the time but he had given me the names and phone numbers of several prominent birders in Austin. I decided to phone Miss Mary Ann McClendon, who had three years before given me information about the Golden-cheeked Warbler.

We stopped at a phone booth outside a drug store and pooled our loose change for the pay call. There was $1.75 in quarters and the usual amount of dimes and nickels, surely ample for a short call to Austin. I could hear the phone ringing and a woman's voice answered but then, of course, came the expected voice of the operator—"Deposit $3.50, please." I asked the operator to hold on for just a minute while I frantically gesticulated to Marybelle to go into the drug store and get more quarters, two dollars' worth. Very strange, I thought, that a call to Austin would cost so much. I could have called home for that amount, I thought. When the bong, bong of those fourteen quarters finally subsided, I heard again the feminine "Hello" at the other end. I plunged at once into my tale of frustration and woe: "My wife and I have been looking for two days on the Del Rio golf course for the Green Kingfisher and we haven't had one bit of luck. Do you know whether the birds are still here? Have you been on the golf course recently yourself? I'm sure we would have seen one if the birds were here. We're at our wits' end. Can you give me any suggestions? Do you think we should spend any more time on the golf course?" I don't recall my exact words or their sequence, naturally, but this was the substance of my jeremiad. "I do not play golf," was the first rejoinder. And then, "I know of no Del Rio. Why are you asking me all these questions, anyway?" And, finally, as my bewilderment increased over these disjointed and seemingly zany remarks, "Besides, I have never seen a Green Kingfisher. I'm sure it must be a most uncommon bird about Boston." Boston! My God! I had been talking to some unknown woman in Boston! Where else in the United States could one get not only the wrong party but the wrong city and obtain a halfway intelligible answer about a specific bird! I explained the mistake as best I could and added that I supposed my poor Texas accent was partly to blame for the operator confusing Austin with Boston. The lady from Boston was not overly amused by my feeble attempt at wit for she hung up without further ceremony. I couldn't face even a remotely possible repeat of this farce so, after the operator returned my $3.50, I gave her Edgar Kincaid's number and repeated the word Austin several times with my best imitation of a Texas accent. At last I got Austin and, finally, Mr. Kincaid.

Mr. Kincaid exhorted patience and more patience and so we had another try at the Devil's River; I was sick of that golf course. Patience and time are obverse sides of the same coin, however, and the one cannot be separated from the other. We did not see the Green Kingfisher at Devil's River on that second try, so we headed on west for Arizona and Mexico.

And now the last act of this little drama, in yet another part of the forest. We returned from our brief Mexican trip via Reynosa. Although it would not have added to our North American list of birds, we had assumed that we would surely see the Green Kingfisher in Mexico. But in eighteen hundred miles of travel we did not see a single kingfisher. So, there was nothing for it but to try Del Rio and that infernal golf course once more.

A momentary whim to spend a few hours at Bentsen State Park on the way to Del Rio was our salvation. The wife of the superintendent told us that Falcon Dam was one of the most likely places in Texas to see the Green Kingfisher and it had the advantage that it was on the route to Del Rio if we couldn't find it at the dam. We stopped at the dam and within ten minutes we had seen our first Green Kingfisher, on the U.S. side for good measure. It was just as simple as that. I wished the austere woman of Boston could have been there to share our jubilation. The next time someone phoned her, she would have had the answer.

The Green Kingfisher was number 557 and the brief winter trip to Texas added three more—Whooping Crane at Aransas Wildlife Refuge, Olivaceous Cormorant at Rockport, and the Harris's Sparrow on the Lewisville, Texas, Christmas Bird Count. We were guests of Professor Warren Pulich, his son "Bobby," and Bruce Mack on the Lewisville count and it was both fun and good experience for us to be a part of a Christmas count far from our customary domain. The cormorant, thirty-three Whoopers, and the ninety Harris's Sparrows, eighty of them in one bush, now made our AOU area total 560. Thus ended 1965.

East Canadian Trip, 1966

The addition of one more new bird—Henslow's Sparrow, seen at Eliot Island, Maryland, in April 1966—had now brought our total North American lifer list to 561, 39 short of our goal of 600 birds. The East Canadian Trip, insofar as the acquisition of lifers is concerned, started at Acadia National Park on Mt. Desert Island, Maine, with the Black Guillemot. We saw only one of these birds, close in toward shore and almost obscured by the heavy fog. We took the Bluenose Ferry from Bar Harbor to Yarmouth, Nova Scotia, seeing two more lifers en route, the

Sooty Shearwater and Wilson's Petrel. Both of these birds breed in the southern hemisphere but roam the open Atlantic in our summer as far north as Labrador. From Yarmouth we traveled along the southern side of Nova Scotia to its eastern end. From North Sydney we took the ferry to Port aux Basque, Newfoundland. Back in Nova Scotia, our route led westward along the northern side and, finally, southward through eastern New Brunswick and back into Maine to Muzzy's Upper Camp for eleven days. This is the outline of our itinerary, and it now remains only to describe briefly the trip to the Bird Islands off Cape Dauphin, Nova Scotia, and our adventure of the Cabot Strait. All our remaining lifers were seen during one or the other of these two spans.

Nova Scotia in the early June of 1966 was a delightful place to be. It was an exhilarating experience after the sun and heat of Mexico and the southwest. The lifers were not many, a total of eleven for the entire trip, but we had known beforehand that this would be so. Still, there were a number of pelagic birds common to these northern waters that we wished very much to see, and we had already been west a number of times. In the two birding trips we have so far taken into Canada, it is the railroads, strangely enough, that have intrigued us. I don't mean the railroads per se, of course—the iron rails, noisy locomotives, and ugly boxcars, those galley slaves of commerce—but the whole early twentieth-century atmosphere of those bygone days, before the ascendancy of the internal combustion engine and, later, the flying machine. The greater authority and prestige of the Iron Horse in Canada was to us symbolic of those quieter if not necessarily happier times. I frequently experienced the indelible nostalgia of my early boyhood when the automobile was not yet a necessity and the steam locomotive spoke of power and distant horizons. I recalled those still nights, lying half asleep in my bed by the open window, when the hoarse, mournful wail of the midnight express to Chicago was heard over the muffled sounds of a city asleep. The whistle of those old Monon trains was indescribably sad and they affected me then as does now the honking of northbound geese high above in the darkness. Certainly I am aware that Canada has huge airports, too many automobiles, racial problems, and all the other modern inconveniences, but in Nova Scotia, at least, I sensed that the Iron Horse had not quite yet been put out to pasture. It was still a vital force, not a relic on the scrap heap of man's ingenuity. And so we loved the railroads. Not so much for what they were but for the memories they conjured up.

Mr. Ahle of Big Bras d'Or had some overnight cabins and, what interested us more, a boat in which he would pilot birders out to the small, rocky Bird Islands off Cape Dauphin. The Great Cormorant, Razor-billed Auk, Common Puffin, Black Guillemot, Great Black-backed Gull, Common Murre, and Leach's Petrel nest on these Islands. Our party of birders that day saw all of these but Leach's Petrel, and the first three of these were lifers for us. Leach's Petrel nests in burrows on the grassy tops of the Islands and leaves its nest only after nightfall to range the ocean for several days before again changing places with its mate. Consequently, we did not expect to see this bird in the vicinity of the Islands. We must have seen at least thirty puffins and they are always an amusing and joyous sight. We had very likely seen the Great Cormorant in winter off the Jersey shore, but without its white flank patch, seen only in breeding plumage, it is not easily distinguishable from the common Double-crested Cormorant and we had not felt justified in counting it. The Razor-billed Auk is an alcid found only on the Atlantic coast and, except for its bill and a few other things, resembles the Common Murre, which we had first seen on the Pacific coast.

It was a most gratifying trip as far as the list was concerned but alcids and their ilk always leave me with a feeling that I have been to the zoo. Pelagic trips, despite their informality and fun, are a soulless type of birding. I have only seen the Hermit Warbler twice but I know this bird much better than the hundreds of Puffins or Shearwaters I have seen—in the latter two cases, naturally, I speak of numbers, not species. One reason is obvious, of course; I do not live on the coast and have been on only a dozen or so pelagic trips—I have no familiarity with ocean birds. There is a more subtle and basic reason, though, for estrangement. It is the ocean itself. The ocean is never intimate, always remote. One does not make friends with Mother Carey's chickens; one only sees them.

The principal attraction of the 1966 trip was the *Cabot Strait*. I refer to the boat, not the ninety-odd miles of water connecting the Atlantic Ocean and the Gulf of St. Lawrence. We had decided upon a boat trip from Nova Scotia to Newfoundland as a further means of increasing our sea bird lifers. The ferry runs between North Sydney, Nova Scotia, and Port aux Basque, Newfoundland, and takes two days for the round trip. This meant that we should have to stay overnight at Port aux Basque. The car would be left in a parking lot at North Sydney. We had our reservations for June 5 and 6 several days in advance. The *William Carson*, a large and relatively new boat, was to begin its first run of the summer season at that time. It was not yet in dock but would be at North Sydney on June 4. This ferry system is owned and operated by the Canadian National Railway.

It was a thirty-mile trip from where we were staying to North Sydney but we were at the ferry office well before the appointed departure hour. But there was no *William Carson* at the wharf, or anything else that remotely resembled the picture we had seen of this fancy-looking craft. To my amazement, we were told that the *William Carson* had not yet arrived from her more southern moorings, that not one word had been heard from her captain and that, apparently, she was lost! This startling piece of intelligence caused us no little dismay, but the ferry personnel appeared almost more pleased than otherwise: to them it was an unexpected break in the otherwise monotonous routine. "Don't worry. We'll see that you get to Port aux Basque," we were encouraged. "The CN won't let you down." And it didn't.

The ticket agent picked up our single bag and told us to

follow him. We must have walked a quarter of a mile at least, threading our way around freight cars, up and down over loading platforms, and across innumerable tracks. By the time we reached our wharf, the ticket man was huffing and puffing and I was thankful he had insisted on carrying the bag. There she stood, or nautical terms to that effect—the cargo ship *Cabot Strait*! She was a much smaller boat than the *WC* and although everything on board was neat and shipshape, her exterior and decks gave every indication of the rough life she led. It turned out that Marybelle and I were the sole paying passengers aboard. There were, in addition, only three "deadhead" employees of the CN, and the crew. We had that whole boat to ourselves and it was a perfect craft for our purpose, big enough to ride steadily through all but the choppiest of seas and small enough to be close to the water. It was love at first sight and we blessed that errant captain of the *WC* who had failed in some inexplicable way to make port in time.

Some of the crew invited us in for coffee before we "sailed" and after we had been served the Captain came over and sat a spell at our table. We told him the purpose of our voyage was to see birds. Understandably, Captain Brown was not thinking of birds and misconstrued "birds" into "bergs." His boat, or should I say ship, had just returned from coastal Labrador, carrying on its outward voyage about seventy-five Indians returning to Labrador for the summer fishing. They had sighted several icebergs on that trip and, naturally, under those circumstances, icebergs would have been uppermost in any captain's mind. We got this misunderstanding straightened out before long but I was sorry we wouldn't see any bergs on this trip. Bells began to sound and the whistle to blow and Marybelle and I hastened out on deck to make sure the ship was weighed properly.

The run to Port aux Basque took about nine hours and we reveled in every minute of it. It was cold but not bitter and the sun was out most of the time. All we lacked was an expert on oceanic birds to make it the most perfect pelagic trip we have ever taken. We may have missed some birds, but even so we kept the leaves of our Peterson Field Guide fluttering in the breeze and if we did miss some birds, we did not miss the expert. I have a bad habit of not making lists of all birds seen on trips and so cannot give you a complete account of the species we saw that fifth of June. As we approached Newfoundland, we came near enough to the Great Bank so that large numbers of birds were seen. Our lifers for that fifth of June were: Skua, Fulmar, Greater Shearwater, and Red Phalarope. In addition there were Gannets, Black-legged Kittiwakes, Sooty Shearwaters, Wilson's Petrels, and several species of tern and gull, none of them lifers for us. We were on the lookout for an Ivory Gull but did not see one. The Skua was definite. We first sighted him in the water and there he remained until the *Cabot Strait* was abreast of him, within a hundred feet. He then flew parallel to the ship until he was only a speck on the horizon ahead. We had more than ample time to observe all field marks well: dark, chunky body; very rusty underparts; stubby, dark tail *and* the conspicuous white patches at the base of the primaries. It was amazing, considering his apparently laborious flight, how soon he outdistanced the *Cabot Strait*—another field "mark" for the Skua. I wrote to Dr. Harrison F. Lewis of Sable River, Nova Scotia, giving him all the particulars of this sighting of a Skua. He generously agreed that it was, indeed, a Skua. Incidentally, I almost forgot to mention that there were four, not three, "deadheads" aboard that day. A short way out from North Sydney, we discovered a female Parula Warbler on board and the bird remained with the ship the entire voyage. We could only hope she would find a mate in Newfoundland. There are few, if any, records of the Parula in Newfoundland.

We ate the noon meal with the three "deadheads," very interesting men, and the Captain and his officers ate at the adjoining table. It was the same for the five o'clock meal, an hour or so before we docked. I hated to leave the decks, for I was certain another Skua or perhaps an Ivory Gull would top the horizon the minute I went inside, but I was ravenous and both meals were superb—good solid food and plenty of it, besides lots of relish and pickles. Later in the afternoon, Captain Brown took us up on the bridge and explained the working of the ship. Marybelle remained for coffee but I went back to my "watch on the quarterdeck." It was then that I sighted the first flock of Red Phalaropes flying fast and low over the water. I was in a frenzy because Marybelle had missed them; I need not have worried. By the time Marybelle was on deck again, flock after flock went careening by and the next day on our return we must have seen hundreds. I hated like sin to disembark and had I been a younger man, I believe that then and there I should have asked to be read in as one of the hands.

Since it was Sunday, the hotel restaurant at Port aux Basque was closed, but we wheedled two sandwiches out of the management, delivered to our room. I was in an exalted state after the *Cabot Strait* and the Skua and I tipped the sandwich girl lavishly. Too lavishly, for she had no sooner gone than she was back, saying I had given her a two-dollar tip. I bethought myself of the Canadian railroads and this almost vanished era in the U.S. Where today in the United States could one find such probity! I told her to keep the two bucks, with a magnanimous gesture of some sort or other. She was not impressed by my prodigality, however, and backed out of the door with a look that said only too plainly, "This man is crazy." Next morning at breakfast I was to be confirmed in my appraisal of that look, for she steadfastly ignored our table while every so often casting covert glances at the madman. It was somewhat embarrassing, but before long I regained my composure in contemplation and ready dispatch of the excellent bacon and eggs eventually brought to us by the other waitress. I made a resolve that in future my largess should be regulated by circumstances. Anyway, one does not see a Skua every day or even decade and the girl was probably correct; I must have been temporarily delirious.

I phoned the CN office and was told that the long-lost *William Carson* had come in last night. Presumably, the Captain of the *WC* must have thought the boat was to go first to Port aux Basque instead of North Sydney. The proprietor of the hotel, in keeping with the geography of the place, owned an immense Newfoundland dog called Carlo, and this half ton or so of fur, bone, and muscle was wedged hard against the outside of the hotel doors when we tried to leave. He gave no evidence that my puny efforts to dislodge him were even felt. The proprietor called to him and rapped on the door, but he merely swung his massive head and looked at us reproachfully. But when the little daughter of the proprietor was summoned to our aid, Carlo got to his feet with an amazing alacrity for so big a brute and whined to be let in. In he came with a vengeance when I opened the door, and I barely missed being trampled to death. If his little mistress had not been on hand, we should in all probability have had to decamp through one of the windows.

The *William Carson* was whistling when we reached the wharf but did not leave for almost an hour. I shall say little about our return trip to North Sydney except that the *WC* was not the *Cabot Strait*. It was the usual semiplush tourist boat—too big, too crowded, incessant canned music, and the decks too high for observing birds. We wished we were back on the *Cabot Strait*, leaving soon for Labrador parts. We did see at least three Leach's Petrels, though, when we were off the Newfoundland Bank, and this unexpected good fortune mellowed us considerably. There were lots of Wilson's about and we took great care to distinguish between the two. Our Leach's all had dark feet and the peculiar, butterfly-like method of flight; the forked tails were harder to make out but we saw this well on at least one of our three birds. Leach's Petrel was our last and eleventh lifer on the 1966 Canadian trip. The rest of the trip was good birding and great fun but I think you and I have about had it. Right?

We flew to Monterey, California, in December 1966 and spent our Christmas vacation birding around Pacific Grove. We also made a trip on Christmas Day to Merced National Waterfowl Sanctuary and saw several thousand Ross's Geese. We participated in the Monterey Peninsula Christmas Bird Count and also took a private pelagic trip off Monterey Bay in the company of two local hotshots, Dr. Ronald L. Branson and William Reese. All told, we added another eleven lifers to our even dozen garnered that year. The total of North American birds was now 583. We were within striking distance of the 600 Club and the next summer would find us in Alaska.

At long last, we have come full circle back to that bleak day at Cold Bay in August 1967 and the climax of all our efforts: St. Paul Island in the Pribilofs and six hundred-plus North American birds. Admittedly, the first part of the 1967 Alaskan trip has been ignored, but this omission, in part, will be remedied by incorporating such incidents as are germane in the brief sketch of our subsequent trip to Alaska. You and I, and Marybelle, of course, have journeyed long and far, seen many birds and have known the spell of those siren voices of the desert, mountain, and sea. Let's rest our weary bones momentarily and I'll tell you about Gradyville and what little I know about the mannerisms and customs of the amateur birding Brotherhood.

IV

Gradyville

Ever since we discovered Gradyville in June of 1960, it has been
our favorite birding place. Many, if not most, birders have had a
similar experience. There is one piece of land, some special terrain, a bit of shoreline, some mountain slope or other haven that
one comes to love, either because the birding is exceptionally
interesting or because it is the most readily available spot where
one, like Antaeus of old, may renew one's strength by contact
with the good earth. Our Gradyville is a tract of approximately
twenty-five hundred acres of Pennsylvania woodland and old
farms about eighteen miles west of Philadelphia and a fifteen-
minute drive from our home. A stream, Ridley Creek, runs
through it and there are numerous wooded ravines, hills, and
fields now mostly feral. Gradyville is a flagrant misnomer, of

course. At present its official name is Ridley Creek State Park and before that it was the old Jeffords Estate. The actual Gradyville is a crossroads hamlet to the west of our birding domain. I suppose we began calling our retreat Gradyville because few people we knew had heard of the Jeffords and we could best direct other birders to the spot by calling their attention to the location of the village on the local maps. After that it became a habit. So, we would no more think of calling it Ridley Creek State Park than you would refer to Grant's Tomb as the National Monument in Commemoration of Ulysses Simpson Grant. Gradyville, then, in these memoirs, is a parcel of land—fields, woods, hills, stream—not the little hamlet at the crossroad dreaming of revolutionary days and the tinkle of sleigh bells in the blue twilight of wintry evenings.

The history of this eastern Pennsylvania countryside is no doubt interesting; however, not being an antiquarian but a single-track birder, I cannot relate it. On the summit of Hunting Hill, the highest spot at Gradyville, there is a tiny graveyard, walled off by stone, in which deaths as long ago as 1838 are inscribed on the fallen and broken slabs. We have often rested on this stone wall and listened to the insistent song of the Cerulean Warbler high overhead in the big tulip or oak trees or turned our faces toward each other in amused recognition of the covert, hatchet-like sound of the Pileated Woodpecker tearing chunks of wood from an old dead beech tree far down on the southern slope. Jessie Lamplugh, an old birding acquaintance of ours, now dead these past ten years, has relatives buried in this spot, and he once told us that the Master of the Hunt in those bygone times was buried standing up with his face to the west, where he could watch the hounds and horses top the rise as they thundered by. It seems to me that I have heard similar tales about similar people in other places. But let it pass—who am I to say what transpires on moonless nights atop Hunting Hill? At any rate, we have seen the fox hunt many a time in broad daylight pass over and beyond the hill, with riders in picturesque scarlet and hounds yapping in the forefront. But the Hunt is no more at Gradyville.

Some years ago the Rose Tree Hunt Club folded up its tents and silently stole away. But there are still foxes and that is all that really matters. A vixen had her litter of pups north of the creek over from Hunting Hill last year. So much for the rude annals of our forefathers.

The recent history and future of Gradyville are all too clear. In 1966 the Commonwealth of Pennsylvania took it over from the Jeffords for a new state park. It was to have been named the Jeffords's State Park but the Jeffords, six months prior to the legal consummation of the deal, sold timber rights to the chain-saw bandits and, in consequence of this somewhat shady procedure, Gradyville was named Ridley Creek State Park. I recall all too vividly this rape of a woodland. It proceeded for six months without letup. I leave you to imagine the havoc that was wrought. I have counted over ninety fresh stumps on Hunting Hill alone. As I am writing this, Gradyville is not yet open to the public. But there are only a few more months of grace in which Marybelle and I will be able to enjoy its solitude. And so to us, the end of an era is approaching. We have been fortunate indeed, however, for the Superintendent gave us permission to continue our bird studies, which we've done through the entire six or seven years since the State took over. No wonder we have come to regard Gradyville as our private domain. We cherish every rod of its 2,489.3 acres—even that last three tenths. In truth, I suppose we should be thankful that the State did buy up the land. The old Jeffords Estate could not have remained intact much longer with all those kids in the back of all those station wagons you and I have seen over the past years. No, it would have succumbed and a giant Levittown or worse would have been the result. But when the rioting hordes do finally invade our sanctuary, I shall feel as though the ancestral estate was going under the auctioneer's hammer. I can visualize it only too clearly. "What am I offered for this shattered old hickory tree standing there all by itself, lonesome-like against the sky? What, no bidders! Put it aside, Hank, I guess no one wants that sort of thing nowadays. What, then, about this sleepy old hillside basking in the afternoon sunshine, with here and there a clump of briar or wild apple trees clustered about some gray, lichened boulders! What do I hear? What do I hear? Nothing! Put it back, Hank. I guess maybe a ski run would be more saleable." And so it will go. I do not have the answer. I doubt if there is one. Some three thousand years ago Homer sang in cadences measured of the good old days. All is relative. But that is poor consolation. Perhaps endless futility is the true and proper sphere of the head primate. It would seem so.

The two of us have recorded 169 species of bird in the past dozen years at Gradyville. We have never seen or heard a Barn Owl there but we know from other sources that this species has been seen or heard within our time. Undoubtedly, too, Saw-whet Owls must occasionally winter at Gradyville because they are reported from adjacent areas now and then. All told, the list could probably be extended to 175 or 180 if more people systematically birded there. But 169 birds is not too bad for only two people, particularly since Gradyville, like any other relatively small area, has a limited variety of habitats. There are no lakes or natural ponds and the marsh area is very small. The latter has become even more restricted since the building of a parking lot along its upper reaches. The chief habitats for birds at Gradyville are woods, former grazing pastures, thickets, and the like. Primarily, it is the passerine birds that nest at Gradyville or pass through it in migration. Naturally, there are a number of exceptions, such as hawks, owls, a few waders, two or three shore birds and the like. We have recorded seventy-one nesting species so far and careful surveillance will probably add the Parula Warbler and possibly the Black-and-white and Cerulean Warblers and Traill's Flycatcher as well. The Cerulean and Parula Warblers have been found nesting in other nearby areas and have undoubtedly done so at Gradyville, but we ourselves lack evidence of this. We have observed Black-and-white Warblers as late as June 28 but have no real proof that this species nests there. In the summer of 1971 we conclusively established the nesting of the American Redstart for the first time.

Our most unusual rarities or accidentals have probably been the Black-backed Woodpecker, Bald Eagle (on the ground, not flying), Prothonotary Warbler, and, quite recently, three Black Vultures soaring over Hunting Hill. This more southern of the vultures in the United States seldom reaches Pennsylvania, but there have been occasional reports and there is one nesting record for the extreme south-central portion of the state. The Black-backed Woodpecker, a more northern species, was seen in one of the extensive white pine plantings of Gradyville. It was winter, of course, and we observed it four different times within a period of eight days. To the best of my knowledge, no one else caught even a glimpse of it although we had set the birding grapevine atremble immediately after our initial sighting. As a matter of fact, Paul DeAoun haunted that pine woods for days thereafter and George Spitalny and his chum, Robbie Askins, set up a checkerboard in the center of the woods for two consecutive days and alternately cheated each other at checkers and watched on the side for that woodpecker. Neither party ever saw that particular Black-backed. The Prothonotary Warbler, though usually associated in our minds with southern swamps, actually nests as far north as southern Canada. It is not often recorded from Delaware County, though, and we got a tremendous kick out of our two individuals seen at Gradyville. Both birds were seen in May, two years apart and on precisely the same spot—a small gravel spit in the shallows of Ridley Creek.

With regard to the Bald Eagle, it is perhaps strange that we have seen only one at Gradyville in all this time and that it should be quietly resting in a field instead of circling high in its azure domain. It was not injured, because later we watched it ascend higher and still higher in ever-widening spirals until even with my 9 x 35 glasses it was only the proverbial speck in the blue firmament. Who but a madman or sick fool would ever knock such a creature out of the skies! Do not delude yourself. Madman or fool, yes. But the trouble lies deeper than this, much deeper. Eagle murder is merely a minuscule segment of the human experiment. This experiment has been under way now for nearly three quarters of a million years amid more internecine carnage, bloodshed, misery, and intentional brutality than in any other intraspecies conflict on evolutionary record. Man has always claimed the right to kill when and how it suited his misguided interests, be it the people of southeast Asia, eagles, or the mice you and I set traps for in our pantries. The sheep rancher who hires eagles to be slaughtered by plane probably talks baby talk to his lambs. Man in the aggregate is wholly irrational. The neocortex, with all its fringe benefits, is perhaps nature's single greatest blunder, anthropocentrically speaking. Its self-justification is limitless. And so eagles are killed not because a handful of damned fools decrees it but because the species to which they belong is both damned and foolish. Human intelligence is a myth perpetrated for its own ends—which are probably blind and undoubtedly nefarious. But enough of this neo-existential despair. Let's get with the warblers at Gradyville.

Warblers, as I have intimated before, are our favorite birds. Our warbler records at Gradyville are more extensive than those of any other group. Gradyville is large enough and its habitats sufficiently varied so that all species of migrating warblers are usually seen there, either in spring or fall. There is also a fair contingent of regular nesting species. Thirty-five species of Wood Warblers, family Parulidae, either migrate through or nest in eastern Pennsylvania. One other species, the Yellow-throated Warbler, has been known to nest in Delaware County or is recorded as a vagrant from time to time. We have recorded all thirty-six of these species from Gradyville. In addition, the two hybrid types resulting from mating between Blue-winged and Golden-winged Warblers have also been seen. Brewster's, the heterozygous dominant, has been observed twice, and Lawrence's, the rare homozygous recessive, has been seen once. The fascinating aspect of these hybrid observations is that all three individuals were seen in exactly the same area but in different years. If this is pure coincidence, it is indeed unusual. We have sought evidence of Blue-winged $\times$ Golden-winged matings in this particular area, and elsewhere at Gradyville, but so far without success. The fact remains that no Golden-winged Warblers have ever been observed during the summer breeding season, only the Blue-winged. Genetically, this is not conclusive evidence that either our Brewster's or Lawrence's hybrids were not hatched at Gradyville, because phenotypical Blue-wings could still carry Golden-winged genes. Also, of course, typical Lawrence's hybrids do not result from pure Blue-wing × Golden-wing mating but occur only in the second generation. However, all three hybrids were seen in either spring or fall and this fact, in the absence of summering Golden-winged Warblers, is suggestive. It is, therefore, probably pure coincidence that these hybrids were all seen in the same restricted area. Eleven species regularly nest at Gradyville. We suspect that the Yellow-throated Warbler also nests occasionally at Gradyville but our personal evidence is so far entirely circumstantial. Four warblers—Prothonotary, Orange-crowned, Yellow-throated, Mourning—we have only seen two or three times. It is always a red-letter day when one of these rarities shows up at Gradyville. Furthermore, the Connecticut Warbler, seen in the east almost always during fall migration, is rather spotty in its appearance. The most we have ever seen in one year at Gradyville is three and some years there are none, meaning, of course, that they were probably there but we weren't. I believe our May record for a single day is twenty-eight warblers. I could verify or revise this figure by laborious reference to our notes and recorded dates, but since such a figure has utterly no scientific value and since I should suffer minor deflation of ego if I found it were, in fact, less than twenty-eight, let us be charitable and grant me my "big day" in warblers at Gradyville as twenty-eight species. In any event, twenty-eight species of warblers seen in one area only, in one state, by two observers in one party may be a record, under the conditions set forth. David A. Cutler, Grand Birding Vizier of the Middle Atlantic States, recorded thirty-one Warblers in a single day in May 1957 and thirty-two the next year. However, on each of these occasions Cutler's party consisted of four people, birding in three states, and covering

127 air miles. Gradyville and its warblers need apologize to no man.

Our lifers at Gradyville are, understandably, very few—a total of six to date. We had been birding for exactly three and a half years before Gradyville swam into our ken and, obviously, it is not a place for shore birds, marsh birds, most ducks, or alcids. The initial impetus that determined our destiny at Gradyville came from our old friend Paul DeAoun. He breezed into Tinicum one day with a tale about a Blue Grosbeak that Charlie Price had seen near some bridge or other on the Gradyville Road. Paul had immediately investigated, because a Blue Grosbeak in the Philadelphia area is more or less of an event. For the life of me I can't recall whether Paul saw the bird but Charlie Price is one of the Delaware Valley Ornithological Club's distinguished birders and we had no doubts concerning the authenticity of the report. We clamored for directions, and Paul gave them to us. I shall never quite comprehend his side remark, though, as he squatted there in the road tracing out our route in the thick dust. "You know what?" he said. "I'm just going to be mean enough to tell you where it is." Now what on earth did he mean by that? I could have asked him at the time but I didn't and now Paul wouldn't even remember this enigmatical utterance. Well, we didn't find the Blue Grosbeak ourselves, but as regards Gradyville it was love at first sight. We saw two lifers there that memorable day—Warbling Vireo and Acadian Flycatcher—and one week later saw our first Cerulean Warbler, mirabile dictu, low and only a few feet away. Thus we were launched at Gradyville.

But time is running out. Gradyville as we have known it will very soon be only a nostalgic reminiscence. In a few months the area will be open to the public—before you read this, no doubt. Gradyville will then have ceased to exist but Ridley Creek State Park will remain. The long, cool shadows of early May mornings and the silent snow-clad fields of February will be shattered by the screams and yells of thousands of frantic souls seeking escape from the artificiality of television. Jeremy Bentham may have had reason on his side but to my mind his simple doctrine lacks common sense. The greatest good for the greatest number may possibly have made sense two hundred years ago but today it can only result in an excruciatingly small amount of individual pleasure. But I do not animadvert upon the people; I, too, upon occasion, find myself part of the lonely crowd. The fate of Gradyville is only one of many Hobson's choices that we have to face today at every turn of the glass—in this case, a park or nothing. The bird life will probably not suffer too much, only the Piatts and their frequent companion and mentor of wild flowers, John Wolf. Before the ravenous picnickers and ski addicts descend upon us, therefore, let us take a quiet ramble or two over the fields and woods of old Gradyville.

The main entrance to the hospital and medical school of the University of Pennsylvania used to have huge iron gates under an ornamental arch of the same material. In the center of the arch, wrought in large, bold letters of iron, was this injunction— Carpe Diem—"Seize the Day" in literal translation, but, as Horace originally appended, with an intimation not to place too much trust in an uncertain future. I never passed under that arch without raising my eyes to this stark admonition. The gates and arch are now long gone and only the heedless multitude passes between the entrance pillars, oblivious of any necessity to capture time's arrow in its flight. Now I am fond of exhortations of this sort, especially when I can construe their hidden import in a manner best suited to my own preferments. More times than I should wish to acknowledge have I risen from my bed at the first faint hints of dawn and said, first to myself and then to Marybelle, "Let's Carpe!" Marybelle requires no verbal amplification of this household idiom. She has heard and used it too many times herself. It means that I can't bear the prospect of wasting such a glorious day in the city. In plain, forthright language it means to hell with work; let's play hooky and go birding. And most of our "carpeing" is done at Gradyville. So come along with us, friend, before those long morning shadows I mentioned earlier are betrayed by the jealous sun. But stay, wait a bit! May is not the month to introduce you to Gradyville. I should have shot my bolt before we commenced. You would expect more wonders on our second visit and I should be unable to produce them. Those who have feasted on Olympus with the gods are never afterward content with plain, mortal fare. So let us return to the house for warm wraps, boots, and gloves—for suddenly it is winter.

There is no snow, but it is very cold and a vicious wind is blowing down from the north and roaring through the treetops on Hunting Hill. It is December 18, 1971, and we are out to do our customary stint at Gradyville for the Audubon Christmas Bird Count of the Glenolden area.

The first arbeit will be in Chain's Woods, an extensive stand of white pine intermixed with a few red pines and deciduous trees. As we get out of the car there is a flurry of small birds in the neighboring brush and we have recorded our first White-throated Sparrows of the day. They are quite numerous this year at Gradyville and by the end of the day we shall have recorded a total of sixty-five, not a large number for other places within the count area but about par for our territory. A female and two male Cardinals are chipping nearby and they are the first of the sixteen we shall eventually see. In one way, it is too bad that the Cardinal is such a common bird in the east. No matter how exquisite or gaudily beplumed a bird, we unconsciously tend to denigrate it when it is ubiquitous and with us the year round. If the Cardinal's winter home were in Peru and it nested only in boreal Canada, we should greet it each spring with at least as many hosannas as we do the Scarlet Tanager—probably more, since it would not be with us in summer either. I distinctly recall my wonderment and exhilaration when we spied a pair of Cardinals at Red Rock, New Mexico, along the Gila River. I had not expected Cardinals that far west and although

Red Rock is a kind of oasis in the desert, it still surprised me. Those Cardinals were almost the most exciting birds we saw at Red Rock. But, as usual, I am squandering our time with my incessant divigations. We are in the pine woods now and just as we start along the trail the trilling note of a Carolina Wren is heard. How often would this bird be overlooked if it did not sound off! I have often wondered whether George Apley and his birding companion, Clara, first heard their Carolina Wren or actually "spied it first." Our total of Carolina Wrens for today will be four, but we will not see a single bird.

We are well into the pines by now and stop at frequent intervals to listen for that thin, tinny bleat of the Red-breasted Nuthatch. Chain's Woods is the prime place at Gradyville for this elegant little bird whenever it condescends to winter in states south of New England. Last winter we did not see or hear a single Red-breasted Nuthatch, but this year for the past few weeks we have counted six every time we have been in Chain's Woods. And there it is! The sound, I mean, not the bird. It is a duet and we soon locate the pair high in an old red pine. Farther along the trail and up the slope we find the rest of the Nuthatch contingent. But lo and behold there are six, not four, and our day's total is eight, not the six we had anticipated. Blue Jays are screaming overhead from time to time and through this raucous din comes faintly down the forest aisles the cheerful but subdued voice of an old, old friend—the first of our eleven towhees is greeting us. Far off White River, Walker Valley, and not so far off Furness's. Poignant memories come flooding in to overwhelm me with their wistful, yearning desire for old faces, old times. I take out my handkerchief and blow my nose. You and Marybelle have walked on a few steps and do not see. Besides, the cold and wind are most conducive to nose blowing and I should have had my excuse ready to hand. I have caught up with you now and we three stand close to a massive tangle of honeysuckle that has all but engulfed several big pines. Marybelle and I exchange glances and shake our heads ruefully—no Great Horned Owl. All the while we have been treading the forest path Marybelle and I have been listening and hoping for an outburst of that wild, obdurate frenzy of the crow mob harassing their immemorial foe, the Great Horned Owl. It is one sure way to locate and put up this marauder of the night. But none of our day's thirty Common Crows is even in the vicinity as yet. And then, just as we take our first reluctant step forward, there is a sudden snap of a dead branch in the honeysuckle tangle. He is off through the closely set trees and out of sight before we can raise an arm to point or utter a sound. It was the huge form of the flying tiger, the Great Horned Owl. We have been successful after all and Bubo is in the bag. Almost always we can put up the Great Horned Owl in one of Gradyville's pine woods and often the owl flies just as we resume our walk, rather than at our approach. With regard to Great Horned Owls, I must ask my friend Angus Cameron if he knows why crows never—in our experience—molest these owls as long as they are on their nest but always raise bloody hell when one is spotted perched in a woods by day. For two successive years, from late January until April, we observed a Great Horned Owl and young in their nest. Not once did any crow or crows take the least notice of the owls although they were plainly visible in the high crotch of the big red oak. Angus has recently written a marvelous book about owls, *The Nightwatchers*, and it is superbly illustrated by Peter Parnall.

We have left Chain's Woods far behind and are now beginning the circumnavigation of the base of Hunting Hill. It is in this field at the end of the southern slope that we shall see most of our sparrows. And, sure enough, Song Sparrows are thick in the wild rose thickets and fallen stalks of joe-pye-weed and golden-rod, some thirty individuals before we are done. The Song Sparrow is another of those birds that suffers through too much familiarity. We seldom pay him deference, for we listers do not really know this bird. In fact, we do not know it at all. To paraphrase Edna St. Vincent Millay, Margaret Nice alone has looked on beauty bare. Her lengthy and meticulous study of the Song Sparrow, published some thirty years ago in a two-part treatise, shows the average lister how really ignorant he is. As we approach the western end of the south field there comes ever so faintly the soft, bell-like twittering of Tree Sparrows and we estimate seventy individuals as a conservative figure. The Tree Sparrow is always a winter delight to us. Their soft notes and restless movements over the fields make these old winter barrens come alive. But here, too, this bird does not belong to us. We scarcely know it. Ask Marguerite Baumgartner, though. She will tell you. She has studied it at Churchill, Manitoba, and many places elsewhere. And, as Marguerite has written to us, she may even count up her lifers some day. Marguerite is not one who eschews the list. She has a doctor's degree in ornithology and is just too busy to give the list much thought.

We continue our route toward the western edge of Hunting Hill after laboriously checking off four Field Sparrows, our day's total take of this trim little songster, now quiet of course, and a very poor count for winter at Gradyville. We know there are more but they seem to elude us today. And now just as we are about to leave the south slope for the higher reaches of a neighboring field, it happens. A flock of six birds flies over us and before they alight in the dogwood trees at the edge of the woods we recognize their sweet, melodious notes. Six Bluebirds, eastern of course, and we feast our eyes on them. Just as the six take to the air again, three more pass close to us and we have seen nine Bluebirds in less than two minutes! With the exception of two individuals in October, these are the first Bluebirds we have seen at Gradyville in over a year and a half. We almost never see them in summer, although I once put up a Bluebird house near the bridge, but always in late fall or winter. It is the most exciting adventure of the day and helps to warm us and clear our watering eyes buffeted by the constant blasts of the wind.

We have reached the locust tree grove on the southwest side of the hill. For years this has been one of our favorite sections of Gradyville in winter. It is protected from north and west winds, faces the south, and offers excellent shelter for wildlife on cold, windy days. This is the spot where we often see deer, sometimes as many as six or eight at a time. William Potter, Park Superintendent, estimates at least thirty deer at Gradyville. But today the deer are either quietly bedded down or elsewhere, for we see none. A Flicker flies by and alights on an old dead elm, not three feet from another. Both of them are soon off again and we follow their white rump patches until the curve of the hill blots them out. There are more Towhees and White-throated Sparrows and a sizable flock of Juncos. Scanning the sky from time to time, as we have done all morning, we are finally rewarded. The pair of Red-tailed Hawks that have nested here for the last few years are at last airborne, wheeling upward in ever-widening circles. I suspect they have been having trouble with the wind. Our real quest in this unexposed spot, however, is the Myrtle Warbler. Every time we have been here during the last few weeks there have been three of these birds feeding on the dark blue berries of the honeysuckle that festoons almost all the locust trees. There are not many berries left. The Cedar Waxwings and Robins have been taking a heavy toll of late and we hope they have left enough to carry the Myrtles through today at least. The Myrtle Warbler has a distinctive chip note that Marybelle seldom fails to identify. She signals us that she has heard it now and we move in toward the sound. It does not take long to spot two of the birds, and a minute or so later another joins the pair. The Myrtle and the Yellowthroat vie with each other for the distinction of being our most common eastern warbler and the former often lingers well into the winter in southeastern Pennsylvania because much of its food consists of berries and the like; it is not so dependent upon the presence of insect life as are most warblers.

We continue around the west and north sides of Hunting Hill and now once more receive the mailed fist of Boreas full in our faces. Some Carolina Chickadees and a few Black-capped, White-breasted Nuthatches and Titmice are our only birds on this stretch. It is entirely deciduous woods, mostly second growth, and most unproductive in winter. The homestretch lies along the east base of the hill and adjacent to a long, straight reach of the creek. This part of Gradyville above all others is my favorite haunt. It was here we found our first Acadian Flycatcher nest and saw our first Worm-eating Warbler. Here it was we had the adventure of the squinting fox. We had been standing quietly watching with our glasses two fawns halfway up the hill when we noticed a fox trotting down the path toward us. We were in deep shade; the fox had the full glare of the sun in its face. We were downwind from Reynard, and as he drew near the dark patch of shade in which we stood we could clearly see that his eyes were almost closed. He was squinting if ever fox did. Just as he crossed the transition zone between light and shade, he gave one tremendous leap into the air, turned at right angles before he hit the ground, and was off up Hunting Hill as though the law of gravity had been temporarily rescinded.

A hundred other memories of similar discoveries and adventures crowd about me every time we come this way. Over this stretch of its course the creek flows smoothly and placidly and Hunting Hill rises sharply against the western sky, content and everlasting. Surely this is the place of all places where one can walk beside still waters. There is a huge flat-topped rock projecting out over the creek at one spot. How many times over the past dozen years have we sought this refuge on hot July days and rested in the shade of the old red maple tree. There is a deep pool beneath our rock and sometimes we bring dried crusts of bread to crumble into the water for the sunfish and minnows. But mostly we converse in quiet tones about not much or, best of all, do absolutely and utterly nothing. It is as close to nirvana as Occidental man may approach. But the strident rattle of a Kingfisher suddenly breaks my reverie and I hasten to climb back into the world. Marybelle spots a Brown Creeper probing for its noon meal on the rough trunk of a shagbark hickory—the first we have seen in almost a month. We are reminded of our own empty stomachs by the intense activity of this prototype of all "little brown birds." Back to the house, then, for a hasty snack and a bottle of good cold ale. Marybelle doesn't like the stuff but I heartily recommend it at noon with a cold beef sandwich.

There is no real reason why we should take you back out again into the cold for the afternoon. You will recall how we listened and searched in vain for the Pileated Woodpecker. There was just too much wind and these big woodpeckers don't like that. We roamed the southern half of Gradyville, never too good for birds in winter, till dark. You will recall the three Purple Finches near Sycamore Mills Road and the eighty-odd House Finches bickering in the ivy-clad walls of Park Head-quarters, formerly the Jeffords' big house. Also, I recall a Ruby-crowned and several Golden-crowned Kinglets. It was not a good day as Christmas Counts go. Our total was just forty species, seven less than the preceding year. The entire total for the Glenolden count area was also an even dozen less than the 1970 count, ninety-seven species in all. The high winds were un-doubtedly the chief deterrent but, also, perhaps I talked too much. We can be proud of our nine Bluebirds and three Myrtle Warblers, though, for no one but we three saw either of these two birds that day. But most of all, we had fun and adventure. Come back again in four or five months when the geese fly high. We shall show you a different set of birds then.

It is still December as I sit here writing. Next May seems eons off, only a remembrance of things past and an unspoken promise of the future. I know, I invited you to join us birding come May and the invitation still holds. But if I am ever to finish this book, we cannot wait for future Mays that may never come. It is often said that time is simply a fabrication of man's mind stuff so let us take advantage of this suppositious artifice and step backward seven or eight years into the so-called past. It is, after all, a common and well-worn device for thwarting time's tyranny. You may join us and welcome. It is May 10, 1964, then, the day of the annual DVOC bird census of the Delaware County area. I am not a member of this bird club, and you are probably not either. Marybelle, being born female, is forbidden to join. Nevertheless, Johnny Miller will probably give me a call next day and ask me what we saw, so our May tenth list will eventually be incorporated into the final big picture. Besides, unofficial status has a great advantage. We shall do what and go where we please and squander time as it suits us. We may actually get no farther than the sycamore grove. It is not a "century day" for us.

We park the car off the road well up the grade, east of the bridge that spans Ridley Creek. It is six o'clock and the sun is not yet above the trees. There are long, long shadows in front of us, just as I had foretold. They reach for hundreds of feet, almost to the creek. No need to hurry. It will be warm enough anon, for the foliage of the black walnuts and some of the other trees is not yet mature. Besides, those loud-mouthed crows and whickering jays have given me an idea. Let's see if we can identify forty or more birds before we cross the bridge or descend into the sycamore grove that borders the creek. Forty species is exactly the number of birds we shall see on the Christmas Count seven years from now and it will be fun to see if an entire day's extensive walk in December can be condensed into an hour or less in May, strolling down five hundred feet or so of shady road. Cast your mind far ahead into the future and you may recall that other day so long hence. It can be done.

The ubiquitous jays and crows are already in the census bag. We must estimate their numbers, to be sure, but we shall not bother our guest with these trifling calculations. A Field Sparrow sings its sweet, clear song somewhere over to our right and almost directly overhead a Prairie Warbler is tripping lightly up the scales. The indescribable song of the Blackpoll Warbler—a sort of insistent teakettle steam hissing that softly swells in volume and then dies away—comes from ahead of us. Marybelle spots him and we all have a good look. There may be more decorative warblers but all God's chillun got wings this morning. There is a Redstart or two sounding off, and a Catbird yodels from a thicket. Someone is cautiously opening a creaking door and we hastily scribble Rose-breasted Grosbeak on our pad, for this is one bird we want to see. His song is pretty but undistinguished and his rusty eke note which we have just heard is totally without merit. But, like the Scarlet Tanager, his long suit is his apparel. As a matter of fact, there are three males, and each in turn is given his proper kudos. As we have been ogling the trio of Grosbeaks, several other well-known sounds have penetrated our consciousness: Chimney Swifts overhead with their electricity-like tickings; "old faithful," the Carolina Wren; the loud, clownish zweep of the Great Crested Flycatcher; and a White-eyed Vireo is "picking up the beer check" with all the frenetic elisions customary to this querulous toper. The first time Marybelle heard the White-eye's song she likened it to a drunken Towhee, a slanderous imputation for our "spark bird." As though in gentle reproof, a Towhee begins to drink his tea from a tangle of nondescript little trees by the side of the road. I'll warrant his tea is not spiked either. The familiar flight notes of Goldfinches are heard as they dip and fly, dip and fly. And we have not moved fifty feet from the car as yet!

As we move forward down the road a Yellowthroat Warbler sings atop an old rose bush. The name Yellowthroat is a stupid baptismal mistake for this bird, especially when another common warbler is called the Yellow-throated. The Yellowthroat should be called the Black-masked Warbler as was his name in the old bird book we used to have at home, *Fifty Common American Birds*. I do not recall the author of this book but his nomenclatural instincts were sound. We are approaching the bridge and are almost but not quite beyond my beloved shadows. I hear it faintly as over the hill and far away and turn to watch Marybelle. You have heard it also; I can tell by the way you turned your head just now. But I can see that Marybelle has not. I dwell overlong on this trifle because it never fails to astound me. Marybelle is far sharper than I on most bird calls but she seems to have what Veblen dubbed in another context "a trained incapacity" for early recognition of this particular bird call. It is none other than the Bob White. To be sure, he is only saying

Bob at this moment but we have been on first-name intimacy with Mr. Robert White for some years now and this is no time to be formal. Marybelle gets it now, of course, and we laugh and walk on, out of the shadows and into the morning sun.

At this instant two things happen simultaneously. We hear, and see, a pair of Wood Ducks fly up from the creek. They are soon lost around a bend of the stream. Also, a sizable shadow glides swiftly across the glaring white concrete surface of the bridge. We look up and behold four Turkey Vultures in the sky. No, we are wrong. There are only three TVs; the fourth is a Broad-winged Hawk. The hawk is far away but, nevertheless, we are most culpable. Thanks for the correction, old friend. This is not a migrant bird but one of the pair of Broad-wings that have nested for several years in south Gradyville. In a few years Red-tailed Hawks will supplant these Broad-wings and although the former will be with us the year round, we shall still miss our nesting Broad-wings in the summer.

We are on the bridge now and Rough-winged Swallows sweep under and over it in their tireless pursuit of insects. Two things catch our eyes at the far southern bend of the creek—a Great Blue Heron and a Solitary Sandpiper. The heron lets out one great squawk, flaps his giant pinions, and lifts laboriously into the air with stately grace. The sandpiper, apparently taking alarm too, passes under the bridge and is soon out of sight. We are abreast of the sycamore grove now but still on the road. A Blue-winged Warbler gives his buzzy squeak, like a dry cork twisted back and forth in a bottle neck, and two Yellow Warblers flash by. We would rather have heard the song of the Yellow Warbler than that of the Blue-wing but right now the former are too absorbed in their own liebesspiel to favor us with a rendition. But later we shall hear them from a half dozen sites up and down the creek. A few White-throated Sparrows are still with us, and one of them is in full voice. I love the plaintive minor of the White-throat, descending after that first rise. It is the first bird song that aroused in me a yearning to learn of every bird its language. If the Rufous-sided Towhee is my spark bird, the song of the White-throated Sparrow is assuredly my spark sound. Through much of all this we have been hearing, almost continually, Cardinal, Titmouse, White-breasted Nuthatch, and Song Sparrow. And also, I regret to say, the bubbly, rather vapid courtship song of the cowbird. Dale Coman, a friend and colleague who worships at the same shrine, has remonstrated with me over my irrational dislike of cowbirds. "*C'est la nature,*" he often remonstrates. "Do not meddle with the natural order of things." I don't and I won't. But I still say the earth in its sidereal sweeps would move more light-heartedly sans Cowbirds.

I apologize for the long sojourn upon the road when inviting groves and distant hills beckon. But give me just twenty more minutes, seven o'clock, and let's see if we can realize our goal of forty birds. A Ring-necked Pheasant is cackling over yonder right now and that was surely a Red-bellied Woodpecker that lit on the walnut tree. Marybelle has walked a little farther up the road and now returns to report a Chat and two Phoebes. And you are absolutely right. That vireo with the Scotch burr must be the Yellow-throated. Yes, they nest here but not so often as they will later. The song of the Yellow-throated Vireo calls to mind one of the most whimsical and delightful of all typographical errors. Get out your A. C. Bent volume on Wagtails, Shrikes, Vireos, etc., and turn to page 285. Bent is quoting from Francis H. Allen on some little-known bird songs. In speaking of the Yellow-throated Vireo, Bent says: "The song consists of several repetitions of a high-pitched note with rising inflection, suggesting the Goldfish's call note . . ." And I quote Bent and not Allen directly because in the latter's article the word is "Goldfinch's." Whether this amusing error is perpetuated in the Dover transcription of the Bent series, I cannot say. If you own a copy, check and see. At this juncture, as a fitting climax to all foibles suggestive of the Goldfish's call note, a Baltimore Oriole sounds off. Of all local bird songs, perhaps the double talk of the Baltimore Oriole's so-called song is the most nonsensical. It always reminds me of a second-rate orchestra tuning up before the overture, which never is played. But what need for music when one's exterior is nonpareil. There is the thin sissing of the Blue-gray Gnatcatcher and we follow the trim little bird to its nest athwart the slender sycamore limb some thirty feet or more above our heads. It is always difficult to determine whether gnatcatchers are building or dismantling their nests. One day they appear to be in a constructive mood, the next they turn vandal and pull the nest to pieces. One mitigating thing that may be said for this Jekyll and Hyde role is that they use the materials of nest one to help build nest two. Perhaps they are perfectionists. This is the most charitable view to take of a dubious performance. And at last! We hear a Chestnut-sided Warbler almost the same time that a Parula begins its rapid, buzzy trill. The Chestnut-sided should have sung long before now; they nest in the sycamore grove. But our time has expired and we are still one bird short of our coveted goal of forty. I shrug my shoulders in resignation and start down the sharp incline into the grove. But before Marybelle and you can follow, we hear the one song above all others that we have been straining our ears for—the Warbling Vireo. It is our fortieth bird heard or seen from the road! This sycamore grove is one of the very few spots in southeastern Pennsylvania where the Warbling Vireo nests. In many respects it is our prize summer bird at Gradyville. This species is nowhere nearly as common east of the Appalachians as it is west of these mountains and our Gradyville Warbling Vireos have served as lifers for a number of eastern birders. Our young friend George Spitalny first saw the bird here, a singing male on its nest. Bird, song, nest—that is the way to see a lifer.

Our tour de force is over. We can now loaf along, enjoying this beautiful spring day and adding birds to our list from time to time. I freely confess that our forty birds, in one hour, along a short stretch of road, is a literary contrivance to glorify our favorite birding haunt. But now listen to this, and do not raise your eyebrows when I tell you that no penciled record is extant to substantiate my claim. One May morning—Marybelle says 1965 but I think it was 1966—we spent exactly an hour and a half along this identical stretch of road, six hundred feet at the most, and recorded forty-six different species of bird. This is fact, not fiction. In essence, therefore, my artifice is no deception but simply a transliteration of events from the original script to the imaginary one. I could, in all justice, have kept you on that road thirty more minutes and added six more birds. But the quality of mercy is not strained and I cheerfully present you with this additional half hour to do with as you choose.

Our long day in May is over. I am pleasantly weary and I know you must be too. We have done great things together and seen much of different climes and countries. Our list is ninety-three birds—again, fact not fiction, for I have the written record dated May 10, 1964, before me. Of the six possible vireos we have seen five, and twenty-five warblers out of the total list of thirty-six, and one would not expect to see the Connecticut here in spring. We have seen sixteen Scarlet Tanagers, eight Baltimore Orioles, one Orchard Oriole, fourteen Ovenbirds, eighteen Canada Warblers, seven Parulas, eight Kentucky Warblers, etc., etc., etc. We also took time to spy out some spring flowers, listen to the rush of water over boulders, and rest for a spell on our big rock. It has been great fun here at Gradyville. But the road calls, those other roads so far away, and the lure of the list forever beckons. So let us leave Gradyville to its long shadows and its dreams. Besides, the enchanted salve with which I have anointed your eyes will soon be spent and Gradyville to you may, then, after all, seem only an ordinary but very nice place to spend a day. The magic of Gradyville belongs to Marybelle and me alone. We cannot impart this priceless gift to others. It is both a heritage and a creed.

V

... of Shoes and Ships

And the Walrus was right. The time has come to talk of many
things—namely, the organizational aspects of birding and perhaps, in a later chapter, some of the various problems and
dilemmas which confront the amateur birder and North American lister. Before telling you the little I know about the American Ornithologists' Union, 600 Club, Audubon Christmas Bird
Count, American Birding Association, and maybe one or two
other organizations that affect the Brotherhood, allow me to
explain and justify, if possible, the raison d'être of this book.
Admittedly, confessionals of the author belong in a preface. But
whoever heard of anyone reading a preface except the author
himself? Do not misunderstand me. I offer no apologia. Only the
truly great or famous can risk self-incrimination. No, like Walt

Whitman, I shall continue to sound my barbaric yawp over the roof tops unashamed. But, as I have scribbled on, a nameless sense of guilt has crept upon me like the thief in the night. My colleagues query me from time to time about the progress of my research. My answers are of necessity evasive, brief, and full of guile. "Well enough," I mutter, and hurry on down the hallway. Little do they know that I have temporarily forsaken *Amblystoma* for the fleshpots of "popular" writing. For the restoration of my good name, therefore, it is essential that I lay bare the whole lengthy, demonic plot that has reduced me to this low estate. I do not hope for expiation; simple compassion will suffice. As someone has said, to know all is to forgive all. Undoubtedly, a stronger man might still have thwarted such an evil destiny, but so intransigent have been the forces which have beset me that I now lie feckless with straining gills, a weary flop or two and all is over. Art is feebler far than destiny, wrote Aeschylus, and so I have succumbed. How, then, did I ever get into this mess in the first place? I shall answer, I shall tell you.

Once upon a time, some thirty years ago to be exact, I was besieged by an implacable antagonist who had the misfortune to be an editor and publisher of books. I was importuned almost daily, month by month, year after year, decade upon decade to write a popular book on experimental embryology. I studied under Ross G. Harrison at Yale, one of the all-time greats in this field, and this, naturally, is my own field of research. No purpose would be served by regaling you with the details of that relentless conflict between editor and recalcitrant author. It is our own private Thirty Years War, and shall thus remain. Once, and only once, during the early days of the skirmish I was foolhardy enough to engage my good friend the enemy closely. It was almost my undoing. I was routed horse, foot, and artillery. In the temporary cessation of hostilities that ensued, I was forced to sign capitulation papers—a thing called a contract— and given a small solatium to recompense me for defeat. I retired from that stricken field licking my wounds but with a desperate resolve to again rally my forces for a counterblow. The victorious enemy, naturally, relaxed his vigilance and at the expiration of three months by herculean effort I succeeded in breaking through his lines and won back my freedom with honor. The short duress of thralldom made me canny to a degree and never since have I directly assaulted the main body of the enemy's troops but ever skulked along his flanks. These Fabian tactics have been strategically sound—for as yet no popular book on "eye of newt and toe of frog" has issued from my left-winged quill. But no victory is complete. There is this book, for instance.

My good friend the enemy, though, was as pertinacious as the bulldog and as canny as his foe. He adapted his own strategy to conform with mine. If I refused to write about something which it was presumed I understood, why not, then, write about something of which I knew nothing—birds. In short, speak with the pen of the amateur, not the professional. You will perceive immediately the invidious implication of this master stroke, and the diabolical cunning with which it was implemented has forced even me to grudging admiration. You see, if I were to write about experimental embryology, I should feel impelled by professional pride to meticulously dot every i and cross every t with precision. And who is there that enjoys a busman's holiday? If, on the other hand, I were to scribble as a rank amateur, a picker-up of shells along an unknown shore, I could relax. Who would ever be so exacting and unsporting as to blame me for my errors and omissions? So a compromise was reached. I would write about birds, but actually much more about birding and birders. In the event it became necessary to state a bit of factual information about the bird itself, I should have several avenues of escape open to me. And thus it was arranged. Besides, my friendly enemy knew only too well my Achilles' heel. A man will work for his profession but he will die for his hobby. And in one sense, writing a book is to die a little. Good, bad or indifferent, profound or ludicrous, something is gone that shall never be again.

As to my credentials, I have none—except that I am Mr.

Average Birder. And the average birder has his tale to tell as well as the professional or expert. It is far less informative or authoritative but just as valid a segment of the birding world. Furthermore, there is often no perceptible demarcation between the professional ornithologist and the amateur birder. Each supplements the other. The world of birds is one in which all kinds of people mingle together in an infinite series of graded expertise and knowledge. It is probably true that most amateur birders never discover anything new about a bird or birds but simply acquire from year to year the same repertoire of knowledge that their predecessors learned in their turn. But this is not to disparage. When I was a young man first embarking upon embryological research, I would admit no one in the fraternity of the true scientist who had not made an original discovery of merit and published the same. Today I am not so certain that original discovery is the sole trademark of the scientist. So be it with birders and birding.

American Ornithologists' Union

The American Ornithologists' Union (AOU) is perhaps the most important and influential organization of birders in North America. Its Fellows and Elective Members constitute the elite of North American ornithology—the key professional personnel and scientifically minded cadre. In addition, however, ordinary membership is open to any person interested in birds, irrespective of his merits or attainments in the field of ornithology. The AOU, therefore, is an aggregation of both the professional scientist and amateurs of all shades. It is probably true, however, that even the amateur contingent of AOU is a degree or two above the typical membership stratum of most local bird societies or garden clubs. There are few, if any, "window watchers" among the AOU clan. The AOU was initiated in August 1883 by three of the foremost ornithologists of the day:

J. A. Allen, Elliott Coues, and William Brewster. Its formal
birth date is September 29, 1883. The aim of the AOU is the
advancement of ornithological science. From a charter membership of 23 Founders, the total membership has increased to 3,142
(1971). Its regular publications are three in number. *The Auk* is
the official periodical organ and is issued quarterly. It consists
primarily of original scientific contributions. The second publication, *Ornithological Monographs*, is issued at irregular intervals and consists of long articles of book length. The third
publication, *Check-list of North American Birds*, is a systematic
list, arranged in phylogenetic sequence, of all species and subspecies known to occur north of Mexico, including Baja California, Greenland, Bermuda, and the islands of the Bering Sea.

Five editions of the Check-list have been published, the first in
1886 and the current Fifth Edition in 1957. Preparation of the
Sixth Edition is under way and will probably be published about
1975, according to Dr. Alexander Wetmore, Chairman of the
current Check-list Committee. Each edition, of necessity, re-
flects the taxonomic outlook of the coeval interval and, naturally, changes and alterations are numerous in each succeeding
edition. This AOU Check-list is regarded by the entire hierarchy of the Brotherhood as the ornithological counterpart of
the Mosaic Law. And woe be unto him that flouts it! Verily, he
shall be cut off from the Tabernacle, his children accursed and
wanderers all upon the face of the earth forever. The current
Fifth Edition is the directive of the North American lister, as
described below in the account of the 600 Club. In another
chapter, I shall discuss the impact of changing avian systematics
upon the defenseless North American lister, as formalized by the
AOU Check-list. Without this Check-list, the amateur birder
would be as spindrift blown hither and yon over a tenebrous sea
of uncertainty. It is the sine qua non of the lister, but, like all
indispensable things, it has its dour side.

The 600 Club

To the best of my knowledge, there exists no formal or official publication setting forth the history, precepts, regulations, and membership requirements of the 600 Club. The modus operandi of this unusual and exclusive Club is strictly *lex non scripta*. My account is based on the following sources of information: (1) common knowledge; (2) a few published articles; (3) personal correspondence with Earle R. Greene, the Club's present Secretary; (4) chitchat among birders; (5) the fact that Marybelle and I are members. If, therefore, I sin on the side of either omission or commission, I trust the reader and the Brotherhood will show clemency.

The 600 Club had its inception with an article written by G. Stuart Keith for *Audubon* Magazine (vol. 65, no. 6, 1963) called "The '600 Club': America's Top-Ranking Birders." This article itself had its origin in an earlier publication by Mr. Keith (*Audubon* Magazine, vol. 63, no. 5, 1961), in which he stated, referring to Roger Tory Peterson and himself: "I know of no other birders who have seen more than 600 North American species in the Check-list area. . . ." The statement was the substantive summary of a highly entertaining account of Keith's success in beating Peterson's annual record of North American birds by 22, a total of 594 species for the calendar year of 1956. This assumption of Keith that he and Peterson were the only two people who had seen six hundred or more birds in North America caused a minor flurry among the higher echelons of the birding world. He received several letters informing him that there were others besides himself and Peterson in this rarefied category. At Keith's request, therefore, *Audubon* Magazine (vol. 64, no. 1, 1962) published a notice entitled "Honor List Nominations Open" asking for information from all those who had six hundred or more birds on their North American list. The key article of 1963 by Keith, mentioned above, was the result. In it, he lists nineteen birders who by 1963 had seen six hundred or more species in the AOU Check-list area. These nineteen birders constitute the "charter members" of the 600 Club and the article itself its inauguration.

Stuart Keith, originally a Britisher, is the "father" and first unofficial Secretary of the 600 Club. His professional duties as Associate in Ornithology at the American Museum of Natural History, together with his frequent periods of fieldwork in Africa, left too little time for Keith to handle the paper work of the Club. Earle R. Greene accepted this rather onerous task and, at this writing, is the Secretary of the Club. Mr. Greene has had a lifelong experience with birds and has written a book with much the same title: *A Lifetime with the Birds*. He is also the author of numerous other publications dealing with the habits and distribution of North American birds. In short, Earle is one of the more knowledgeable birders in the United States and an indefatigable correspondent—both necessary qualifications for the Secretary of the 600 Club.

Recently, Mr. Greene published a brief resumé of the Club's history, rules, and objectives in the *Western Tanager*, the official journal of the Los Angeles Audubon Society. He remarks, among other things, that there are no stated meetings, no officers, and no dues. The motto is: Cooperation not Competition. This means, of course, that members are mutually helpful in directing attention to new birds or localities where prospective lifers may be found. In our slow and laborious climb up this Jacob's Ladder we have often been materially aided by other members. For instance, on May 20, 1971, I received a phone call from Joseph W. Taylor, the top man on the 600 Club totem pole, telling me exactly where and when he had seen the Curlew Sandpiper, a lifer for him. Two days later, Marybelle and I found this bird in the exact spot where Joe had seen it. In our turn, we then drove over to Tuckerton, New Jersey, where we had reason to believe Marion and Russell Wilson of California were on the prowl for this same species. We were able to show them "our" bird at Brigantine before it left; they had waited in vain for three long days at Tuckerton. The guiding light in this nexus of relayed information was P. William Smith of New Jersey, who rules the birds of the Jersey shore with a heavy hand. Smith, Taylor, Piatt, Wilson was the chain, and it did not end there. When we finally left Brigantine, the Wilsons were pointing out this obligingly sessile bird to yet other birders. Oh, there is a fine camaraderie among the Brotherhood, despite an occasional petty jealousy or tricky "back field play."

Membership in the 600 Club is open to anyone who has identified at least six hundred full species within the territory included in the Fifth Edition, 1957, of the American Ornithologists' Union *Check-list of North American Birds*. This area consists of the following regions: conterminous United States; Alaska, including all Bering Sea islands of the United States; all of Canada; Greenland; Baja California; Bermuda. If a European bird, the Ruff, for instance, is seen in England, it does not count toward the 600 Club. If, on the other hand, a Ruff is seen in any of the areas named above, it does count toward membership in the Club. Contrariwise, if a North American bird, the Brown Thrasher, is seen in England, it does not count. It is not the species but the territory in which the bird is identified that is the criterion of the 600 Club list.

There are also rules governing the conditions under which a bird may be listed:

(1) Full species only. This means that in any polytypic species (two or more subspecies) only one of the subspecies may be listed, even if some are readily separable in the field (most of them are not). My first Song Sparrow was seen in summer in eastern Pennsylvania and, therefore, belongs to the nominate subspecies (first named), *Melospiza melodia melodia*. There are approximately thirty other subspecies of Song Sparrow recognized in North America but, having seen *M. m. melodia*, I can

count no others. In monotypic species (no subspecies) this consideration is, of course, nonexistent. A Bobolink seen anywhere in the Check-list area can be counted toward the 600 Club; there are no subspecies.

(2) Chickens don't count. This, my own small pleasantry, means that only birds in the wild state may be counted. If I see a flock of Turkeys in farmer Brown's barn lot, they are taboo. If, on the other hand, I am in Myakka State Park in Florida and a flock of Turkeys blocks the entrance road, I can count the bird—even though these wild Turkeys often appear less "wild" than do the barnyard kind. Precisely what conditions and environment constitute a "wild state" are not always clear. There are certain conventions, however, that are more or less recognized and accepted by most of the Brotherhood.

(3) No caged or confined birds. This rule is more or less a corollary of point 2 above but applies to wild caged birds as well as domesticated. This means, naturally, that no zoo birds can be counted. Furthermore, if someone obligingly catches a Boreal Owl and places it in a cage for my inspection, I can only drool, not list. The person who caught the owl, however, could count it because he first found it in the wild state. (Personally, I should like to waive this restriction as applied to the Boreal Owl. I have come to the reluctant conclusion that only under such circumstances shall I ever be able to see this species.) If I go to a National Wildlife Refuge and a flock of Pintails is temporarily penned for banding purposes, I cannot count these birds. If they are released the next day and I see them in a nearby pond, I can count them. This leads to point four.

(4) No escaped birds. This rule generally has reference to zoo birds, imported waterfowl, or caged pets. The Pintails mentioned under point 3 would not come under this rubric because they are wild birds that were only temporarily confined: they are not escapees in the ordinary sense. All species of birds not native to the area of the AOU Check-list, especially waterfowl, are usually suspect and, if banded, should definitely not be counted. I have seen but not counted Egyptian, Gray-lag, Red-

breasted, and Bar-headed Geese: these birds were either banded or were very probably escapees.

(5) Introduced species can be counted only after successful maintenance and breeding in the wild state for five or six years. This precept was first advocated by Roger Tory Peterson in a letter, July 29, 1964, to Mr. Greene. This so-called "Peterson policy" has been more or less officially adopted by the 600 Club membership although I sometimes wonder if all prospective 600 Club aspirants are guided by this convention. The period of time is, of course, quite arbitrary but, obviously, some such restriction is necessary. Otherwise I could go to a pet shop, purchase a Toucan, take cage and bird out into the street, open the cage door, and count the bird as it stepped onto the sidewalk.

Twice a year the Secretary of the 600 Club sends each member a revised and readjusted list of the membership, stating the present number of North American birds that each has recorded to date. These lists usually come out in the spring and fall. The current list, April 15, 1972, lists seventy-two living members and three deceased, almost four times that of the charter member list of nine years ago. Joseph W. Taylor of Honeoye Falls, New York, is our Abou Ben Adhem with 693 species. Other illustrious names of the birding world are Ira N. Gabrielson, 673; Stuart Keith, 658; Roger Tory Peterson, 656; Allan D. Cruickshank, 622; Richard H. Pough, 618; Clarence Cottam, 607; Alexander Wetmore, 603. There are seventeen members with 650 or more; five with 640+; six with 630+; thirteen with 620+; thirteen with 610+ and eighteen with 600+. There are sixteen women and six husband-wife teams among the current membership. The Club is growing rapidly. When Marybelle and I were first "initiated" in 1969 there were only thirty-nine members.

And now just a word or two as to the rationale behind the name. Why the 600 Club? Why not a 500 Club or 700 Club? With a moment's reflection, of course, the answer is obvious with regard to a 700 Club. No one yet has seen 700 birds in North America, although the 1957 AOU Check-list records about 740 species.* The effort, time, and expenditure required to see seven hundred or more full species are all in themselves considerable hurdles; their cumulative deterrence is formidable. Many birds are unpredictable, or rare accidental species that do not breed in the Check-list area and will probably never be seen by ninety-five percent of the Brotherhood. Finally, it takes elaborate and careful planning in advance to make any extensive birding trip pay off in number of species or rarities. As of the present date, a 700 Club would be eminently nonsensical—a Club with no members. A 500 Club is perfectly feasible, of course, as would be a 200 or 100 Club. There is the single obvious objection—numbers. For every person who has recorded 600-plus birds, there are probably three or four who have seen 500 or more species. For each one in the 500 category there are probably at least ten who have seen 400 species. There are undoubtedly thousands, if not tens of thousands, who have seen at least 300 birds. Considering how rapidly the 600 Club itself is growing, a 500 Club would very soon become unwieldy. Whatever prestige or consequence there may be in belonging to the 600 Club would soon be dissipated if the figure were to be lowered to 500 or less. To put it another way, an angel in heaven is no one in particular.

The future of the 600 Club would seem to be assured but, personally, I have vague misgivings. In the end it will most likely receive the kiss of death from well-intentioned but lethal organizational tactics. Man's propensity for organization is, apparently, unlimited. The panacea of over-organization is always more organization. The soulless doomsday that Roderick Seidenberg has predicted for the over-all affairs of mankind in his seminal discussion, *Anatomy of the Future*, will apply to baubles like the 600 Club as well. Secondly, the allocation of a specific taxon as a species or only a subspecies has been based from the Club's inception upon the 1957 edition of the AOU Check-list. All lists have been compiled under this aegis. Very soon there will be a

* As of October 1972, Joseph W. Taylor has seen 706 birds north of Mexico.

new edition of the Check-list and all lists will have to be adjusted accordingly. For instance, if I cannot recall when, where, and if I saw all the former subspecies that will be raised to species rank in the new Check-list, my list will suffer. There will be a number of us in the same boat and there will inevitably be grumbling and dissent. The converse of this imbroglio—the demotion of former species to subspecific rank—will pare our lists but otherwise occasion no difficulty. Those who have seen all four dark-eyed juncos and all three flickers will simply deduct three and two birds, respectively, from their lists. This commutation may run smoothly but, with my inveterate pessimism, I doubt it. And bear in mind that a seventh edition will ineluctably follow the sixth edition, and a new set of adjustments will be necessary. The Heraclitean doctrine of ceaseless change is nowhere better exemplified than in systematics. The taxonomy of any group of plants or animals is, of necessity, in continual flux. Lastly, there is the jet age and the expanding population. In the not too distant past when most of the older birders were compiling their lists, time was an important deterrence. One could not rush in a few hours from New York to Alaska or Baja California. Travel took time. Now any aspiring high school student with the right connections and drive can see over six hundred birds in one year. I know one, Ted Parker for instance, who has already accomplished this feat. There is an ever-increasing number of the exuberant young swelling the ranks of the Brotherhood—and time is on their side. The 600 Club will be the inevitable victim of the jet and the population explosion, as is the rest of the world right now.

National Audubon Society

There are few who need an introduction to the National Audubon Society (NAS). Everyone has seen *Audubon*, the magazine of the society, or hiked the trails of its sanctuaries. Unless you are an active birder, however, the chances are that you haven't heard of *Audubon Field Notes* (*AFN*) or have any conception of the key role this publication assumes among the ranks of the faithful. *Audubon Field Notes* has recently been incorporated under a new format and rechristened *American Birds,* but I shall continue to speak of this periodical by its original name, *AFN*. I grow weary and provoked by the present fad of renaming things. I shall never forget the mild shock I received some years ago when Old Dutch Cleanser, a household necessity in my mother's home, appeared on the market as NEW Old Dutch Cleanser. Can minor insanity conjure up a more ridiculous antinomy? It is youth's privilege, I suppose, to continually pour old wine into new bottles, but it is also the privilege, nay the obligation, of the old to save their old bottles and transfer the stuff back where it belongs. So *AFN* it shall be.

Audubon Field Notes, published by the NAS in collaboration with the U.S. Fish and Wildlife Service, appears bi-monthly. The six issues are as follows: (1) Christmas Bird Count; (2) Fall Migration; (3) Winter Season and Winter Bird Population Study; (4) Spring Migration; (5) Nesting Season; (6) Breeding Bird Census. Four of these issues, numbers 2 through 5 above, report the seasonal occurrence of birds throughout North America. Special emphasis is placed upon unusual birds or rarities for the area concerned, but the habitual and routine bird populations constitute the great bulk of each report. The United States and Canada are divided into approximately twenty areas and each has its own regional editor and his coterie of collaborators. These separate accounts are collated by a central staff of NAS editors and distributed to the Brotherhood—for a price, of course. These four issues of the *AFN* are an invaluable aid to the vagrant lister. Close perusal of several consecutive, yearly accounts will indicate fairly well the spectrum of species he may expect to find in a particular region at any of the four seasons. Of course, if he wishes to see a Bachman's Warbler, an Eskimo Curlew, or an Ivory-billed Woodpecker, he soon learns that a reverential pilgrimage to his favorite oracle will be more efficacious—endangered species are not reported, and rightly not, too. What chance would an Ivory-billed Woodpecker have if five thousand crazed birders trampled his fleeting domain! The true authentic value of the *AFN*, quite obviously, is its scientific value as a long-time, minute record of the seasonal distribution of North American birds.

The Christmas Bird Count (CBC) is by long odds the most popular and ecumenical enterprise of the Brotherhood. If *AFN* consisted of nothing but the CBC, it would still remain the single most cherished publication of the amateur birding world. It is the challenging, competitive nature of the CBC that endears it to the collective heart of North American birders. Birding is a sport as well as an enthralling hobby to thousands and the CBC is the apogee of this subdued frenzy. The annual Christmas Bird Census, as it was originally named, was inaugurated by Frank M. Chapman in 1900, a truly twentieth-century project. Only twenty-five reports were submitted in the first CBC and just twenty-seven birders participated. It must have been a rather lonely occupation in those dear, dead days beyond recall but better, to my mind, than the Lonely Crowd of today. Seventy-one years later, there were 903 reports published and a Brobding-nagian 16,657 participants. There remains small doubt that the increased coverage afforded by so many observers imparts to the current CBC a thoroughness and reliability impossible to the earlier counts, but much of the mystery is gone. We now know what birds spend Christmas on the snowy tundra and dumps around Nome as well as those seen amid the slush of the Bronx. A total of 561 species were reported on the seventy-first Count. Cocoa, Florida, led with 205 species and Nome, Alaska, brought up the rear with just three birds—Willow Ptarmigan, Common Raven, and McKay's Bunting. Despite Cocoa's 205 birds, I should have preferred to be with Bill Foster and his sturdy little band of seven at Nome. Scanning that almost interminable list of birds reported by Allan D. Cruickshank and his legion of eighty-eight birders, I recognized no lifers; at Nome, the McKay's Buntings seen there would have been a lifer for me. This Bunting is almost unobtainable to all but a very few favored birders since it breeds only on inaccessible Hall and St. Matthew Islands in the middle of the Bering Sea. If Foster's McKay's Buntings keep on frequenting that dump at Nome in winter, I'm going to see them if it's the last bird on my list!

The rules and regulations of the CBC are reasonably simple and soon told. (1) All count areas must fit within, preferably fill, a fifteen-mile diameter circle. No overlapping of areas is permitted. (2) Counts must be made during the official period, announced a year in advance by the National Audubon Society through *AFN* (*American Birds*). This period is about two weeks' duration and always includes Christmas Day and usually New Year's as well. (3) Counts must cover only one calendar day. (4) Only full species receive official recognition although often unusual subspecies may be mentioned. (5) Dead birds are verboten. (6) The compiler of each count must adhere to a rigid format in his report and include a number of items such as weather, temperature, winds, terrain, longitude and latitude, names of all participants, party hours, etc., etc. This is quite necessary and precludes carelessly prepared reports and maintains a standard of scientific accuracy. I can speak easily and with conviction on such matters because I have never been a compiler but simply one of the free spirits collecting my species and invariably ignoring the reading of the mileage on my car speedometer. Over the years, though, the compiler of our home count area has slowly impressed upon my stubborn mind the importance of the unimportant. I now check the car mileage the night before count day so that my exuberance of the early morning will not blind my eyes to the glorious instrumentation of the dial panel. (7) And oh yes, I almost forgot, each participant must pay a fee of one dollar to help defray publication expenses of the CBC issue of the Field Notes. It is the outstanding bargain of the century, even if the ante is raised, as it probably will be. Nowhere can one buy so much spiritual, physical, and, yes, moral fun for one depreciated U.S. dollar.

Our own CBC area is Glenolden, Pennsylvania, with its center in Wallingford. I haven't the foggiest notion where Glenolden is or, in fact, what it is. Each year when I report our bird list of the day to Ted Rigby, our area compiler, I vow I'll ask why the name Glenolden instead of Wallingford, the hub of the count and, incidentally, our own Post Office address. But I never do. There is always too much bird lore to discuss. Despite the fact that Glenolden has for some years led the state of Pennsylvania in numbers of species seen—last year we set a new state record with 109 birds—it is a relatively small affair, twenty-one participants on the seventy-first Count. Often only half that number, or less, rise early before the dawn to seek adventure.

The biggest counts are always in Florida, California, or Texas. Cocoa, Florida, and San Diego, California, are deadly rivals and almost always log over 200 species. The campaign for these big counts are planned days in advance and every bird in the area mentally recorded for der tag. Even so, several species usually manage each year to elude these human bird dogs on count day. Such intransigents are recorded as seen during the count period but not on count day and do not contribute their luster to the final numerical tally. The year Marybelle and I were permitted by the Monterey Peninsula satraps to join their CBC we had spotted three Black Brants in exactly the same locality at Pacific Grove three successive days preceding count day. This species would be our own contribution to the count day list, we told ourselves. No Black Brants were recorded on count day, either by us or any of the local experts. No doubt they were the three Evil Sisters in disguise, cackling downwind at our chagrin. In 1970, however, in our own dooryard, we fared better. A Wood Thrush, an exceedingly rare winter bird anywhere in the United States and doubly so as far north as Pennsylvania, was present in our yard from Thanksgiving to December 26, the latter being the Glenolden count day. Unlike the three Black Brants of ill repute, we had not seen the Wood Thrush for the three days preceding count day and dolefully recorded him in our minds as a quitter and renegade. But on count day, as we were hastily cramming down our frugal lunch, the phone rang and our neighbor told us the Wood Thrush was at her side door eating the bits of apple she had thrown out to lure him in. One minute later we were on the spot and our Wood Thrush was still there munching his apple. Neither Mrs. Swisher nor we ever saw him again. Wild things do not often so order their lives to accommodate the vagaries of the top primate.

American Birding Association

The American Birding Association (ABA) is, contrary to the Preacher, something new under the sun, at least that sun which warms the North American birder's world. As I write this, the ABA is less than three years of age. So young an organization can scarcely be evaluated by its traditions or past performance but enough water has flowed over the dam since its inception to cast a reasonably accurate horoscope of its future impact upon the Brotherhood. Its avowed major objective is to "promote the hobby and sport of birding." This goal, together with the uncompromising spirit of intent articulated by its founders, is a true line of departure from other major birding societies. Its uniqueness lies precisely in the emphasis on birding as a non-scientific pursuit. Any and all types of birders are welcome to membership in ABA but in this house of many mansions all and sundry must first deposit in the ample cloakroom portfolios, slide rules, and the pomp and circumstance of scientific hocus-pocus. In the words of ABA's President, Stuart Keith, "The common denominator is that birding is his hobby, his form of recreation, the thing to which he devotes much of his spare time. Therefore, the one essential ingredient to birding is that it should be FUN." At last the ordinary bird watcher—I use the latter, odious term advisedly but sorely, against my finer instincts—has come into his own. He now has at his back an organization with the courage to state positively and categorically that listing and field identification are honorable destinies, sui generis, ding an sich—and he need not even apologize for his Latinized and Germanic flummery. This, at least, is our hope.

The ideational father of ABA is James A. Tucker, secretary and editor of *Birding*, the official organ of the Association. Jim writes: "The idea of the ABA was conceived by me in 1968. At that time I proposed to call it the American Birdwatcher's Association and call the magazine the *Birdwatcher's Digest*. Actually, I never intended to start anything as imposing as has resulted. I just got tired of writing the same letter to all my birding friends giving them all the news that I had accumulated, so I set up a plan whereby we could share information, and you can see what happened. Little did I realize how ripe the birding fraternity was for such an organization. Actually, while I suppose I provided the catalyst for this thing, I feel certain that it would have come about by spontaneous combustion sooner or later and I really cannot take too much credit." Stuart Keith and Arnold Small were almost simultaneously engulfed in the vortex of the storm engendered by Tucker, and the former is now President and the latter First Vice-President. Robert W. Smart of New Hampshire, a most knowledgeable birder and 600 Club member, is Second Vice-President. Joseph W. Taylor, at the present writing just seven birds short of seven hundred, is the recently appointed Treasurer (see updated figure, p. 136). Six additional officers at large, all highly skilled birders, conclude the roster of officers of ABA. With no advertising other than by word of mouth, ABA has now reached the thousand mark and is still burgeoning. There are members in all fifty states (Idaho was the last holdout), six Canadian provinces, and eight countries. More incredible still, there are now over thirty Life Members at a hundred dollars a throw. Since this amount would cover membership for twenty years, a number of the Brotherhood, as Jim Tucker put it, "must think we are for real." Apparently, ABA is firmly launched and fast beating out to sea with a good land breeze and flying colors. The phenomenal growth of ABA and the almost Corybantic enthusiasm of its devotees is the manifest culmination of the American birder's long struggle for adulthood. Just as there are no longer yokels who careen by golf courses yelling "Fore" at the hapless victims of this insidious sport, so there are few louts among the nonbirding world who now tap their forehead or snicker at the sight of the birder with binoculars. When barbarians cease to scoff at that which is foreign to them, it is a sure indication that the erstwhile object of their ribaldry has come of age.

The publication *Birding* offers an exhilarating outlet for the exchange of ideas, points of view, and all the other manifold cares and joys of the Brotherhood. Today, however, perhaps the most popular feature of *Birding* is that department which deals with bird finding. One of the prime problems of the lister is where, when, and how to look for his desiderata, or, in plain terminology, what he "needs." Two books by Olin Sewall Pettingill, Jr. have been the indispensable vade mecum of the itinerant birder during the recent past: *A Guide to Bird Finding East of the Mississippi* (1951) and . . . *West of the Mississippi* (1953). Both are still valuable aids, but because of the relentless and accelerated destruction or alteration of much of our countryside, many sections of these guides no longer represent things as they are today. Tomorrow both volumes will be even more outdated. A more recent book by Pettingill, *The Bird Watcher's America* (1965), has sought to amend the situation to some extent by updating birding areas and regions in a more general and less detailed manner so as to make the information less susceptible to the corrosive effects of time. In addition to these three books, Pettingill for years published bird finding articles, for a specific region or bird, in the *National Audubon* Magazine, but this popular column was abandoned a few years ago when *Audubon* Magazine ceased to cater primarily to birders and became a general nature and conservation mouthpiece. ABA has taken over where *Audubon* Magazine left off and each issue of *Birding* now includes bird finding information in the form of maps and detailed instructions as to where and when to look for rare or hard-to-find species. Announcements of pelagic trips and other related data are also included. For instance, Marybelle and

I had been trying for several years to get reliable information on ways and means to get to the Dry Tortugas. An announcement of a boat trip to these small islands, seventy miles west of Key West, by Bird Bonanzas was recently published in *Birding* and our difficulties were solved. We took the trip in the summer of 1971, and added five lifers to our North American lists. Apparently, a successful future for the ABA is assured and it will undoubtedly continue to answer the needs of the nonprofessional birder and lister. There are, nevertheless, several small, dark smudges on the horizon. Whether any of these will materialize as prominent thunderheads remains to be seen. Let's take a quick look at just two of them.

The ABA had scarcely pipped its shell with its precocious egg tooth before two categories of membership were created—regular and elective—shades of the AOU. Thus, almost as soon as the caul was removed, a hierarchy was established. Now for an organization with the avowed purpose of promoting birding as a hobby and sport this is a sorry beginning. If one's hobby is birding and one makes a sport (defined in my dictionary as: "diversion; recreation, pleasant pastime") out of it, how can one be graded for this voluntary commitment? It is as though I stationed myself at some spot along the Appalachian Trail and ticked off the hikers as they passed. This fellow has a sturdy stride and keeps his eyes fixed upon the distant hills, ipso facto he shall be an elective member of the Trail fraternity. This dawdler, on the other hand, often stoops to examine a flower or slips his pack from his back and rests awhile on some lichen-covered boulder, his eyes half closed in dreamy contemplation. He does not seem to be working as hard at his fun as number one, therefore, surely, he is fit only for regular membership. It is possible my analogy is unsound, but I think not. In other words, to award a higher status to John because he plays harder than Joe is a reductio ad absurdum. A person's profession or work is, perhaps, a different matter. In an essentially professional organization, such as the American Ornithologists' Union, if I have made no scientific contribution, I cannot expect to become an elective member. It would be an absurdity to reason otherwise. But in the ABA, an organization conceived to meet the needs of the average birder, where is the necessity for higher and lower echelons? The officers, to be sure, will rightfully always be picked from among the more knowledgeable and active birders. But is it necessary or even wise to first create peers of the realm? I do not wish to be an elective member of ABA and have not sought this dubious distinction but neither do I wish to be a second-class brother. In my own professional organization, American Association of Anatomists, there is just one class of membership. A fortiori, there should be only one class of membership in a communion dedicated to FUN.

Quite recently, the Secretary of ABA explained to me that the prime purpose of an elective membership is to guarantee the perpetuation of the present persuasion, fun in birding. The founder and officers do not wish to see ABA become the mouthpiece of yet another conservation group or degenerate into a scientifically oriented junta looking askance at the plebeian mention of "tail feathers" instead of that gloriously descriptive word "rectrices." I can only point out that good intentions are often like a double-edged sword: they may sometimes cut in the opposite direction from that intended. It is entirely conceivable, for instance, that when the old order changeth yielding place to new, the latter may stage a palace revolution and lead the defenseless populace down the dreary road of scientific quackery and the interminable measurements of rectrices. But I was born several millennia too late. Isaiah or Jeremiah would have been only the running dogs of Pollyannaism by comparison. So let us put our trust in Jim Tucker and his merry men and, in the words of someone or other, hope for the best.

My other reservation concerning ABA is not a criticism but a prophecy—and I sincerely hope I may be proved a false prophet. It is that perpetual curse of numbers. If the membership continues to increase at anything like its present rate, ABA will lose the intimate and personal appeal that has so far endeared it to the Brotherhood. It will then be in danger of becoming an unwieldy, amorphous miscellany with no more soul or spontaneity than the American Association for the Advancement of Science or the Republican Party. This will not be ABA's fault but society's. Nonetheless, ABA will be the helpless victim. There is no point in laboring this old chestnut further. Philosophers and sages from Heraclitus of Ephesus to Hegel and the dialectical materialists have told us that quantitative accretion invariably precipitates qualitative changes. We read about it today in the altered behavior of animals subjected to overcrowding in the laboratory and we see it in the violence of our urban jungles. Everyone understands and laments. So much for the obvious. Maybe there won't be any birds left by then anyway and ABA will die aborning.

There are a number of other professional or semiprofessional societies devoted exclusively or in part to ornithology, but I have little personal knowledge of them and no useful purpose would be served by extending the list. There are also numerous local Audubon Societies, local bird clubs of note, and a few state-wide bird clubs, such as the Texas Ornithological Society and so forth. Altogether, the Brotherhood has evolved a formidable array of organizations with which to channel its various activities and aspirations. But ever above the confusion and din of battle sounds the rallying cry, the mot du guet—Good Birding!

VI

The Pelagic Trip

Sooner or later every birder, especially the rapacious lister, must take a pelagic trip. And when I say a pelagic trip, I do not mean, of course, just one trip but many, at least ten or more if most of the truly oceanic species are to be seen. The average nonbirder, whatever such a category may denote, and the average beginning birder are seldom aware of the great number of birds that either inhabit the oceans exclusively the year round or that spend much of their time on or near the seven seas. Thanks to Coleridge and the Midway Islands of the "last" war, everyone has heard of the Albatross and knows it is a large sea bird and the name storm petrel is a household word to most folk. However, by and large, robins, cardinals, bluejays, and other strictly land birds represent the world of birds to those who carry their binoculars only to the racetrack. The novice birder, naturally, soon hears of shearwaters, murrelets, auklets, murres, puffins, and the like but by that time he has probably ceased to be a novice. Also, if he lives in Wichita, Kansas, or Winnipeg, Manitoba, it may take a few months or years before the breath of life is blown into those pictures of shearwaters and alcids that clutter up the beginning and middle pages of his field guides. There are two large groups of more fortunately situated birders, of course—those who dwell on the east or west coast—and they, for all I know, may have cut their birding eyeteeth on Black or Pigeon Guillemots instead of crows and robins. Whether my asseveration that most people are unaware of pelagic birds is true or false, the incontestable fact remains—namely, that your corner pharmacist and the man feeding pigeons in Fairmont Park have never heard of the fine distinctions between Pink-footed and Pale-footed Shearwaters. I'll even venture a more sweeping generalization and wager that neither has heard of either.

I have just made a rapid and somewhat unsystematic check of the truly pelagic species of bird that may occur in either the eastern Pacific or western Atlantic Oceans, as well as "semi-pelagic" species—my own unscientific rubric—that usually inhabit the coastal waters of North America for all or part of the year. This tabulation for the most part does not include rare or accidental species. On the Atlantic side there are: Shearwaters and Fulmar (6); Storm Petrels (2); Frigatebird (1); Gannet and Boobies (4); Alcids (6)—total 19. On the Pacific side are: Albatrosses (2); Shearwaters and Fulmar (7); Storm Petrels (4); Frigatebird (1); Boobies (3); Alcids (15)—total 32. The total number of species for both the Atlantic and Pacific Oceans bordering North America is 40—the reader will readily understand that east and west totals are not additive because the same species may occur off both coasts. Then there are the four Jaegers—one of them called Skua in the United States—found on both oceans and seldom coming ashore except during the nesting season. In addition to the above more or less truly pelagic birds, there are: Loons (4); Grebes (3); Tropicbirds (2); Pelicans (2); Cormorants (6); Sea Ducks (9); Phalaropes (2). This heterogeneous group of "semipelagic" birds either winter or spend part of the time in ocean waters. Finally, there are the Gulls (18) and Terns (16) that habituate the coastal waters, migrate along the coast, or are found only on offshore islands during the nesting season, like the Sooty and Noddy Terns of the Dry Tortugas. All of the species tabulated above add up to a grand total of 107 North American birds that are either entirely oceanic or usually found in coastal waters during some part of the year.

One word of caution. Do not quote any of the above figures except as an acknowledged approximation. No two specialists in oceanic birds would concur with my figures nor would they probably agree between themselves. The self-anointed "expert" would most certainly disagree if for no other reason than to exhibit his superior knowledge. It is not a question, you see, of whether I have consulted the right book or books; it is a matter of judgment, in part. Pink-footed and Pale-footed Shearwaters, for example, are considered conspecific by some authorities and distinct species by others. Also, a Kermadec Petrel was once sighted at Hawk Mountain, Pennsylvania, on October 3, 1959, and photographed by Donald S. Heintzelman. The normal range of this pelagic bird is the South Pacific. Should it be considered among the North American bird fauna? Of course not. But suppose as I write this someone is recording it off Cape San Lucas or the San Diego coast! What then? Incidentally, Marybelle and I missed this bird by one day; we were at Hawk Mountain on October 4, 1959.

If you have borne with me this far and scanned the equivocal figures and attendant caveat, you will assuredly be longing for a breath of tangy sea air to dispel the cobwebs I may have engendered by my unauthoritative disquisition on the number of North American sea birds. But wait, do not attempt to embark yet. We must first procure a boat. Before you can feel the heave and pitch of the deck under your feet and brush away the myriad sea birds that will darken the sky with their vast numbers, we must commandeer a ship by fair means or foul. A cutting-out expedition might be best, for then we could pick and choose our vessel with some consideration for its intended mission. But, alas, few birders know how to shake out a topsail on a moonless night and perhaps none has ever climbed back downward up the futtock shrouds. No, it will have to be an ordinary fishing boat, power driven, chartered for the day. And it is not always an easy matter to convince the captain of such a craft that a horde of birders clumping and reeling about his beloved boat is not a degrading enterprise or downright sacrilegious. In any event, fishing boats that are for hire must be chartered weeks or months in advance of the proposed date. I know, for I once took it upon myself to arrange a small pelagic trip and it took several weeks' negotiation and as many more of waiting. Be patient, then, and in the meantime thumb carefully through your field guide so that when the great day arrives you will not bring disgrace upon yourself and embarrass the entire company by shouting, "Shearwater," when it is only a tern swooping low over the waves, or claim, as I once did, that the bird was a Leach's Petrel instead of Wilson's because it had yellow feet.

Marybelle and I have taken a number of pelagic trips but even so there are scarcely two other people in North America who know less about the identification of shearwaters, petrels, murrelets, and their ilk. One reason for this glaring lacuna in our bird lore is that probably half of our trips have been on routine ferry runs by ourselves, without benefit of other birders to help in spotting or experts at hand to point out the salient differences between one species and another. Field guides are an inestimable help, naturally, but oceanic birds do not flap lazily alongside your boat permitting minute inspection of bill color, length of legs beyond tail, size of white neck patch, or baffling vagaries of wingbeat. No, most of them fly like the proverbial bat out of hell, small bullet specks half a mile away hidden three fourths of the time by the wave troughs. And when your field guide tells you that the flight of the Manx Shearwater is fast, that the wingbeat of Audubon's Shearwater is fastest of all and, finally, that the flight of the New Zealand Shearwater is lighter than the Manx—what does all this really mean, apropos of identifying your bird? And supposing you have never seen a Manx Shearwater! What then? Correct and rapid identification of oceanic birds requires far more expertise than the ordinary birder possesses. Let's put it another way. Suppose your total experience with all the warblers of North America, approximately fifty-six species, was twelve days of field work. How swift and accurate would your identifications be? Add to this the proposition that on some of these twelve days only two or three species showed up and at intervals of several hours apart. Warblers are much easier to identify than most oceanic birds but I doubt if you would consider yourself an authority on the Parulidae under the conditions I have imposed.

You will readily perceive that I am going all out to defend my ignorance of oceanic birds. It is almost as though I protested too much. In any event, whether I have exculpated myself or not, I give you freely the benefit of my experience with the pelagic trip, meager as it is. It will have to be chiefly of people and circumstances, though, and not birds. Also, if in the following condensed account I appear somewhat vague concerning dates, names, and places, you will understand it is in the interest of anonymity or, if you will, cowardice. I neither wish to be garroted on some black night in an unfrequented street nor do I wish to stoop to petty, personal aspersions. Besides, nothing really shocking or despicable ever happens among the pelagic brethren. They are just like people, only more so.

A pelagic trip is very much like a cocktail party except for two relatively unimportant differences; namely, no distilled spirits are served—although a few desperate souls may smuggle a flask or two on board—and the hours are a trifle unconventional, usually six in the morning or midnight. If it is winter, there is only the faintest intimation of paling in the eastern sky at six A.M. and even if it is California there is apt to be a nippy breeze blowing off the water. We grope our way along the uneven wharf and mark a few bobbing lights at the far end. That must be where the boat is moored; or else, perhaps, it is the press gang. Admittedly, I have been indulging myself with too much Hornblower of late but at such an hour one tries desperately to inject a parcel of sodden humor into the enterprise. Yes, it is a boat, but make certain it is the one your group chartered. Other boat crews and their passengers are also abroad at this hour and all of them but yours will be off for sailfish or albacore. On one occasion, I watched a young couple scramble aboard the boat opposite ours. They immediately sought the highest and most remote part of the prow, where they seated themselves and gazed dreamily out across the darkened inlet toward the open sea. "Thinking of the big ones they are going to catch," I mused. But when the leader of our birding group began to call the roll, down came an answering hail from the other boat and the Carters frantically gathered together their gear and left that fishing craft as rats are said to desert a sinking ship. If the fishing crowd had sailed first, the Carters would have had a sorry day of it. Or would they? I know what some of my ardent fishing friends would answer: "Serve the bloody bird watchers right!" or "Probably have some real fun for once in their dull lives." Regardless of the respective merits of fishing and sea birding, lesson number one for all concerned is to find your own boat and crowd.

We stand awhile alongside on the wharf until we have seen by binoculars, telescopes, and so forth that this one is surely our boat. A familiar paperback bird guide in the hip pocket of one of the boarders is our irrefutable assurance that we have indeed found our boat and we stumble on board with the others. Most of the people seem to know one another and we envy their jaunty repartee and wide-awake salutations. A rather short, plump woman of nondescript age in a long, loose-fitting dress, the only female so garbed, catches her foot on the last step of the ladder and pitches headlong into a pile of coats, bags, and birding paraphernalia amid much merriment on her part and sympathetic chucklings from the rest of us. This unfortunate female will bear watching, for she is a type found on every pelagic trip. She has simply come for the ride. We look about for the most advantageous place to stand or sit but all, presumably, are taken so we place ourselves against the stern railing and inhale great draughts of the Diesel fumes coming inboard from the idling engine. There is no roll call this time and perhaps it is just as well, for to establish the identity of everyone on board would have taken another half hour. I had noticed a large, permanent sign on our boat to the effect that twenty-two passengers was the limit for fishing. I learned later from the leader that our group numbered about forty. The lines are at last cast off, the boat swerves away from the wharf and we are off for the briny deep. The "Goodwin Lights" are soon far astern and the business of watching the horizon for birds will soon begin. As yet, the light is still too poor and, besides, only junk birds will be present this close to shore—common gulls and terns, an occasional Cormorant or Grebe and a low-flying line of Brown Pelicans. Let's take a look at our companions on this voyage.

In age they range from a young girl of about twelve to grizzled old men like myself. That lean, stringy fellow over there gesticulating to his neighbor is probably even older, say about seventy or so. There are more men than women but not preponderantly so. There are, also, always several well-defined types on any authentic pelagic trip. Most conspicuous and vocal are the teenagers and young men. These are the true spearhead of the expedition, eager hounds straining at the leashes. They gravitate to the upper forward deck as if by some compelling, positional tropism. There amidst the flying spray and the roll and pitch of the vessel this vanguard maintains its constant and relentless vigil for winged specks on the far horizon. A few hardy oldsters usually mix with this "masthead lookout" but they are always in the minority. Most of the birds seen on any trip are first sighted by this energetic and sharp-eyed avant garde. If it is your first pelagic trip, you will quite naturally wish to place yourself in the midst of this forward deck lookout, this fountainhead of advanced tidings of joy. It is a mistake that you correct long before the end of the trip. In the first place, the forward end of the boat is much livelier than the sides or stern and it takes a very good pair of legs and eyes to keep your bird in focus. For the most part you see heaving billows and sky and little else. Secondly, the bird, always sighted at a distance, never eventually flies past your side of the boat but invariably cuts across to the other side when it gets within range. There is the mad rush to the other side and now you are faced with a double line of backs and broad shoulders, not even an interstice to view the sea or sky. In one such melee, I finally gained a point of great vantage to the rear of the swaying mass only to have a mad-dened youth hop on the bulwark I was leaning on, directly in front of me. His back blotted out sea and sky as effectually as a board fence. I finally saw the birds from the stern after a hasty retreat down the ladder that led to the lower deck. When the excitement subsided and nothing but blank sea again presented itself, I sought out that inconsiderate lout who had deliberately blocked my view. Before I could say one word he turned to me, the "newcomer" on the upper deck, with rapture in his voice, "Did you get the terns? Did you get them?" What could I say except, yes! No, never bird from the forward deck on a pelagic trip unless you are young and sturdy or a recognized authority who can command deference and, what is more to the point, elbow room.

Next in importance is the small group, usually two or three, of pelagic experts who, apparently, have sailed all the seas for seven years and a day and really know their birds. Of course, such authorities are the real sine qua non of any trip but ordi-narily the foredeck mob is relatively well informed and the adjudication of their elders is seldom required. Then there is always one individual, not necessarily a woman, but usually so, who would rather gab and gossip about his or her birding ex-periences of last year or a decade ago than bear down on the birds at hand. This often forlorn type of "social birder" is by no means limited to pelagic trips but on board ship with things happening in the wink of an eye and the need for close attention and lightning action this type is maddening. Even with my limited experience, I have learned to spot these characters the minute they climb through the companionway and it has become second nature to avoid them, even at the risk of mounting again the forward deck and its overpowering confusion. Marybelle with her less misanthropic outlook and greater forbearance is a sitting duck for these lonely souls. But she too is learning fast.

There are yet two other types who play minor character bits upon this tossing stage. Invariably one person, and oddly enough usually only one, is seasick the entire voyage and lies green and groaning in or near the scuppers or the rail. The trip for him is a watery-eyed torment. If the Wandering Albatross hove into view two points abaft the larboard bow, he would not so much as flicker an eyelid or contract a single fiber of his stapedius muscle. The sea is too much with him late and soon. If this miserable wretch records any birds on the trip, it will be only Herring or Western Gulls as we leave or reenter port. It is always heartening, however, to observe these individuals just before the boat docks. They are usually munching on some kind of provender and the light and hope of future days is beginning to dawn upon their pasty features.

The other bit actors in this saga of the sea are the diametrical opposite of our seasick friend. These people are sucking on a candy bar as they climb aboard and their mouths are full of the joy of eating during the entire trip. They usually carry a capacious paper bag in one hand and a huge thermos of coffee in the other. They find a protected nook shielded from spray and wind and to them the voyage is one continuous picnic, untroubled by clarion hails from the prow or flying specks on the horizon. Oddly enough, these masticatory prodigies always have binoculars hanging around their necks and even languidly raise them from time to time. But I strongly suspect it is to dislodge the crumbs that cover the top lenses rather than to scan the wave crests. Watching this anaconda type of pelagic birder, one speculates uneasily about the destiny of western civilization.

But the dramatis personae of the pelagic trip are not all freaks, as my hyperbolic account thus far would lead one to believe. Quite the contrary. At least three quarters of these birders are intensely normal, dedicated birders. Many of them know their oceanic birds well and are always ready to help the novice. They are not pushy, probably eat less than I do, and their single-minded purpose on board is to see as many species as possible. Knowing my limitations so well, I seldom volunteer specific opinions concerning any bird that is sighted at a distance. On the few occasions when my discretion has been superseded by an unhealthy exuberance and I have yelled, "Three shearwaters!" and my shearwaters resolve into gulls or terns, no one has ever berated me for this folly. Some are even so humane as to lie and tell me they often make the same mistake themselves. So now, having reinstated myself in the good graces of the company, let us make a few remarks about the birds themselves.

As I have repeatedly stressed to the point of surfeit, my experience of pelagic trips and birds is too limited to give you a rounded picture of the number of species and individuals usually seen on these trips. Obviously, this varies tremendously depending upon the time of year, the ocean, the latitude, and the distance from shore. On one midsummer trip off the Jersey coast we were out for almost twelve hours and saw only a single individual, a Gannet, that couldn't have been seen from shore. And when I say "saw" I use the word indiscriminately, for both Marybelle and I missed that bird. On another occasion in the same waters we saw hundreds of Wilson's Petrels, no Leach's, and thirty-six Cory's Shearwaters—but nothing else. In early June off the Portlock Bank near Kodiak we saw several thousand Slender-billed Shearwaters, perhaps a hundred or more Fork-tailed Petrels, and three Kittlitz's Murrelets. In July between Key West and the Dry Tortugas, we saw just three Bridled Terns and one Audubon's Shearwater. In winter off Monterey Bay, California, there were a number of Fulmars, Ancient Murrelets, Rhinoceros Auklets, one Pink-footed Shearwater, and one Pomarine Jaeger. In all these trips, the greater part of the time was spent searching empty ocean and sky for birds that were not there. It should be made clear, however, that the species I have mentioned above represent only those forms seldom seen from shore. There are almost always the more common gulls, terns, ducks, cormorants, pelicans, and so forth.

Probably the most disappointing pelagic trip we have taken to date was a late February trip out of San Diego. Let me give you a list of the possibilities that were presented to us, without bothering to indicate which species one would have expected to see and which ones would be problematic or rare: Common, Arctic, Red-throated Loons; Pink-footed, Manx, Sooty, Pale-footed Shearwaters; Black, Leach's, Ashy Petrels; Cassin's, Rhinoceros Auklets; Pomarine, Parasitic Jaegers; Fulmar; Xantus's Murrelet; Common Murre; Kittiwake; Tufted Puffin; Black-footed, Laysan Albatrosses. It is just possible that if Captain Horatio Hornblower had given the same studious attention to his sea birds as he did to his whist game, he might have seen all those species by the time he had hoisted his broad pennant. At any rate, it is a list that might arouse the acquisitive instincts of even Joseph Taylor or Ira Gabrielson, the two top men of the 600 Club. Marybelle and I flew all the way from Philadelphia to San Diego and back in a single weekend just to take this trip. Despite the fact that our North American lists at the time stood at an even 640 birds, there were seven lifers for us on that list of sea birds. There are still five.

This trip was scheduled to proceed to the Cortez Bank, ninety miles offshore, but fate played us a scurvy trick. West winds that day were so strong that the boat's speed was reduced to the point that the Captain decided we could never complete the round trip of 180 miles during daylight hours. Also, the sea was very rough. I recall vividly one distraught moment when the Captain turned the boat about to head back toward the mainland. The deck must have canted at least seventy degrees and I felt for a brief second or two that we were all doomed to Davy Jones's Locker. The startled glances of our companions showed me that I was not alone in this wild surmise. Consequently, we did not even pass San Clemente Island but reversed our course in its lee; thus the round trip was approximately 120 miles instead of 180. All told, we were fortunate at that. I discovered later that because of the weather the Captain had been reluctant to even leave port and for awhile the trip itself had hung in the balance.

Our failure to reach the Cortez Bank was undoubtedly the chief reason for the paucity of lifers that day but it does not explain the almost total lack of bird life over those waters we did cover. As I sat hour after hour on the lockers or restlessly moved at frequent intervals from larboard to starboard or from prow to stern, I bethought myself of those simple words from the immortal verse of Lewis Carroll: "No birds were flying overhead—there were no birds to fly." The words kept trickling through my head like water through a sieve until I was almost bordering upon a self-induced trance. Needless to say, no Albatross was sighted. There was not a single Petrel of any species. There were no Jaegers. There were no Loons. There were no Puffins or Kittiwakes. There were no Auklets. There were no Pink or Pale-footed Shearwaters. Not one lone Fulmar ever dented the horizon. In all that vast expanse of sea and sky not a living thing moved for hour after interminable hour. I have never seen the ocean so bereft of bird life. Nothing short of a malevolent conspiracy could have produced such a void. No birds were flying overhead—there were no birds to fly.

The details I have just stated are perfectly true (to the best of my knowledge) but, of course, as we have been told so many times we almost believe it, nothing is ever pure black and white. About midway between San Clemente Island and the shore on our return trip, two Xantus's Murrelets were seen at close range, both in the water and flying. At about five P.M., as we were approaching the long breakwater that shelters the harbor, three Manx Shearwaters were sighted. Both of these species were lifers for Marybelle and me. Actually, unless one has phenomenal luck, or has just begun to bird, two lifers are about all one can expect on a single pelagic trip. I have no valid kick so far as lifers go. I was not really so naïve as to think we would see even half of the birds "advertised." Certainly the good and true, well-informed birders who planned this trip did not anticipate any such good fortune I am sure. All such pelagic lists represent possibilities, not probabilities. It was just that things were so damned, deadly dull—except for that turnabout in the lee of the Island—for just about eleven hours and forty minutes. So, as the chill February dusk creeps into the still waters of the harbor and we begin to disembark, take stock, dear friend, concerning sea birds and their ways. Pelagic trips are like Pope's Pierian spring —take deep draughts or don't meddle with the stuff. "If you'd go to Mother Carey . . . where she feeds her chicks at sea," do not fail to go often. You may not find the spot the first time.

VII

...and Whether Pigs Have Wings

Throughout this discursive chronicle of lifers and listers there are frequent allusions to the Brotherhood, the implication being that birders are a monolithic clan, so many toy soldiers standing all in a row. This is far from the truth. Diversity of approach, aptitude, and application characterizes the birding world as well as other human pursuits, once one has delved beneath the veneer of uniformity. We habitually speak of the professor, the banker, the farmer, etc., as though our calling or profession made stereotypes of us all. We know this is not so but for convenience' sake we inveterately suppress those intimations that run counter to false generalities or demand reorientation of preconceived notions. I know for a fact that there is no such animal as *the* college professor. Some are scholars; others are atrocious dilettantes. Some, a very few, speak with the tongues of angels; others, the majority, slobber out their plebeian speech with at least one solecism for every disjointed sentence. Some are near alcoholics; others would stagger or reel if the fumes from an empty champagne bottle were to reach them across a crowded room. Some are dull beyond belief; others are brilliant—but even their brilliance is occasionally duller than the dullard's dullness. Many are blatant extroverts, to a degree that would make a first-class Rotarian shy away in terror; probably the majority are introverts, many to a degree that almost transcends any meaningful distinction between outer and inner. Some are fat or gay; others are lean or morose. But enough of professors. They are a sorry lot at the best and unbearable at the worst. Diversity among birders is our present theme.

I strongly suspect that both Marybelle and I would have become enamored of birding long before we actually did if it had not been for Dr. H. She is dead now but perhaps anonymity should still be the watchword. There is a small botanical garden with a refreshing pool of water in its center that adjoins the grounds of the medical school at Pennsylvania. It has attracted many birds to its green seclusion over the years, less so now with the prevailing edifice complex of the University. Marybelle and I saw our first Lincoln's Sparrow in this oasis, amidst the howling wilderness of brick and mortar. Many a late spring evening we have listened to the bullfrog's sonorous churrump blustering in from the pool through the open windows of the stuffy laboratory. A Fish Crow was a frequent visitor to the garden for several years and long before we knew there was more than one kind of crow we enjoyed his nasal, monosyllabic harangue. We dubbed him "Dagwood" after that inane laugh of Arthur Lake, the comedian who portrayed this comic strip character on the screen. It was a perfect replica. But into this small Eden crept the serpent in the guise of the good Dr. H. Marybelle suffered more than I because Dr. H. sought out her own sex, usually, for these garden excursions. Dr. H. was a distinct birding type and unquestionably the Delaware Valley Ornithological Club (DVOC) had this type in mind when they excluded women from membership. Needless to say, they have their own male Dr. H.'s and a more garrulous bunch of old frauds I have never laid eyes upon. Anyway, it was Dr. H. that chilled us on birds for years. She used birding as a ploy for gossip and companionship, and always with herself in the driver's seat. She would gabble on incessantly but when I occasionally sought to interject my own philosophy of life, she would immediately spy an ovenbird, or whatever was handy, and all conversation was instantly terminated until she had once more gained the ascendancy and recaptured the monologue. One time I boldly attempted to beat her at her own game. I interrupted the talk to ask why our "Dagwood" sounded so much different from the Indiana crows I was used to. And believe it or not, she launched off into a panegyric over the Ruddy Duck! It was the "cute" way he wiggled his "little tail" over and over and on and on. I admire the Ruddy immensely but it is in spite of Dr. H., not because of her. Dr. H.'s type is not peculiar to the bird world; it may be found as the compulsive prattler in any and all walks of life. Lest I offend where no offense is intended, let me hasten to add that Dr. H. was really a good soul. She was also a dedicated teacher and a distinguished scholar in her own field of tissue culture. But as a birder she was something beside you quacking in the wilderness. She represents the epitome of the social birder—the kind that talks about birds as a last resort. They are legion on the lowest rung of the birding ladder. I don't know why, but Dr. H. and her birding always calls to my mind that cadenced but incomprehensible non sequitur of the Preacher, ". . . and he shall rise at the voice of the bird, and all the daughters of musick shall be brought low." It was impossible to hear the voice of the bird and in the botanical garden the daughter of music was never brought low.

There is another variety of birder hardly less reprehensible than Dr. H. and even less comprehensible. This is the birder who seemingly manifests genuine interest in birds but who never troubles to use binoculars or buy a field guide. Year after sterile year they see birds as through a glass darkly. I have two individuals in mind, both of whom frequented Furness's. Whenever our paths crossed, one of these birders was almost certain to stop us and describe a bird she had just seen. She was most humble about the whole affair and invariably sought guidance from our superior wisdom. Usually, the description was so garbled and devoid of crucial data that we were seldom able to identify her bird. It was, of course, always either "a little brown bird" or a bird "about the size of a robin." Little else of much value. After one of our numerous failures I recall grumbling to Marybelle, "If that old bat (she really wasn't old but middling young and rather pretty) saw a crow, she couldn't tell you its color or size." Just one week later, after my hyperbolic outburst, I had my comeuppance. The "old bat" stopped us near the bridge just as we were leaving Furness's to tell us about her latest unknown. My mind instantly went blank, an acquired protective device, and I listened despondently to her tirade. When she finished, I shook my head in that perplexed but intensely interested attitude I always assume on such occasions. Since Marybelle offered no solution either, we left her. When we were about halfway up the "old road," I came to a sudden and embarrassed halt. It was slowly dawning upon me that this woman had given us one of the best and most accurate descriptions of the American Redstart I had ever heard or read. And we had responded like dummies! What must she be thinking! A warbler that every eastern beginner learns at a glance and seldom confuses thereafter. It was a superb example of hearing but not listening. I have never felt more like a damned fool. Surely she must have known all along what the bird was and was merely having fun with the "experts." This was my disconcerting conclusion at the time. Later, the next time I met her, I was, happily, not so sure. She was describing what I instinctively knew to be a Brown Thrasher but, from her account, one could have as readily deduced a Belted Kingfisher.

Miss W. in some respects was the opposite of the redstart lady; she was confidence personified. She professed an exaggerated knowledge of the local birds based entirely upon her own mine of misinformation. Seemingly, she never verified her assertions but drew upon an inexhaustible store of innate, congenital knowledge. She held some vaguely defined, unofficial position at Furness's Upper Bank Nursery and, consequently, was always handy with her advice. For some reason or other we seldom see Winter Wrens at Furness's, at least not as often as at Gradyville or the Tyler Arboretum. One late November I saw a Winter Wren on two successive days at Furness's. In a heedless moment, I volunteered this information to Miss W. "We call them Carolina Wrens around here," said this fount of all knowledge. I did my best, believe me, but to the day of her death I'm quite sure Miss W. stoutly rejected that phantom bird, the Winter Wren. It was fairly obvious that she had probably seen only two kinds of wren in her life, the Carolina and House. On another occasion she handed me a copy of the annual Delaware Valley Bird Census, sponsored by the DVOC. This, she intimated, would lead my erring feet into the paths of righteousness. For some years now, even though neither Marybelle nor I is a member, we have contributed to the compilation of this census. So much for the dregs of the birding world. Many there are in the Brotherhood who would deny any status whatsoever to Dr. H., the redstart lady, or Miss W. This, I feel, would set a dangerous precedent. There is undoubtedly a much greater disparity between my own ornithological knowledge and that of an Ernst Mayer, Alexander Wetmore, or Frank Pitelka than between the redstart lady and myself. Let us be merciful, else we all perish through our own vanity and vexation of spirit.

There is next to be considered, briefly, the type of birder who contemns the list. Almost without exception, these individuals are the nonperipatetic sort. They may walk about, to be sure, but they seldom stray far from home. Of necessity their lists are relatively small. They are, for the most part, active and enthusiastic birders and often know more about the local birds than he who wanders afar. They are keen on lifers but if you question them as to how many birds they have seen, they are either evasive or scornful. All this is natural, maybe, and more power to them. To them a list is a means, not. an end—a most laudable attitude. To me, though, this posture is too rational and cold-blooded. Also, it has a distinct touch of Tartuffian piety about it. A man who does not know how many dollars he has in the bank is either extremely wealthy or a liar. Yes, I know, there may be exceptions but I have never had the good fortune to meet one of these rarities, and I doubt if Diogenes the Cynic ever did either. I suspect that the majority of "nonlisters" secretly list. Their lists are small because they have failed to enlarge their horizons and, to speak plainly, they are jealous. Anyone who has the leisure to bird almost always has sufficient funds for travel, at least within the United States. He may not be able to go en prince but he can manage. The birder who makes a virtue out of not listing is almost always the sour grapes type.

The backbone of the Brotherhood, to which I hope I belong, needs little characterization. It is what this book is about. As an anatomist and birder, however, perhaps it is just as well to point out that the vertebral column is not the head. The column supports the head but the head directs the movements of the column. I state this simplistic principle lest my self-inclusion within the backbone group be misinterpreted as "headism." The average, well-intentioned, eager birder belongs here. He makes the Christmas Bird Counts and supplies the data for *Audubon Field Notes*. Most of his spare time is consumed in birding and he has a passionate regard for his hobby. He is fairly knowledge-able in his own domain or "specialty," but not necessarily an expert, and he also can tell you how many birds he has seen, be it in his own state, North America, or the world. He does not harbor any false illusions that the list is the alpha and omega but he does believe it is at least the alpha. He may have seen only 331 birds but he is proud of it and intends to keep right on. He may never have heard the screech of a Barn Owl but is familiar with at least half a dozen sounds of the Blue Jay, can instantly recog-nize a Carolina Wren through all its vagaries of note and song and, if he is an easterner, can identify a Wandering Tattler or a

Surfbird the first time he sees either on the west coast. If he is from the west, he will be able to distinguish between Piping and Snowy Plovers the first time he sees the former, or recognize a Wilson's Plover as distinct from a Semipalmated. However, it is not his stock of bird lore that characterizes the backbone birder, for this varies considerably among individuals, but his ardent desire to augment his fund of knowledge. He is ever prey to the conflicting stimuli induced by both competence and inadequacy. He glories in the speed with which he identifies fall warblers but the next moment is berating himself for letting that "drab" in the big red oak elude him. And last of all, perhaps his most distinctive attribute is his relentless propensity to bore the hell out of his nonbirding friends. Our good friends Harry and Kay Bailey could relate countless episodes that would compel gestures of purest empathy from a granite statue of Bismarck.

There are a great many people who "window watch." That is, they put out feed for winter birds or, in the west, sugar water for Hummingbirds. They recognize those species that come to their feeders but little else. I should hesitate to include this diverse group in the Brotherhood but perhaps I do them an injustice. Rare species, for the area, occur at feeders from time to time and all is grist for the mill. There is also a rather well-defined class whose members are part of every bird walk but who seldom are afield by themselves. These people are primarily social birders and do not differ significantly from our paradigm, Dr. H. They are always more concerned with people than birds. At the opposite pole, of course, is the top birding clan, frequently those individuals with the biggest North American or world lists. They are the influential elite who edit magazines, serve as officers for the larger bird clubs, contribute to bird-finding guides and usually write articles or books. It is a limbo in which the distinction between professional and amateur is largely obscured. There is no fundamental difference, though, between the top birding clan and the backbone group. The top clan, naturally, possesses a greater knowledge of birds and their field experience is usually more extensive. The difference, however, is one of degree not kind. At first glance, and probably second and third also, there is so much difference between your scrivener and an Allan Cruickshank or Stuart Keith or Roger Tory Peterson that we might seem to inhabit different worlds. It is not so, though. All four of us are confirmed fanatics and my ready stock of ignorance does not alienate me, as acolyte, from the temple. The first-class private is just as much a soldier as the five-star general.

As a small boy I had the chore of walking every other evening to the Siedams' for our two quarts of milk. Even in those antediluvian times Indianapolis was a fair-sized city, but we lived on the northern outskirts and in many respects it was more like the country than not. The Siedams kept a small herd of cows and although Pasteur would have winced at their milking practices, we never found a trout in my milk pail. In summer, when the days were long, I used the alleys and a pear orchard as a short cut between their house and ours but in winter I was constrained to abandon this route because it was pitch dark and I could not see my way among the trees of the orchard. For two blocks, I walked Thirty-eighth Street, which bordered Crown Hill Cemetery. It was not a route conducive to a leisurely stroll when one is very young. The dim street lights reflected eerily from the polished surfaces of the tombstones and cast a shifty radiance far beyond my range of vision. It was not that I was afraid of seeing ghosts; I was afraid of what I might not see. In my early teens I often climbed the cemetery fence on warm summer nights and walked across the graveyard to the summit of the hill, the highest point in Marion County, where lay the Hoosier bard, James Whitcomb Riley, in peaceful repose. I had conquered my little boy's fear of the unknown and was yet too young to fear the known. Oh blessed interlude! Sprawled on the huge granite slab that capped Riley's grave I searched the winking stars and heard the music of the spheres. Oh, Jim and I have shared great moments there together on that lonesome hilltop under the scudding clouds of night. And when, late at night, I strode down the hill and across the graveyard toward Thirty-eighth Street and home, I often thought of that elegiac couplet of Riley's: "Heaven portions it thus/the old mystery dim/It is midnight to us/It is morning to him." And what has all this to do with birding? Everything—as the Hoosier bard could have told you. It was on one of these nights that I heard my first Whip-poor-will! Not the drawn-out, plaintive legato I should have imagined from that old ditty we oldsters used to sing when kids in school but the rapid, staccato insistence of a throbbing, pulsing creature of the night. Thirty-eight years later I saw my first Whip-poor-will, by flashlight, resting on a rotten stump in Pocomoke Swamp, Maryland. Could the boy at Riley's grave have counted that bird? Was the bird any more a Whip-poor-will because the man saw it, more as a small huddle of dried leaves than a bird? This quandary is one of the perplexities that perpetually confronts the birder and lister. Let us explore it a bit.

In the May–June issue of *Birding* for 1971 there is a cartoon that illustrates most effectively the core problem of sight versus sound as regards placing a bird on one's life list, or any other list for that matter. It depicts a desert landscape, with a flat-topped mesa in the background and a Cactus Wren with bill agape perched on a prickly desert shrub in the foreground. A man is leaning far out of a telephone booth nearby with the instrument to his ear and gesticulating. The caption reads: "So what if you are in New York? Even if you only just hear him you can count him you know." Can the birder in the badlands canyons of New York City count this familiar sound of the desert as a lifer—in other words, the Cactus Wren? A very few might say yes; a great many more would say no. The hypothetical cabal of realists that answer "yes" would point out that almost any lister has one or more birds on his life list that he has identified by sound alone, even a glimpse of the bird having been denied him to date. They would argue further that such being the true state of affairs in the birding fraternity, the actual presence of the birder's body in the near or remote vicinity of the singing bird is an incidental irrelevance. The "yes men" would conclude by stating that the "counting" distance between bird and man can never, in the last analysis, be anything but a self-imposed, arbitrary dictate of an arbitrarily formulated set of rules. Those who would answer "no," and this group would constitute almost all birders, would maintain that the "yes men" were the real casuists in this debate. They would indignantly affirm that there are plain, self-evident, common-sense ways of looking at things, i.e., a birder must be *trying* to see his bird and the "count" distance is a finite function of the strength of his optical equipment or, in the case of hearing, his unaided aural acuity. They would add with considerable asperity that if "telephone birds" can be counted, then the next logical absurdity would be to play over all the recordings of bird songs that one could lay hands on and count any bird on the records not yet seen as a lifer. For my money these "no men" offer the only sane, operational reaction to the purposely synthetic and satirical implication posed by the cartoon. And, obviously, even the most "non" of all nonbirders realizes by this time that the absurd extremity postulated by the cartoon is merely a concrete hyperbole, not an issue that actually concerns the Brotherhood. In point of fact, there would be no "yes men" at all for "telephone birds." There are, though, well-defined and real problems facing the lister with regard to the means of identification he must employ with his birds, particularly lifers. From here on we are not dealing with "telephone birds" but shall trod the earthy paths of the actual birding world.

The dilemma of sight versus sound arises from the fact that Dame Nature—the biologists call it speciation—has decreed that two birds may look alike but actually have descended from different gene pools and, therefore, constitute separate species. In other words, certain species of birds cannot be distinguished or identified in the field by sight alone. Their markings, size, or proportions are not sufficiently different inter se for recognition. And even if one species tends to be more yellow or buffy than the other, this is not a safe means of identification because there exists overlapping of color intensity between the two species. Even the extremes are generally differences of degree only. The group of small tyrant Flycatchers belonging to the genus *Empidonax* are the outstanding and oft-cited example of this annoying situation in North America. There are other closely allied species groups throughout the rest of the world that present similar problems. In the Delaware Valley region, for instance, four species of *Empidonax* either nest or migrate through the area every year. Only one of these, the Yellow-bellied Flycatcher, can ordinarily be distinguished by sight alone, and even this can be a risky proposition. The other three—Traill's, Acadian, and Least—cannot safely be identified unless the song or certain characteristic notes are heard. Furthermore the nests and habitats of the three are different. To complicate matters further, one of these three, Traill's, sings a different song in the eastern part of its range than conspecific individuals in the midwest. There is even considerable gossip among birding gurus to the effect that eastern and western Traill's are distinct species. And so it goes. Sight identification alone of most species of North American *Empidonax* is not acceptable to the Brotherhood. Therefore the bird's song, call, or nest must be the deciding factor. This being the case, a number of the brethren question the expediency of actually seeing the bird as well. And they have a valid point.

There are numerous other examples throughout the world and several in North America that parallel the *Empidonax* predicament, but the problem of sight identification is less acute. The Long- and Short-billed Dowitchers look so much alike that not too many years ago they were considered to be conspecific. Now they are foisted off on the guileless lister as distinct species and, ergo, must by hook or crook be separated in the field. Their breeding ranges are fairly well separated, but much of their winter ranges and migratory routes are not. Here, too, sound is probably the safest identification character, since their respective calls are more or less diagnostic. Two other shore birds, Greater and Lesser Yellowlegs, though usually distinguishable by sight, often create identification problems, especially for beginners or birders unfamiliar with shore birds. But their call notes are different, usually, and offer confirmatory evidence for field identification. When a small flock of either species flies rapidly overhead or at a distance, it is the flatness or sharpness of their call notes and the number given that identify the birds. Sight in such instances is of little value.

In addition to similarity of appearance, there are yet other problems to be met in deciding how and when to list one's new bird. Certain birds are extremely difficult to see yet present no special problems once seen. Rails are notoriously secretive, habitually inhabiting marshy terrain that defies all but the stoutest heart and lungs. The Yellow Rail is a very small, wretched bit of brownish-yellow fluff that is almost impossible to see well, not only because of its well-nigh impenetrable habitat and reluctance to flush but also because its breeding areas are limited and localized. Sight identification often is a real problem in the case of the Yellow Rail, not because visual clues are lacking but because visual opportunity is about nil. In a small, circumscribed marsh near Waubun, Minnesota, Marybelle and I finally saw three Yellow Rails. But I seriously doubt if it was worth the effort. At fifty-nine years of age I could just as well have had a heart attack and then what would my sight record have profited me! The day before we had heard very close and often—it was a dark, rainy afternoon—a number of Yellow Rails. A graduate student from the University of Minnesota was camping on the spot and was making a study of the nesting and breeding habits of these rails. He verified our sound identification. We even stomped about in the wet, tussock-ridden marsh in the drizzle for over a half hour but never saw or flushed a Yellow Rail. Prompted by the information that three other birders had actually seen the bird later that same day, we tried again the next evening and were successful. It was an anticlimax. We were both so wet, exhausted, and ravaged by mosquitoes that the mere sight of those damned marsh chicks left me in a distempered rage. Our real thrill had come the preceding day when we heard them for the first time and knew it was the toc-toc, toc toc toc of the bird we had waited so long to "see." And I use the "toc" advisedly rather than the customarily employed designation "tic" because it sounded like toc to me and it was the Yellow Rail that spoke. Marybelle, perversely, insisted it was "tic." You see, I'm still in a foul mood.

The small Black Rail offers almost as great a problem as the Yellow Rail—it is about as hard to see and, unless the time is spring or early summer, can be confused with the hatchlings of some of the larger rails. The young of most rails are, naturally, small and some are also black. Furthermore, the call of the Black Rail is easily confused, chiefly by the uninitiated, with other voices of the night, especially the small marsh-dwelling frogs and orthopterous insects. I have heard the Black Rail only a few times and seen it just once. But that was some years ago and I would not be sure of the sound today, particularly since males and females are reputed to have different calls. Because of my herpetological apprenticeship, perhaps I am better qualified than the average birder to distinguish calls of the Hylidae from that of the Black Rail, but I do not trust myself. A marsh at night is full of weird noises. But a number of listers have undoubtedly included the Black Rail by virtue of sound alone. And I do not blame them. It is a tour de force to see some birds and usually unrewarding in the case of the Black Rail.

For those who virtuously insist upon sight records as an indispensable requisite for inclusion in the life list, there is also the puzzler as to how well the bird must be seen to be counted. In Maine and Pennsylvania I often heard the Barred Owl and occasionally saw it or its silhouette against the night sky or dark background of the forest. I had identified the bird by sound and, technically, I had seen it too. Should I have counted it? But suppose the shape I saw was not the Barred Owl but a nearby Great Horned Owl? It's most unlikely that two such large predators would share the same hunting territory, but it's not impossible for a brief time. Could I then have heard one owl and seen another? Since the owl I did see could not possibly be identified by sight (in the dark), am I justified in thinking it the species I heard? There is no absolute proof one way or the other. Sight in such cases resolves itself into a ritualistic farce. If I hear a Poor-will in early summer in the Chiricahua Mountains and see a dim shape flitting through the gloom, can I be certain the bird I "saw" was not a Whip-poor-will? And what value does the shape add to the identification? Williamson's Sapsucker has a very characteristic method of tapping or drumming. If I hear this woodpecker sound at the correct place and season but see it fly only at a distance, can I count the bird? And what about those African or South American birding safaris where the leader ticks off a different bird every other minute and the ignorant followers can scarcely write the names down before another species is seen. Is this sight identification? For the leader, yes; for the led, no.

Recently the Rules Committee of the ABA held a powwow over the vexing problem of sight versus sound in species identification. Opinions and views of the membership at large were also solicited. The Rules Committee itself came to no consentient conclusion and the general membership was about equally divided as to whether one's life list should include birds heard but not seen. The following is part of a letter I wrote to James Tucker, Chairman of the Rules Committee, and which was published, in part, along with the comments of others. "It may surely be taken for granted that any normally motivated birder would rather see his new bird than just hear it. Most of us who began birding 'on our own' without the field companionship of experts always identified our birds visually; the awareness of sound discrimination came later. I well remember the unprecedented numbers of 'Least Flycatchers' my wife and I saw that first spring birding during the height of the Ruby-crowned Kinglet migration in southeastern Pennsylvania, as many as five or six in one tree! What I wish to emphasize is that sight 'identification' is not ipso facto any more reliable than sound 'identification' in the hands of the uninitiated—and all of us come under this rubric when we see (or hear) a bird new to us. Why then place so much more reliance upon the occipital than upon the temporal lobes of our brains? In my opinion it resolves itself into a simple matter of conventional precedence and, perhaps, prejudice. If a person in the correct area, habitat, season, etc., hears the song of the Ruby-crowned Kinglet *and* learns from an *unimpeachable* source that this sort of effervescent sound is made by a Ruby-crowned Kinglet, he can put the bird on his life list for all of me. It is as legitimate as spotting this diminutive bit of fluff at the top of an eighty-foot hemlock in winter. One is as valid as the other for an identification *IF* the eye or ear has been correctly programmed for this bird. I'd almost rather hear a sunrise chorus of Chachalacas than see one but I should hate mightily to only hear a Green Jay. At all events, don't permit your Committee to come up with some sweeping ukase to the effect that every life bird must be *identified* visually. Stated thus, it just can't be done with every bird in the field by most birders; sound or other characteristics are sometimes essential. If we maintain the prejudice that all lifers, like the children of yore, should be seen and not heard, then let's leave out the word 'identification.' "

Birding and listing are intensely personal concerns and no fiat handed down from on high will settle the matter satisfactorily. This, too, was the essence of the decision arrived at by the Rules Committee of the ABA. Before concluding this little exegesis on the relative merits of sight versus sound in bird identification, I should wish to point out that we have been concerned, in the main, with life lists, not day by day routine identification. There are almost no birders who would insist that every Carolina Wren or Wrentit appearing on a Christmas Count should have been seen. Probably at least a fourth of the species Marybelle and I place on our daily lists are identified by sound alone. In spring or early summer, when every species is singing or calling, the unseen birds average considerably more than this. As a matter of fact, many experts in their own bailiwick seldom use their glasses at all. There is no need. What most birders object to is not the primacy or practicality of sound identification in certain cases but the aesthetic loss when a bird is only heard and not seen. In spring migration, I try to see all my warblers—and so does everybody else with any gumption. Finally, it should be mentioned that sound is almost invariably the key to sight. Walk through an eastern woods in June sometime when all the birds are calling and then again late in summer or early fall, by which time a number of nesting species have ceased to sing. Compare the number of individuals seen on the two occasions. Unless you make a heroic effort, the number of individuals recorded on your August or September list will be less than the June list. But they are still there. The song calls attention to the bird, and without sound many individuals go unnoticed. This past summer at Gradyville, for instance, at least eight singing male Acadian Flycatchers established territories, indicating sixteen adult birds. By the end of August, most of them had stopped calling and although we occasionally and accidentally saw Acadian Flycatchers at the different locations, we did not record more than three or four birds in any one day. To quote the much overquoted Preacher yet again: ". . . the eye is not satisfied with seeing, nor the ear filled with hearing." We need them both, especially we of the Brotherhood.

In the preçeding section I have attempted to delineate some of the problems that torment the conscientious lister when a new bird is seen and/or heard; namely, what set of conditions constitutes adequate identification of species in the field. Hairsplitting, dubiety, and indecision, yes, but so far we have dealt only with the relatively simple matter of how designated species are distinguished from one another by the ordinary birder. Certainly the fateful decision rests with him alone: he has either seen/heard a Gilded Flicker or he has not. There is no middle ground, no third choice. Logicians call this kind of unencumbered proposition the Law of the Excluded Middle, *tertium non datur*—A is either B or it is not B. But now, at long last, we come face to face with a much more fundamental problem: the granddaddy of them all; namely, what *is* a species? In the realm of systematics—the classification and ordering of plant and animal kingdoms—*tertium non datur* denotes three bad words. There is always middle ground in systematics. Taxonomists dote upon the "Law of the Included Middle"—in other words, that vast intermingling gene stuff that may encompass the entire continent, engulfing everything within its path. Three Flickers may become as one; one Sapsucker may become as three. It all resides in the mind stuff of the taxonomist. Today, for instance, the Gilded Flicker is officially recognized as a separate species, *Colaptes chrysoides*, and any eastern birder making his first trip to the southwest may list it. Tomorrow, on the other hand, he will, in all probability, not be able to list it, for the Gilded Flicker will have ceased to be a separate species. It will then be merely a subspecies, *Colaptes auratus chrysoides*, and our befuddled eastern birder has already seen *Colaptes auratus*, the Yellow-shafted Flicker, in his own back yard. Perhaps, after all, such dictates are consonant with the Law of the Excluded Middle. The whole mess is frightfully mixed up and unclear. But, for that matter, so are the tenets of taxonomy. Why should I be accused of inconsistency in an imbroglio not of my making? Let's all make a valiant effort and see if I can be more lucid.

During my brief and frenetic apprenticeship in systematics during the days of the Great Depression, I read several books and many learned treatises and articles on the "species problem." I explored with the unflagging assiduity of the budding scholar the intricate maze of subtlety and half sophistry that constituted the literature of the late twenties and early thirties on the distinction between species and subspecies. Each writer's argument was plausible, if somewhat confused, but there was no real unanimity of opinion. What, after all, was this elusive thing called a species? I asked my professor, Dr. E. R. Dunn, who was recognized as one of the more up to date and brilliant of the younger taxonomists. He gave me one of those characteristic grins, half humorous, half sardonic, and said, "A species is what a competent taxonomist chooses to call it." This Pantagruelian definition is the only one that will stand the test of time. And yet, like so many other profound remarks, it turns out to be a Barmecidal feast in the end. Also, those same mischievous logicians have a name, too, for this sort of thing. It is called *petitio principii*, the assumption of that which in the beginning was set forth to be proved—in everyday parlance, begging the question. But in God's name let us have done once and for all with these devious logicians in order that reason and clarity may finally prevail. Bear with me for one more fit or two and perhaps that dim light at the cave's entrance may brighten apace.

Let us start at the beginning and proceed rapidly, for most of this is rather dull. The entire Animal Kingdom is subdivided into categories of decreasing rank, starting with the phylum and ending with the subspecies. Thus every individual, or group, has a pedigree both in time (Evolution) and contemporary lineage (Phylogeny). Omitting most intermediate categories, our Gilded Flicker is first an animal (Animalia); second, a chordate (Chordata); third, a bird (Aves); fourth, a Woodpecker-Jacamar-Toucan-Barbet type (Piciformes); fifth, a Wood-pecker-Wryneck type (Picidae); sixth, a Woodpecker (Picinae); seventh, a Flicker (genus, Colaptes); eighth, a Gilded Flicker (species, chrysoides); and finally ninth, if you see it near Tucson, Ridgeway's Gilded Flicker (subspecies, mearnsi). Barring the improbable discovery of some ancient typographical error or nomenclatural squabble, the Gilded Flicker will always be an Aves, a Picinae, and a Colaptes but, in the near future, it may well cease to be a Gilded Flicker in the sense of a distinct species—*Colaptes chrysoides*. It will then be only a subspecies of the nominate (earliest described type) form *Colaptes auratus*, the Yellow-shafted Flicker. It will then bear a trinominal name, the hallmark of a subspecies, *Colaptes auratus chrysoides*. This newly created subspecies will undoubtedly still be referred to as the Gilded Flicker in the common vernacular of the Brotherhood but no longer as a full or distinct species. It may no longer be counted by the lister if he has seen either the Yellow-shafted or western Red-shafted Flicker first. The latter will also suffer the same fate as the other two and be simply a subspecies, *Colaptes auratus cafer*. If this change in classification within the genus *Colaptes* is sanctioned by the Nomenclature Committee in the next edition of the AOU Check-list, there will be only one flicker in North America insofar as the amateur lister is concerned. He may, if he chooses, denote each of the subspecies he has seen but it will not enhance his numerical status on the lister's totem pole by one decimal. What transformation has taken place since 1957 in the scheme of things that has deprived the helpless lister of these two goodly birds? Have flickers changed during the past two decades or so? Or has the mind stuff of the taxonomist altered? It requires no great sagacity to surmise the correct (nearly) answer. That gallimaufry we call men's minds changes every minute. It takes somewhat longer to change a bird.

Ernst Mayer in his treatise *Principles of Systematic Zoology* defines a species thus: "Species are groups of interbreeding natural populations that are reproductively isolated from other such groups." Most modern taxonomists agree with the essential tenets of this definition. They regard a species as a fluid or transient (in time) population of individuals all descended from the same gene pool but, of course, no two individuals having identical genes. The old Linnaean concept of fixed, immutable species has long been abandoned by systematists and the only substantial difference in point of view between the taxonomists of yesterday and those of today resides in the increase in technical methodology employed by the latter (population genetics, mathematics, etc.) and, in addition, the augmentation of relevant data over the years. Professor Dunn, if he were alive today, would revel in the numerous subspecies of salamander, frog, lizard, and snake that were either not known or not recognized when I was a student of his in the early thirties. A salamander with a zigzag dorsal stripe was considered a full species in those days and distinct from another having a straight stripe. Today, it is known that extensive hybridization occurs between those two forms and they are now reduced to subspecific rank. Because birds have been studied longer and more intensively than salamanders and because most birds possess the physical means of wider dispersion, flight, their allocation as species or subspecies is continually changing.

Closely related species are said to be either allopatric or sympatric. Allopatric species occupy mutually exclusive but usually adjacent geographical areas and, consequently, are separated in space from each other so that it is ordinarily impossible for them to get together and interbreed extensively. Sympatric species, on the other hand, occupy the same or greatly overlapping geographical areas. Two species existing in sympatry, therefore, are reproductively isolated from each other not by distance but by other factors such as habitat, inability of sex recognition, gene incompatibility, mutual hostility, etc. If allopatric species can be shown to hybridize freely where their respective ranges are contiguous, they are, in current taxonomical usage, considered conspecific. If, on the other hand, their ranges overlap to some extent and both hybrids and pure parental types occur, they are considered distinct species. Don't ask me why, mine but to do and sigh. Contrariwise, in the case of subspecies being elevated to full species rank, it must be demonstrated that if they occur sympatrically, no interbreeding takes place. In other words, distinct species must be reproductively isolated from each other by geographical barriers or other factors. In short, if two or more taxonomically distinct groups interbreed freely in nature, they are classified as subspecies. If they do not interbreed freely in nature, whatever the isolating factors, they are considered separate species. Shape, size, color, voice, etc., etc. are not in themselves necessarily criteria of species or subspecies allocation. I hope the good Angel of Mercy has had her eye on me the while and that I have not made a complete fool of myself in this brief unveiling of the taxonomist's steely but flexible soul. If by either commission or omission I have misinterpreted or distorted the Mosaic Law of the systematists, I stand thrice damned and lost to even the lesser of the Brotherhood forever. It is the chance one must take when one dabbles in the occult.

What does all this mean to the lister? It is only too plain: he is on the outside looking in. No derisive flattening of his nose against the window glass will alter one spark or flame of that resolute fire burning ever bright in the abode of the Blessed. He must wait patiently for the moldy crusts of bread which are periodically thrust out to him through the chinks of the door by the saboteurs within. Species are not conceived in heaven for his delight. They are conceived in the mind stuff of the systematists. They call the tune, and we listers either mournfully dance to the raucous discords of the lumper (species reduced to subspecies) or flit on winged feet of delight to the silver-toned lute of the splitter (subspecies raised to species). Perhaps all our sorrows stem from that bite into the forbidden fruit of knowledge of good and evil. If there were no distinction between good and bad taxonomy, we listers might still be so happy in our Elysian Fields of typology—no variants exist and each individual is an exact replica of an immutable type. And yet—and yet, maybe things are not hopeless. If we practice forbearance, perhaps after all the lister may inherit that good part. Although listers are sympatrically associated with the avian systematists, we could, by sheer force of will, desist from interbreeding with them and gain full species rank. Their own scrawny puddle of ill-assorted genes would soon lead them precipitously down the path of extinction. We should then erect a statue of Linnaeus as our tribal deity and men like Edward Drinker Cope would be our prophets—Cope was a Latter-day Saint of taxonomy who, so I am told, routinely discarded all specimens that did not fit into his preconceived, typological conception of a species. It would be unscientific but everlastingly glorious! What more halcyon fate could befall the true lister? But to return to sanity, Emmet Reid Dunn's aphorism is still sound: a species *is* what a good taxonomist calls it, but we listers refuse to admit that taxonomists arrive on earth trailing clouds of glory. They are, when all is said and done, merely a specialized offshoot of

Platonic-Kantian idealism. They believe that the idea of the thing precedes the thing itself. To paraphrase the blind bard, nothing is either species or subspecies, but thinking makes it so.

And what of the future? The future of birding I mean. Lamentations reach the ear from all quarters and there is gnashing of teeth and much wailing at the wall. Listen, then, to the threnody of the Brotherhood.

Recently, someone estimated that there are ten million birders in North America. I do not recall the source of this information and I am sure the figure is greatly exaggerated. The exact number is unimportant, however, and would depend entirely upon one's definition of a birder. What does matter is that there are too many of us. If I were to have the ineffable good fortune to see Bachman's Warbler or an Ivory-billed Woodpecker tomorrow, I should be constrained from giving the necessary details to any of my personal birding friends or the Brotherhood at large. Literally thousands would converge on the spot and by their numbers alone endanger the existence or perpetuity of these nearly extinct species. If I go to Brigantine Wildlife Refuge for a quiet morning of shore bird identification, I find hordes of other birders lined up in rows along the dikes and the sandpipers and plovers far out in the impoundments as a consequence. Also, I must drive only in one direction along the dikes because the traffic may become snarled otherwise; I cannot retrace my route to have a better look at some bird that has flown off in the opposite direction. Furthermore, the thrill of discovery will be almost nil. Because of sheer numbers there will always be someone who has spotted the rarity before I come up to it. Finally, if I check the record book in the visitor's booth, I find that three Mute Swans or a flock of Glossy Ibis share honors with a Black-tailed Godwit or Curlew Sandpiper as "unusual" birds. It is as though you were at the Academy of Music listening to Brahms's Second Symphony while on either side of you people cracked peanuts and munched noisily. The ranks of the faithful are becoming diluted at an alarming rate. Snobbery? Perhaps. But as Thackeray once saw fit to remark, the conditions of society make it impossible not to be a snob at times. Birding will soon become, or has already, a mass-directed movement and its charisma will vanish with the advent of the multitude that chants the *Te Deum*. The day may be not far off when birders will be required to pay a license fee, as hunters and fishermen have done for so long. When I see Johnny Miller, an ace birder of the DVOC, with a plaque pinned to the back of his sheepskin coat, "Birding Permit No. 430,891," I shall say a paternoster for the Brotherhood and hang up my binoculars.

Although the adulteration of the birding world by the infiltration of the television and Sunday afternoon crowds is one aspect of doomsday, it is not the only one. There is the converse, the swelling of the ranks by the frenzied, rapacious young—the *enfants terribles* of the Brotherhood. This in itself and on the surface would appear to be a gladsome thing, a wholesome reaction to the mechanized world of the ordinary teenager. But I am an incurable pessimist. Compared to me, Cassandra bubbled over with tidings of great joy. I see these lupine youngsters of today thirty, forty, fifty years from now as aggressive and arrogant satraps of the birding world. Our world has always been competitive but not with the mass, insane frenzy that pervades every minute of our lives today. These kids are different from our Tinicum kids, although separated in time by not many years. Like everything else they experience in life, birding becomes an intensely competitive pursuit. If you are convinced that your scrivener is a birding snob, wait until these joyless bird dogs attain grumpy old age! Oh, of course, they derive extravagant pleasure from each new conquest, but one is reminded more of a speculator making a killing on Wall Street than a birder excitedly counting his beads. Some way, these kids strike one as being more candidates for the Explorer's Club than the 600 Club. There is nothing inherently amiss with these sharp and conscientious young birders. Nothing really that one can give name to. But their attitude and the future of the Brotherhood which they will inherit trouble me. Is my concern simply an old man's jealousy? Is it the generation gap—not the hodiernal gap vaunted by youth of today but the eternal hiatus between knowledge and wisdom? Or, after all, is birding losing its enchantment and appeal through the technological mores of the space age, as personified by the get-there-fast attitude of the capable but complacent young? It is entirely possible that I have created only a mare's nest for my own lugubrious satisfaction. Time will tell. Or will it?

Before I leave the wailing wall, permit me yet one more gloomy foreboding. We shall call it, paying homage to the great Francis Bacon, the Idols of the Squid. The squid, as you all know, makes great progress backward while emitting large quantities of ink. This is exactly what we are doing today in facing our environmental debacle. As long as there are bumper stickers in Alaska saying, "Oil feeds my family," as long as citizens of Nome offer to send all the wolves of Alaska to New York City in exchange for some of the latter's dubious glamour and "culture," as long as leaf burning is forbidden but industrial pollution still fouls the air, as long as we hold world environmental conferences but are powerless to act, there will be less and less hope for wildlife, including that denizen of the city jungles —man the killer. One cannot bird without birds. It is just that fateful and simple. And if anyone ask for my proofs, my figures, my driver's license, he is an even bigger fool than I had despaired of. The portent is all around us—and it is a portent only in our infantile, wishful thinking. Crises do not always come like sudden, sharp pistol cracks. More often than not they are just a long series of slow, sordid occurrences, each accepted already as a fait accompli.

VIII

Interlude, 1968–1969

A discerning and sympathetic reader of this nomadic yarn will have sensed from time to time a vague but distinguishable endeavor on the part of the writer to narrate events in their proper chronological order. Others, no doubt the majority, will dub such an arrogation a brazen piece of impudence. Probably the latter are more nearly correct. After all, this book begins in Alaska ten years after Marybelle and I had started birding. It has shuffled past, present, and future at Gradyville in a scandalous disregard of the Gregorian calendar, or any other. And of late, we have jumped back and forth from one ocean to the other with a calculated omission of dates. Let us then return in all sobriety to the security of Father Time's great horologe. In this short chapter I shall relate the events of 1968 and 1969 so that we may once again pick up the birding trail from the time we departed Umnak Island in 1967 to the time we returned to Alaska in 1970. There are only ten lifers between these dates, so I shall not be overlong.

You will recall that Marybelle and I left the Pribilofs with 603 and 604 lifers, respectively. We added no new birds that year after we reached home; nor did we see any during the first four months of 1968. Early in May, however, we once more set out for southern New Mexico and Arizona. The outbound route took us through western Oklahoma in search of the Lesser Prairie Chicken; the homeward trail wound through eastern Wyoming, the Black Hills of South Dakota, and northern Minnesota. The total trip was 7,794 miles. Most of the time we were not traveling was spent at four of our favorite southwest birding haunts: Silver City, New Mexico; Chiricahua and Huachuca Mountains; and the Patagonia area north of Nogales in Arizona. The lifers on this trip numbered just five named in the order in which we saw them: Lesser Prairie Chicken, Violet-crowned Hummingbird, Varied Bunting, Pinyon Jay, Yellow Rail. We also probably heard the Flammulated Owl, a would-be lifer, in Cherry Creek Canyon near Silver City, but he did not sound off enough for certain identification, and so the Flammulated is still one of our desiderata. I have recounted elsewhere our long delayed encounters with the Pinyon Jay and Yellow Rail and see no reason for reviving old enmities and maledictions at this time.

We saw the Lesser Prairie Chicken near Arnett, Oklahoma— at least a dozen of them. The game ranger of that area, Haskell Moseley, had set up a small blind for observing this rapidly diminishing species and told us to look for it on a small rise two hundred feet or so off a small, dead-end dirt road. We scanned every rise off that particular road and several others for two days without seeing either blind or chickens. On the third day, convinced that some evil spirit of the prairies had thrown a cloak of invisibility over this particular spot, we set out to tramp the area willy-nilly and flush those chickens. We had walked scarcely a hundred feet before we spotted the blind. It had been blown down by the strong winds of the preceding days and now lay flat on the ground, truly invisible from the road. We resurrected its upright position the best we could, crawled in, and waited. We crouched and stooped and stooped and crouched till our aching joints could tolerate no more abuse, but we saw only a few White-necked Ravens and a number of Lark Buntings. The fourth morning we were out before dawn and once more entered that canvas torture chamber. Our perseverance or stupidity, call it what you will, paid off within the hour. It was another of those rare occasions when we have seen a lifer at dawn. It was too late in the season for mating display but the birds were still attracted to the spot and it was like watching barnyard fowl from the kitchen window, but not so comfortably. When we finally staggered to our feet outside the blind, we knew we had a toast for that night.

The Violet-crowned Hummingbird was seen in Ramsey Canyon in the Huachuca Mountains, the place our birding friend from Nogales, Bill Harrison, has dubbed the Hummingbird Center of North America. The Varied Bunting was seen near the famous roadside rest on route 82 south of Patagonia. Neither of these birds was a lifer, for we had seen both near Mazatlán, Mexico, three years before but, nevertheless, we welcomed them ecstatically since it was the first time we had seen either species north of the border. They counted two more birds for our North American lists and, needless to say, two more toasts. I have always maintained that the amenities must be preserved. Not to drink a toast to a North American lifer, just because it was not a world lifer, would be a serious breach of good form.

After our return home, we took a pelagic trip about thirty miles off the Jersey coast on July 30 and saw our last lifer of 1968, Cory's Shearwater. Marybelle's North American list now stood at 609 birds and mine, thanks to my "good ole" Wheatear, was one more. It was just twenty-six days short of twelve months before we saw our next lifer, July 4, 1969.

Early in 1969 we signed up for a summer birding trip to

Chiapas, Yucatán, and northern Guatemala with Crowder Nature Tours. We bought several field guides and bird finding directories covering these areas and carefully checked all the new birds we might possibly see. I made a valiant attempt to memorize key field marks and call notes. It was truly a case of love's labor lost. Some five or six weeks before the departure date, this trip collapsed for want of sufficient numbers. Apparently, few people were willing to brave the tropical heat of southern Mexico and northern Central America. Upon receiving this dreary bit of news, we promptly decided to go to Churchill, Manitoba. I shall not insult my readers, obviously all of superlative intellect, by attempting to explain this volte face of approximately forty-four degrees latitude northward. To a severely logical mind there can be no other alternative to Tapachula or Tikal but the west shore of Hudson Bay. It is simply one of those self-evident propositions that requires no intermediate, Euclidean succession of steps for its comprehension. If one cannot see the Blue-crowned Motmot, then, naturally, one immediately thinks of Smith's Longspur. Genius is like that—bold, swift strokes of the brush and another masterpiece leaps from the canvas.

We drove to The Pas, Manitoba, by way of the most northern route through Ontario. Whenever the mosquitoes and black flies were only a few thousand per cubic foot, we invaded the woods on either side of the road looking for Hawk Owls. Through a series of unfortunate blunders this bird had been denied us in the States, so we hoped for it now in the spruce forests and muskeg bogs of Canada. We also made token searches for the Boreal Owl, a bird we had been unable to find on our 1966 trip to Canada. We had no real expectation of sighting a Boreal Owl all by ourselves but we kept up a barrage of cheery remarks to mask our increasing awareness of the futility of our searches. Hawk Owls, on the other hand, do not have the Boreal Owl's reputation for secretiveness and our confidence in finding one never flagged. We had a firm understanding between us that the nondriver would rigorously inspect the top of every spruce on his side of the road while the driver took care of his side. Fortunately, the traffic along route 11 through most of Ontario was light. We became skilled adepts—I hope the redundancy does not trouble you—in distinguishing between the upright tufts of needles crowning so many spruce trees and a feathered tuft occupying the same position. However, by the time we finally reached The Pas, every feathered tuft we had seen was either hawk, Gray Jay, or some other non-Strigidae. Nevertheless, our faith and ardor remained undaunted through this long succession of disappointments. We surely could not fail to see at least two or three in the almost twelve hundred miles of round-trip travel between The Pas and Churchill. I even hummed a little nonsense tune about the elusive Hawk Owl as I unpacked the car in front of our motel, The Tamarack, at The Pas.

A number of years ago—I had the date written down but that particular slip of paper has disappeared—rail communication was completed between Winnipeg and Churchill. The Pas is about halfway between. The train ride both to and from Churchill was a continuous delight to us. It passes through countless miles of muskeg and birch and evergreen forests. The train stops at practically every Indian village and it takes the better part of a full day and night to go one way. There is plenty of opportunity to watch for Hawk Owls as one rolls sedately along through this magnificent wilderness. As fate would have it, our double window soon gathered enough moisture between the panes so that visibility was reduced to a single small area near the bottom. Fortunately, I thought of the club car. Here, facing the wide, single window directly opposite, one could sip a whiskey and soda for hours while keeping a weather eye out for the tops of the spruce and birch trees. On the return trip our window was clear and probably our heads were much clearer also. But mellow or stone sober, it was just the same. Not one Hawk Owl did either of us see on that long, leisurely ride, either going or returning. I kept up my faith to a degree on the outbound run but on the return trip my vigilance became more and more perfunctory and at last I succumbed to the dread realization that we weren't going to see the Hawk Owl on this trip! I decided that we should have ridden the club car back to The Pas as we had on the outbound run. After all, whiskey and soda is an anodyne of great antiquity in times of acute stress.

Our stay at Churchill was ridiculously brief, the equivalent of two days. Furthermore, the only car I could rent was an ancient wreck; it had glass-smooth tires and the gears frequently froze in either first or reverse. I was afraid to take it as far as Twin Lakes, so all our birding was on the tundra near Churchill and around the shores of the bay. I shall, therefore, stick to a short account of our two lifers, Smith's Longspur and Thayer's Gull. There is yet another reason for not dwelling at length on this fabulous birding area, a personal one. Churchill should be visited *before* one goes to Alaska. To us it was an anticlimax after the 150 miles of tundra stretching south from Barrow and the wilderness surrounding Nome, Kotzebue, and the Aleutians.

The train pulled into Churchill about noon, and after we had engaged a room at the Hudson Hotel I set out to find Mrs. H. L. Smith. This woman is a well-informed and ardent amateur naturalist and an authority on where to find birds in the area. Of course, Smith's Longspur, not named after the lady in question, was our immediate objective and I plied Mrs. Smith with questions concerning its whereabouts. This small sparrow-like bird breeds from eastern Alaska to northern Manitoba and Ontario, and Churchill is about as far south and east as one can usually find this bird in summer. It winters in the more southern plains area but in the few times we have been within its winter range we have missed it. The male in breeding plumage is a handsome little character and, as we discovered, has a pleasing song. Mrs. Smith told us several places to look and we set out in high spirits. The closest we came to Smith's that afternoon was the Lapland Longspur. The male of this latter species is also a strikingly marked bird, but we had first seen the Lapland in winter at the Philadelphia airport, also in central Texas and later, in summer, by the hundreds in Alaska. By nine o'clock that first evening our high spirits had dipped to a new low. Being a lister and not an ornithologist, I can never concentrate on other birds when a lifer is sought. Much of our birding that afternoon was spoiled for me.

The next morning, July 4, was a bracing beautiful day and we set out early. At the first place I stopped our venerable wreck there were a number of big boulders between the road and the narrow strip of tundra that borders Churchill to the east. Right on top of the biggest of these glacial pebbles was a male Smith's Longspur singing. Before we had time to congratulate ourselves, a second male hopped up on the same rock and we had two of them in our glasses at once. The day, the whole trip, the entire world was all at once a resplendent success! I could now relax and give my attention to the numerous Hudsonian Godwits and other birds that we ordinarily see on the Atlantic coast only in migration. Before the morning was over we had seen three more male and three female (or immature) Smith's Longspurs. A Pigeon Hawk had its nest nearby and we could only hope it did not deplete too greatly the supply of Longspurs in that area. One time when I approached the nest too closely, the bird swooped down with a sharp cry and nearly knocked my cap off. I should think a singing Smith's Longspur on top of a boulder would be a shining mark for a hawk, especially a Pigeon Hawk. I recalled that ominous first sentence under "Food of the Pigeon Hawk" in Arthur Bent's *Birds of Prey:* "The Pigeon Hawk is mainly a bird eater." Bent goes on to list thirty-two or more species of bird known to have been captured by Pigeon Hawks. No Longspur is listed but I'll wager this particular Pigeon Hawk could have authoritatively corrected this omission. Then it came to me how Dale Coman would have chided me about this mawkish bit of sentimentality and I decided that Pigeon Hawks have to eat too. As we left this part of the tundra, we could still hear that eerie winnowing sound that Wilson's Snipe creates as it flies high above the ground. It brought back memories of Sprague's Pipit and the faraway plains of North Dakota to the southwest of Hudson Bay.

That afternoon found us at Cape Merry Point, a long tongue of naked rock separating the broiling estuary of Churchill River from Hudson Bay. Mrs. Smith had mentioned that there were still reports of Thayer's Gull in the Churchill area and Cape Merry Point was a good place to observe gulls. This gull breeds in the most northern part of the Canadian arctic and July 4 is a very late date for stragglers so far south of the breeding range. But right now the river and the bay held our attention. The ice in the bay, so we were told, had only broken up about two weeks before. Now there were gigantic pieces careening swiftly down the river and so on into the bay. Offshore about a mile or so these miniature icebergs were jammed together in a jagged green-white ice field and now and then a muffled boom would come to our ears as some huge piece ground into the pack. We marveled at the small Indian boys guiding their boats in and out between these floating monsters. Now and then one of the big pieces would shift its center of gravity and turn upside down with a menacing swirl of green water. At this particular time it was not an ideal river for a leisurely canoe trip. We saw no whales in the bay that afternoon but there was a multitude of seals. Parasitic and Long-tailed Jaegers sailed overhead, mostly the former. Both Arctic and Red-throated Loons crossed the rocky cape from time to time. Gulls were circling about and many more were sitting on the rocky points here and there. I concentrated on the latter and began to look for "Herring" Gulls with brownish or dark irises and less black in the wing tips.

To condense a long afternoon into a few words, I'll simply state that I am reasonably certain we saw at least one typical adult Thayer's Gull; actually, there were probably two at the Point that day. Thayer's Gull in the current AOU Check-list is classified as a subspecies of the common Herring Gull. Of late, however, several authorities have considered it a distinct species. From various sources, I gather that the next Check-list will concur with this view and if so, Thayer's will then officially be a bird one can add to one's life list of full species. And now I must make a confession. Confessions, so we have been told since childhood, are good for the soul. My own soul on that particular Fourth of July seemed in sore need of a restorative, some healing balm or other. So, I added Thayer's Gull to my list of North American birds. I could never adequately convey in mere words the lightness of heart and soul I felt after I had performed this simple ceremony of lustration. If the next AOU Check-list does, after all, retain its present classification with regard to Thayer's Gull, then, of course, I shall delete it from my list. This also will be good for my soul. So, you see, my soul will indubitably profit come what may. I flatter myself that the whole affair has been managed rather well.

One final brief scene and we are back home in Wallingford, Pa. After Churchill we spent a few days at Lake Atikameg, a few miles north of The Pas. The second day at Atikameg we drove up the dirt road to its end at Clear Water, the name of the Provincial Park and the first railroad stop northeast of The Pas. We had been walking along the railroad tracks a short distance when we heard an unfamiliar vireo song coming from the edge of the woods bordering the right of way. It might just possibly be a Philadelphia Vireo—we had never heard its song—so we climbed halfway down the railroad embankment to a big flat rock. Seated on this convenient rest we waited for a recurrence of the unknown vireo song. We did not hear that particular vireo again but very soon we heard something else. It was the unmistakable low rumble of a fast approaching train. It thundered by and, looking up, we watched the swaying coaches as they passed. It was the same train, coach for coach, we had ridden back from Churchill two days before. The end coach was ours. We followed this coach with our eyes till it disappeared from view around a distant curve and, all at once, a great wave of nostalgic longing overwhelmed us. It was our train on its long run back to Churchill and we wanted desperately to be aboard. I have seldom experienced such a forlorn sense of being left behind. Someday, if the nickel deposits at Thompson don't rapidly devastate the northern Manitoba wilderness, I want to grab a Canadian National rattler and journey to Churchill once more. The little bird with the Harlequin face and-the rather commonplace name is going to be lonesome without us.

Just before the old year, 1969, handed over the appurtenances of his trade to his youthful successor, we drove to Cape Ann and nearby Newburyport, Massachusetts. We were looking for two more lifers, Dovekie and Black-headed Gull, to help us celebrate the demise of the old and the birth of the new. There was a combination sleet and snow storm all along the New England coast shortly after we arrived on Cape Ann and cold winds the entire time. I don't believe I was ever so cold and miserable in my life as on that second day we combed the tossing sea for Dovekies from the vantage of Andrew's Point. We spent almost seven hours with telescope that day in a numbing wind and saw only one Guillemot, a few Common Eiders, a small raft of Surf Scoters, and an occasional Old Squaw duck. The third day at Newburyport amidst a glare of ice we slipped and slid to our first North American Black-headed Gull. The next and last day we finally spotted a lone Dovekie off Andrew's Point and were able to watch it for at least twenty minutes. Marybelle's list was now 613 and mine 614 birds. We arrived home just in time to greet the New Year in front of a cozy fire, thaw our bones and count our blessings—and lifers too, of course.

And now let us get on to the land of the midnight sun, our second trip to Alaska. You will recall that in 1967 we traveled with the Crowder Nature Tour through Alaska. On the second trip of 1970, we were on our own. My intention is to dwell almost exclusively upon four or five highlights of the 1970 trip with throwbacks to the 1967 trip when such reversions might be of interest. It may, therefore, be advisable to list in order the places where we birded in Alaska on both trips so that the reader can judge for himself how much of Alaska we saw all told and what new places were visited on the 1970 trip. For the Crowder Tour of 1967 I shall name only those places that were visited after Marybelle and I joined the tour; we did not join the party until it reached Anchorage. The following places were birded in

1967, July 22 to August 14: Anchorage and vicinity, including the Matanuska Valley; McKinley Park; Fairbanks and vicinity; Barrow; Kotzebue; Nome; Katmai National Monument and Cold Bay, both on the Alaska peninsula; St. Paul Island in the Pribilofs; Umnak Island in the Aleutian chain. The following is the list of places we birded in 1970, from June 3 to July 4: Anchorage and vicinity; Kodiak, by round-trip ferry from Anchorage; Fairbanks and vicinity; Eagle Summit; Bethel; Hooper Bay; Nome and vicinity, up to seventy miles' distance; St. Lawrence Island, chiefly Gambell; Barrow.

So let us board a plane going to Seattle, the airline gateway to Alaska from the lower forty-eight, and we shall hope to be in Anchorage about five P.M. the same day. It is a fantastically beautiful flight from Seattle to Anchorage in the late afternoon. But let's be sure to sit on the right-hand side of the plane and pray for a clear day.

IX

Alaska

Our Alaska Airlines plane coasted down to the Anchorage airport late in the afternoon of June 3, 1970. We were in bed by seven P.M. Anchorage time, midnight east coast time. It had been a beautiful trip from Seattle and just as fine a day as on that memorable occasion when we had first flown up from Seattle to meet the Crowder bunch at Anchorage three years earlier. But on this particular occasion, as on many others during our second sojourn in Alaska, we missed the friendly cooperation of the tour gang and its orderly bustle at the airport. There was no Roy Clark to take charge of the baggage, no Isabella Coons to take care of tickets and reservations, no Gene Bleiweiss with apropos caustic remarks, no Al Webb with his ready wit and savoir faire. We were truly on our own and it was just a bit lonesome there in Anchorage, as it was to be in Barrow at the finish of our trip. One thing helped, at any rate—it was the familiar ensemble of the old Anchorage airport that met us that first day. Before we quit Alaska in 1970, we would have either landed or taken off nine different times at Anchorage. And the ninth would be from the new airport building. This was only one of the many changes we noticed in Alaska in three brief years.

I am anxious for you to meet Dan Gibson and the Hawk Owl at Fairbanks so this paragraph is by way of chronology, not adventure. We birded close to Anchorage for most of June 4 and 5. We recorded no lifers but saw over forty birds, many of them such goodies as the Varied Thrush, Townsend's Warbler, and Common Redpoll. On the evening of the fifth we climbed aboard the Alaska ferry *M. V. Tustumena*, bound for Kodiak and back. This vessel was a superb boat for birding and the next two or three days were the most relaxed and tranquil of the entire trip—but for this very reason it makes dull telling; absolutely nothing went wrong. Haven't you always noticed that the best parts of your favorite novel are always when either the hero or heroine is in dire straits, not when fortune smiles on them? So it was with our own trip to Kodiak. We recorded four lifers on this ferry trip through Cook Inlet and the northern part of the Gulf of Alaska—a great many Slender-billed Shearwaters; many Fork-tailed Petrels; three Kittlitz's Murrelets; two Aleutian Terns. We returned to Anchorage Sunday evening untired but very happy. The next morning we flew to Fairbanks. It is monstrous, I realize, to so casually dismiss a scenic trip that made us catch our breath many times, but this is essentially a birding Odyssey and there is no time to pull off the road at every scenic lookout. Besides, Hawk Owls seldom wait on man's convenience and, as I shall soon demonstrate, Boreal Owls never do.

In Fairbanks I lost no time in phoning Dan Gibson. Daniel D. Gibson is one of a relatively small group that really knows its Alaskan birds. Dan edits the Alaska section for *AFN*, has prepared a check-list of Alaskan birds and, as I recently learned, is cooperating with Dr. Brina Kessell of the University of Alaska in updating Gabrielson and Lincoln's voluminous records of Alaskan birds. We first met Dan when he was a ranger at Katmai National Monument in 1967 and he gave our group a more than just interesting talk on the birds of that region. He was due back that day from Washington, D.C., and from our previous correspondence before he left Fairbanks I knew he had two Boreal Owl nests located. He answered the phone himself, glory be, and a half hour later he walked into our hotel room all set to show us the Boreal Owl—if the owls were still at their nest. I'm sure my crash tactics that day did not endear me to Mrs. Gibson for depriving her of her recently returned husband so soon, but all birder's wives must suffer their share of martyr-dom, just as the more publicized golf widows.

The only Boreal Owl's nest that might still possibly be in use was not far beyond College, the site of the University of Alaska, and it did not take us long to reach the area. It was about a hundred feet off a dusty, grass-grown road in a dense thicket of willow, maple, and birch, not evergreens as I had expected from my reading about the habitat of this species. All the way out from Fairbanks Dan had prepared our hungering souls for possible failure. After all, it was late in the season for nesting Boreals. But with a superlative mixture of bonhomie and sober-ing comments he kept our high spirits from waning. Pan or his band of satyrs never lusted after sighing Syrinx as I did after that Boreal Owl! Soul lust is so much more difficult to control than the carnal kind. The nest itself was a sizable hole in a live birch about twenty feet from the ground. We approached it with great caution, on the lookout for any movement at the opening or in the neighboring trees. There was no movement of any sort, if you exclude the thumping of my heart, and after beating on the tree a few times and circling the area we decided to return the following morning. Dan would bring along his climbing irons and then we would know for certain whether the nest held owl or naught.

In the morning Dan strapped on the irons and Marybelle and I waited below with pathetic quietness for destiny to run its course. Dan reached into the hole and drew out not owlet but egg, a round dead thing like a small ping-pong ball. A good night's sleep had prepared me for this final mockery, and there was no wailing or wringing of hands. I believe I took it like a man. But, oh, that horrible gone feeling! We searched the area for a long time but no owls gladdened our lackluster eyes. They were gone. It was Samuel Butler, I believe, who once said that a chicken is just an egg's way of making another egg. That morning I was quite willing to accept that sapient remark at its face value, the primacy of egg over fowl. Why couldn't I count that poor addled egg? It was just as much an owl as a bunch of feathers and yellow bill. Poor, unhappy dolt. Desire plays strange tricks with us sometimes. Anyway, Marybelle and I are probably the only people who have seen a Boreal Owl's egg but not the owl. So be it. "The moving Finger writes; and, having writ, moves on . . ." It was indeed a variation on the theme of Omar Khayyám—Kismet. We went over the surrounding scrub a second time but found neither owl nor trace. We were just too late.

The rest of the morning was spent birding in and around Fairbanks and about eleven o'clock our luck took a decided turn for the better. On the cover of a recent issue of *AFN* there had appeared a photograph of the Hawk Owl. That particular owl had been photographed near Fairbanks and Dan had been the photographer. Knowing this, I had hinted rather broadly that we should like to see a Hawk Owl but it had never occurred to Dan that the bird would be a lifer for both Marybelle and me. He had supposed that I simply meant we did not have the opportunity to see this species very often. When he discovered that neither of us had actually ever seen one and heard our tale of woe concerning our frustration in Ontario and Manitoba of the previous year, he went into high gear. He at once took us to several of his favorite Hawk Owl areas and even showed us the very tree in which his photographed owl had perched. The old dead spruce, however, was a most unsatisfactory ersatz for the real thing and only reminded me of that utility pole in South Carolina near which a Bachman's Warbler had been seen in 1961. Also, as we passed a wide, level field, Dan remarked that a few weeks before dog races had been held here and that above the noise and crowds a Hawk Owl had flown over this field most of the day. This did not especially soothe my taut nerves either for, of course, no Hawk Owl was hunting the peaceful field at that moment. However, just as we were driving by some of the main buildings of the University of Alaska on a paved and relatively well-traveled street, Dan yelled, "Stop!" He had had an experienced and sharp eye out for all the utility poles along our route and this vigilance finally paid off. There, chuckling and peering down at us from this man-shaped artifact, sat our first Hawk Owl. Dan had his telescope with him and we even looked at the owl through it. The effect was more than a portrait, closer to a sudden glimpse of the forbidden. I thought of all those countless spruce tops I had scanned from the train on our trip to Churchill and heaved a deep sigh. But it was a sigh of quiet jubilation, not pique. After all, this owl was an animate beautiful bunch of feathers and eyes, not a rounded, addled egg. It remained in the vicinity all day and Marybelle and I found him again late that afternoon on another pole. It was the end of a long, long quest.

Eagle Summit is high land lying south of the Crazy Mountains about 110 miles northeast of Fairbanks. It is reached by an unpaved road, the Steese Highway, which terminates some miles farther on at Circle. I had first heard of Eagle Summit from Robert Weeden in 1967. Eating breakfast at a hotel lunch counter, some of the Crowder gang were discussing the possibility of Rock Ptarmigan in the Fairbanks area and our conversation was tapped by one of the local men eating across from us. "If you're interested in Ptarmigan, see Bob Weeden. He's studied Ptarmigan around here for years," was the advice he gave us. I called Mr. Weeden, at that time associated with the Alaska Fish and Game Department, and arranged for him to come over that evening to Traveler's Inn where the Tour was staying and talk to us about Alaskan birds. He gave us an interesting and most knowledgeable account of the birds of the region. I still remember his slides of the Great Gray Owl, over which I drooled unashamedly. But most of all he told us of Eagle Summit, his favorite country, which he knows so well. There, he informed us, we would be able to see both Rock and Willow Ptarmigan. Furthermore, Wheatears and Wandering Tattlers nested there also.

Unfortunately, the Crowder Tour schedule did not permit us time to travel that far; it was an overnight proposition. So instead of this promised land, Eugene and Loraine Bleiweiss, Marybelle and I rented a car and birded Wickersham Dome, on another road and much closer to Fairbanks, in the hope of Rock Ptarmigan at its treeless summit. The climb up Wickersham Dome proved to be a mosquito-infested trek that taxed our strength and patience to the limit. On top, where it was bare, Water Pipits were the only birds we saw. On the drive out we had also had a flat tire and discovered too late that we had no spare or car jack even if we had had the former. All told, it was a most discouraging performance for the Bleiweisses and Piatts. Al Webb, snug back in Fairbanks, always referred to our day of mishaps as the "Wickersham Dome Disaster." He never spoke truer words. Marybelle and I vowed that the next time we were in Alaska we would leave the Dome to the pipits and the route up to it to the mosquitoes and take time to bird Eagle Summit instead. The year was now 1970 and it was that "next time" we had promised ourselves.

Before leaving Fairbanks for Eagle Summit, I had talked with Weeden, now Conservation Representative in Alaska for the Sierra Club, and he told me that two young fellows, Jerry McGowan and Terry Bendock, were camped at the Summit engaged in a study of Rock Ptarmigan breeding cycles and nesting. This seemed like a sure thing and so it was, in a way.

We had no camping gear, but at mile 101 on the Steese was a small eatery and gas station and, best of all, the proprietor had a small but cozy cabin that we could rent. There was a wood-burning stove and plenty of wood so we kept warm and toasty during our four days' stay at Eagle Summit. The only other place we could have gotten traveler's accommodations was at Circle Springs, a resort type of place that was expensive and too far from the Summit. If our Rock Ptarmigan and Marybelle's Wheatear would only show, we had it made.

It was June 10 and the days were long. We set out to reconnoiter the birding situation but principally to spot the camp of McGowan and Bendock. We soon found it. It was near an abandoned gold mine, but no one was there so we proceeded on up the road to mile 109, the highest point of the road in the Eagle Summit area. There were trees along the mountain creeks below but the heights were a series of barren, rocky knolls. We stopped the car along the side of the road and got out to try our luck. Almost immediately we heard the song of a male Lapland Longspur, given in flight as the bird hovers and flutters in the air. And then, not five seconds later, we heard a song we did not know but which would become familiar before we left Alaska. The bird was not more than fifty feet away perched on a small rock and when he flew we could see the white tail and coverts with an inverted black T at the tail tip. At long last Marybelle had seen her first Wheatear and our scores were now the same, 619 birds in North America! No longer would it be necessary for me to employ consummate tact in speaking of this trim little thrush. I could gabble about Wheatears from now till doomsday and not once receive that baleful glare from my much honored and respected spouse. It was worth the entire trip just to put an end to that one bird disparity between us. And when, later, we watched Wheatears at several places on the Seward Peninsula, some of them feeding young, I was conscious only of a serene bond of camaraderie between us. Also, I had again become as Caesar's wife. Since that triumphant little episode at mile 109 on the Steese, I cannot recall that my earlier sighting of a Wheatear at McKinley Park has ever once been challenged.

As we drove back down the road, we looked again for a yellow truck at the old gold mine. There was none and we judged that both McGowan and Bendock were still out somewhere in that vast panorama of rolling hills. It had begun to rain softly and we sat in the parked car watching the mile-high streamers of water move across the gray landscape. All at once a large bird soared up from the hillside below us and swept past the car to land on the road behind us. It was surely a ptarmigan, but which one? That most obliging of all birds remained at the edge of the road walking very slowly and sedately for at least ten minutes. It was a male Rock Ptarmigan about halfway along in its summer molt. We could see clearly the black eye stripe, and when the bird finally flew, his wings and much of the back were pure white. So much white on the bird at this season reminded me of those lines in Tennyson's *Idylls of the King*, "The ptarmigan that whitens ere his hour woos his own end." Of course, in early June our Rock Ptarmigan was browning, not whitening, but his remaining white plumage was very conspicuous nonetheless. It had indeed been an afternoon of pure delight, successful far beyond our most sanguine expectations. Marybelle had the Wheatear and both of us now had all three ptarmigans. We did not know then that our first Rock Ptarmigan was also to be our last, to date.

While we were eating our hamburgers at the little restaurant that night, Jerry McGowan drove up. He had been in Fairbanks all day, so that accounted for the missing yellow truck. We made a date to meet him and Terry at their camp next morning and they would take us to one of their Rock Ptarmigan nests. As the crow flies, or perhaps in this case the raven, the nest was not too far from camp but if you have ever climbed a boggy tundra-covered Alaska hill with knee-length rubber boots, you will soon come to realize that distance is decidedly relative. We did get there, though, and both the young men were most considerate and adapted their pace to ours. Mr. Weeden's big black dog had come with us and before we actually approached the nest he was told to heel or sit or whatever so that he would not flush the hen prematurely. This dog had been well trained by Weeden and was invaluable in the Ptarmigan nesting studies because it was he that had pointed most of the nests that were found. He was aptly named Ptarmigan and even more aptly called Tar for short. As it turned out, the hen was not on her nest. However, this was not a shattering blow like the departed Boreal Owls, since we had seen a male Rock Ptarmigan the day before. Consequently, I did not resent those seven live eggs as I did that single Boreal Owl remnant. We waited in the vicinity for only a few minutes; it would not have been wise to remain longer that close to the nest for it was cold and the hen should have been incubating. There were other nests, of course, but all were quite far away, even as the raven flies. Had we not been so fortunate in seeing a male Rock Ptarmigan ourselves, we should most certainly have dogged Jerry and Terry's trails the next two days. But as it was, we were free to roam the less difficult terrain and find out as much as we could about the other birds of Eagle Summit. Lifers always come first to a lister, but then the Rock Ptarmigan was no longer on the red side of our ledger.

We birded the Eagle Summit area for two more days and truly hated to leave when our time was up. I can understand now why Eagle Summit is Robert Weeden's Gradyville. Along the creek near our cabin we heard our first Gray-cheeked Thrush sing. This bird migrates through Pennsylvania every spring but has never favored us with its song. It was also a treat to see a Wandering Tattler in breeding plumage. There were Varied Thrushes, Common Redpolls, Water Pipits, White-crowned Sparrows, many Lapland Longspurs, Snipe, and other old friendships to renew. The greatest surprise to me was the Say's Phoebe that teetered on the bushes near our cabin and snatched at passing insects. Exactly eight years before, to the day, June 13, 1962, we had seen our first Say's Phoebe building a nest on the beams of a roadside rest pavilion in the desert of west Texas. We have seen this bird often in California and elsewhere but for some undefined reason I did not think it nested as far north as Alaska. I suppose this bit of self-inflicted ignorance stemmed from my initial contact with the bird in a desert setting. I wonder how many thousand other misconceptions about birds clutter up my mind. It would be truly appalling if they were all loosed at once. The morning we bade Eagle Summit farewell, we backtracked to mile 109 to say goodbye to Mary-belle's Wheatears. They were there. And so was the whole vast, beautiful wilderness. It had been a second Gradyville to us.

Earlier, when I had gone to the Wein Consolidated Airlines office in Anchorage to adjust our flight schedule to Hooper Bay and Nome, I had been mildly puzzled by the reactions of the two good women behind the counter when I mentioned that we were staying overnight at Leen's Lodge in Bethel. Once there I understood perfectly. Actually, I marveled at their restraint. They had said with wry smiles that it was a hotel—of a sort. And so it was. We were on our way to Hooper Bay, but our flying schedule from Fairbanks via Anchorage landed us at Bethel too late in the day to catch another plane to Hooper Bay. Practically all commerical flights to and from Hooper Bay begin and end at Bethel, which is a town on the west bank of the Kuskokwim River approximately fifty miles above the river's termination in the Bering Sea. Bethel is a jumping-off place for much of the wilderness area of southwestern Alaska and, like all small outposts of civilization, is the epitome of all that is ugly, disorganized, vehicle-laden, dusty, dingy, and drab. It is the smelly, unsightly guts of commercial riparian Alaska. If there is a Bethel chamber of commerce, which I doubt, I ask its forgive-ness for this somewhat uncomplimentary thumbnail sketch of their fair town. I realize that no wilderness was ever conquered without noise, grime, and machinery, but since I have little sympathy with the conquest of the Alaskan wilderness, I refuse to give Bethel a leg up. Leen's Lodge is, after all, perhaps the fairest jewel in its crown. It is affectionately referred to by the businessmen who frequent it as the Hilton Tilton. It is certainly tilting in several places.

We saw no birds of consequence at Bethel. There is a wildlife refuge not far from town but in the few hours of late afternoon left to us we found no way to reach it. We walked through much of the town and along the dusty road leading to the airport but our hearts were not in it. We were thinking only of that plane which would take us the next morning to Hooper Bay. The cot on which I "slept" reminded me of those accounts one has heard of the torture chambers used by the Nazis—places especially designed so that the victim could not stand, sit, or lie down without acute discomfort. But the glorious breakfast next morning did much to revive my instinct for survival. Huge platters of eggs, bacon, toast, and preserves! Whatever deficiencies plague Leen's Lodge, food was not one of them. Our supper and breakfast alone were almost worth the twenty-eight bucks we paid for board and room at the Hilton Tilton.

The cab I had called to take us to the airport was shared, of all things, by some birders from Wilmington, Delaware, practically next-door neighbors it seemed to us here in faraway Alaska. The four of them, Howard Brokaw, his son and two other lads, were also going to Hooper Bay for ten days of birding and then on across the Brooks Range on a walking tour. We had met Mr. Brokaw at a luncheon given by the Stokeses in Philadelphia, at which Pete and Ruth Isleib were also present. Both the Isleibs and Brokaws had searched for the Ivory-billed Woodpecker in the Big Thicket of Texas and since the Piatts were preparing to take up the torch a few days from then, a get together was arranged. As the six of us checked our baggage and gear (they had mountains of it) at the Bethel airport before boarding the Twin Otter plane that would carry us over the extensive tundra to Hooper Bay, I could think of nothing more original to mumble than the old stereotype, "It's a small world after all." Also, I was a bit concerned as to where six Auslanders were to find a haven at Hooper Bay. My own prior arrangements were even at this late date none too certain.

Hooper Bay lies on the shore of the Bering Sea halfway between the deltas of the Yukon and Kuskokwim rivers. It is surrounded for many miles on the land side by tundra, countless lakes, and waterholes. The whole vast area is a paradise for waterfowl, shore birds, and birders. In particular, it is a favorite haunt of the Spectacled Eider and Emperor Goose, two lifers we wanted very much to see. Hooper Bay is a primitive Eskimo village, relatively large but with not a vestige of commercial accommodations for visitor or traveler. At the suggestion of Wien Consolidated Airlines, I had written the previous fall to their agent there, a Mr. Robert O'Brien. Months passed and I received no answer. In desperation I finally wrote to the Principal of the school at Hooper Bay, Bureau of Indian Affairs, inquiring about some place we might possibly stay for two or three days. The Principal, Donald Barta, wrote me promptly that he was sure some arrangement could be made, especially since school would be over and some of the teachers might then be gone. But now I was concerned because it was quite possible that the Delaware gang had also made some arrangement for lodging with Barta. Would there be places for six of us?

The flight of the Twin Otter over the expanse of tundra between Bethel and Hooper Bay was uneventful but impressive. As I watched the never-ending panorama of brown tundra interspersed with lakes pass steadily beneath us I once more experienced that sensation of exaltation mixed with awe that any wilderness encounter inspires. It was easy to see from this aerial view of the land lying between Alaska's two great rivers how easy it would be for one to lose himself for days in the heart of this gigantic prairie. The little Eskimo girl sitting in front of us with her mother kept looking back at us and grinning, and I was reassured. She, at least, would never lose her way. It would only be helpless city folk like me that would ever fear the tundra. I did not consciously or actually fear the tundra, of course; but what one does not fully understand always elicits a subliminal unrest or apprehension.

After our pilot had, by radio, bawled out a small, unidentified plane for lousing up the airways over the landing strip, we put down safely at Hooper Bay. It was foggy, as is usual along coastal Alaska, and an untimely air crash would not have added to the luster of the occasion. The airstrip was close to the ocean some little distance from the village, and it was necessary to load all the baggage onto a flat-topped trailer for transportation up the rutted road. The driver of the battered truck hauling the trailer must have had a date with some Eskimo beauty back in the village or maybe he was just hungry. Anyway, he went hell for rubber up that road and managed to centrifuge a suitcase off the heap onto the road and into a lagoon-sized mud puddle. The bag was mine, of course, and I jumped off the load to retrieve it. By this time the driver had lost his savagely gained momentum and the truck balked at the last small grade. We all unloaded our own baggage and set out on foot for the remaining short distance. The small fry were all around us as they are at practically every Eskimo or Indian village I have ever visited and we asked them to lead us to the Principal's house. This they did with great éclat and with two suitcases and a duffle bag I was sore put to it to keep up with them. As a matter of plain fact, I gave up before we reached the end of the long boardwalk and the kids took over some of our stuff.

Brokaw and his boys had trundled off in the opposite direction and we learned later that their contact at Hooper Bay had been the Catholic priest with whom they shared the "manse" during their stay. We were very fortunate. Don Barta was kindness itself. The Public Health Service Clinic, where he had intended to put us, was already occupied but he let us use the vacated apartment of one of the teachers. There were no covers for the bed and most of the furniture was shoved over in one big, inextricable pile against the wall, but it was luxury beyond compare in this poor Eskimo village. We wished the native population could have enjoyed quarters half so fair and commodious. We were to look back longingly to this privacy and elegance while at Gambell. And it did not cost us one red cent. Strictly speaking, Barta was not empowered to let other than BIA personnel use these quarters. Mr. Barta, however, is no longer at Hooper Bay and after so long a time surely the bigwigs of the BIA will not castigate him for this mild infraction of regulations.

After laying in some hamburger, bread, and canned goods at the Native Store we set out to explore the surrounding tundra on foot. It was not easy going and much of our time was spent in backtracking out of some watery, impassable cul de sac, but the birds were worth it even if we had to crawl. A partial list for that afternoon included: swarms of Dunlin; hundreds of Black Turnstone; Western Sandpiper; Sandhill Crane; several big flocks of Whistling Swan; Black Brant; our old friend the Short-eared Owl; Parasitic and Long-tailed Jaegers in the air everywhere; a number of Sabine's Gulls; Arctic Tern; Willow Ptarmigan in every thicket; Arctic Loon; Common Snipe; Pintail, Green-winged Teal; Old Squaw duck; hundreds of Lapland Longspurs; both Northern and Red Phalaropes with their gorgeous breeding plumage in almost every waterhole; and finally, most exciting of all, three Bar-tailed Godwits and scads of Emperor Geese—the latter two lifers.

The Bar-tailed Godwit breeds where terrain is suitable from the delta of the Kuskokwim to the delta of the Colville River and we had searched diligently for this bird in 1967 at Barrow, Kotzebue, and especially around Nome but without success. Our failure to find this noisy, conspicuous bird on the first trip to Alaska was probably because it was past the height of the breeding season and the birds were dispersed by early August. Whatever the reason, we struck pay dirt that first day at Hooper Bay and the Bar-tailed Godwit was entered in the records as 622. The breeding range of the Emperor Goose is more restricted than that of the Bar-tailed Godwit, but Hooper Bay and St. Lawrence Island are both prime places for this handsome bird. We were puzzled, though, when we saw our first flocks of Emperors flying low over the tundra. Their heads and upper napes were decidedly reddish in color instead of the clear white our field guides portrayed, and the slanting rays of the low sun accentuated this reddish cast. We were soon to discover that many if not most Emperor Geese are so marked, at least in the summer months. No Eskimo ever sets forth on the tundra without his gun, and at Hooper Bay and later on St. Lawrence we were to have ample opportunity to inspect the red-tinged feathers of dead birds. It did not appear to be a stain but actual pigmentation of the feathers. My own limited ornithological library does not help me much on the true nature of this reddish suffusion, so you will have to ask some ornithologist for the answer. Pintail ducks in summer often show the same sort of reddish cast on their otherwise white breasts.

Ted Hunter, the Eskimo guide we had hoped to engage to take us by boat along the coast or far back into the tundra, was on fire-fighting duty somewhere west of Cook Inlet. On our trip to Kodiak we had observed with apprehension the menacing columns of smoke rising from among the snow-capped mountains of this region. Was it man's handiwork or nature's? Man being simply a deracinated child of nature, I suppose the question is largely meaningless. But we had learned from several reliable sources that forest fires in Alaska are sometimes started intentionally so that fire fighters will have a job and, consequently, more money for liquor. Some British poet once wrote, "Better fifty years of Europe than a cycle of Cathay"—but I doubt it. The ancient Chinese probably were no worse than rootless Occidental peoples. At least the former built walls instead of destroying forests. My moralizing is not procuring us a guide, however, so let's get on with the business of finding eider ducks. Mr. Barta again came to our assistance and through him we located an Eskimo guide, a very old man whose weather-beaten, mahogany-colored face might well have been a familiar sight in the village streets of that same Cathay. I think his name was Kopanuk—my ability to recall names is wretched—and because he spoke no English, his teen-aged grandson (or was it great-grandson?) was to go with us as interpreter.

We met both old and young Kopanuk the next morning down at the muddy shore of the inlet. The tide was not yet quite high enough to launch the boat so I pulled my field guide from my pocket and showed the old man the page illustrating the four species of eider ducks. I pointed to the picture of the Spectacled Eider and almost instantaneously his old face lit up with a smile like a cracked full moon rising over the horizon. He jabbed with his finger out eastward over the tundra. So far so good. It looked as though the Spectacled Eider was in the bag. I then pointed to Steller's Eider. Both Spectacled and Steller's Eiders are reputed to be common breeders at Hooper Bay. There was no sign of response on Kopanuk's face this time, however, and I experienced that well-known sinking feeling of the expectant but thwarted birder. He looked at the picture a long time and then pointed out to the ocean where, despite the almost complete absence of even a breeze, the green waves were white-capped and towering. Finally, he pointed in a northerly direction and shook his head. I asked the grandson what the old man had said and what was the import of his gestures; I had almost guessed and was not far from the truth. The Spectacled Eider we could find by crossing the small, quiet inlet and following the main stream back into the tundra. Steller's Eider, on the other hand, we would probably not see unless we traveled north along the coast some dozen miles to Igiak Bay vicinity, and the sea that day was too rough for such a journey. This information did not accord with what I had read in Gabrielson and Lincoln, for that book states that Steller's Eider is a common breeder at both Igiak and Hooper bays. I wondered if the old man could be mistaken or simply did not recognize Steller's Eider and was too proud to admit it. I hoped this might prove to be the case. I was dead wrong. We spent twelve hours that day boating and walking the tundra for miles and never saw a single Steller's Eider. Maybe you will go to Hooper Bay and find this pretty little duck abundant. I can only state that on June 6, 1970, there were no Steller's Eiders on or above the tundra near Hooper Bay.

I shall not dwell in detail on our tundra trip with Kopanuk. It was exciting at the time but in retrospect there is not much to tell. It was not long before we saw our first Spectacled Eiders. We were rounding a bend of the main stream when Kopanuk gave a low cry and pointed ahead toward the far bank. There were two ducks in the water close to shore. With outboard barely turning over, we glided slowly toward the spot. When we were close, Kopanuk killed the motor and we approached the pair in utter silence. It was a beautiful pair of Spectacled Eiders and before they at last took wing we must have been less than ten feet from the birds. I doubt if many birders have ever seen male and female Spectacled Eiders in the wild so close. It was one of those deep-down, soul-satisfying experiences that come to the average birder all too rarely. We saw six more before the day was over but not in the water and certainly not so close. We watched young Kopanuk shoot two Emperor Geese—he was a magnificent shot—and it was a sad experience for Marybelle and me to see those splendid birds crash down to earth, inert dead weight where only a brief second ago in Icarian flight they had been soaring to the sun. However, like so many other city-bred folk in similar circumstances, we thought of the bawling calf and our taste for veal cutlets and were silent. It was terrifically hot, for Alaska, on the tundra that day. The sun shone brightly through a light haze and there was no wind at all, only dense swarms of mosquito-like flies. They did not bite but compensated for this friendly gesture by getting into one's eyes, mouth, and ears. Before crossing the inlet back to the village, we stopped on an extensive mud flat to wait for the tide to rise sufficiently for docking the boat. While there we saw three more Bar-tailed Godwits and watched them for a long time. Just before we reached the village, Kopanuk pointed westward to a low cloud bank hanging over the sea. "Rain," he said. Now I want to know—did he or did he not speak English? Surely this single, meteorological utterance was not his entire repertoire in this, to him, barbaric tongue.

Kopanuk the elder was no mean weather prophet. Beginning that night it did rain and by morning it was coming down in sheets, almost horizontally with a forty-mile-an-hour wind behind them. The rain continued all that day and the next and when it finally stopped about noon of the third day, the violent wind still churned the cold gray waters of the Bering Sea and stormed across the limitless prairies beyond. Nome was our next destination, and rather than make the long triangulation back through Bethel and Anchorage we had made arrangements with Munz Northern Airlines of Nome to fly a special plane directly to Hooper Bay across Norton Sound to pick us up. This would not have cost too much in excess of the scheduled flights via Anchorage. Besides, I had hoped to coax our pilot to detour somewhat to the east and fly low over the plateau that lies beyond Mountain Village and above Curlew Lake. It was on this plateau that Arthur A. Allen and his party discovered the first nest of the Bristle-thighed Curlew in 1948 and where Joe Taylor had seen this bird in 1967. I did not really expect to see Bristle-thighed Curlews from a plane but I wanted to case the entire terrain to see whether Marybelle and I could make the ascent on foot from the lake. Joe Taylor had done it but he is a few years younger than I and probably doesn't smoke.

To condense into a few words what seemed to us an interminable wait, I'll simply state that the Munz plane never came to Hooper Bay. The winds were too strong for maneuvering a small two-engine job. This disappointment was the more devastating when we discovered that another couple had wished to fly from Nome to Hooper Bay, thus halving our flight costs. Our place was at the opposite end of the village from the Wien Consolidated radio contact station—the latter being none other than the house of Mrs. Robert O'Brien, a very pretty Eskimo woman. It is a never-ending source of amazement to me that a proud, self-sufficient people should give up their inheritance to the extent of adopting Irish names such as Robert O'Brien. But at last I found out why the Wien agent at Hooper Bay never answered my letter. He had not been the red-faced, bluff son of Eire I had imagined but a pure Eskimo who probably did not know enough English to compose a letter. In any event, he had died about the time my letter must have arrived. His wife still had the letter but had made no attempt to answer it. But to get back to the geography of the village before this paragraph disintegrates into a house that Jack built sort of thing, let me state that I must have trod that boardwalk between radio station and our place at least twenty times in that drenching rain. I finally learned that the special Munz flight to Hooper Bay had been definitely canceled. So we took the Twin Otter back to Bethel and I contracted a bad case of aerotitis on the too-rapid ascent. We had a four-hour wait at the Bethel airport, without lunch, and were back in Anchorage late that night, weary and disgruntled. The next morning we flew to Nome via Kotzebue. It was decidedly a roundabout way of reaching our goal. We had squandered over three days on that miserable boardwalk and in airports. Such, often, is birding in Alaska.

During the brief stopover at the Kotzebue airport I strolled about and listened for the canine racket so familiar to our ears when we birded there in 1967 and saw our first North American Yellow Wagtails running around the village streets. The airport is not too close to the village itself but I should have heard some dogs at least. I heard not one lone howl. I have read somewhere—I do not vouch for its authenticity—that sixteen hundred human and two thousand canine souls inhabit Kotzebue. This is no longer true since the advent of the abominable snowmobile. From Cape Prince of Wales to far Labrador the sled dog is facing extinction, not perhaps as a species but certainly as a working subspecies. Dogs must be fed and unless they can earn their keep, they become a liability to their owners. There are more dogs in suburban Philadelphia than probably all of Alaska today. I, for one, would gladly undertake to hitch all of them to one huge dog sled and mush to Nome with the serum. Perhaps then they would be too tired to yap all night long. Kotzebue dogs were the genuine article; suburban dogs are as vitiated as most of their owners and almost as nasty. This last waspish invective has done me a world of good and if this book never sells one copy in Greater Philadelphia, it will still have been well worth it.

Nome is my favorite Alaskan town. True, it no longer has its picturesque boardwalks that we trod in 1967, but the whole town exudes a subdued swagger and frontier atmosphere that is a stimulating tonic to an inmate of megalopolis. It would not surprise me too much if I saw the Nome counterpart of Klondike Kate come strutting through the entrance of the North Star Hotel. Also, since we have spent more days birding in this part of the Seward peninsula than any other spot in Alaska, we have come to look upon Nome and its three major roads as our province. But we did not come to Nome for its vintage flavor but for a sterner purpose. So let me tell you as briefly as good form permits about our three lifers at Nome.

There are no car rental agencies such as Hertz or Avis in Nome, probably because all roads out of Nome lead only to local or relatively local dead ends. You cannot drive to Nome any more than you can drive to Hooper Bay or Barrow. So I rented a pickup truck from the Q Trucking Company, owned by Chuck Reader, a real nice guy. Why it is called Q Trucking Company, I have never found out. My curiosity about the contrived world of the human species has never been excessive and when possible lifers are in the offing what residue I possess never rises to the conscious level. "God hath made man upright; but they have sought out many inventions." The wisdom of Holy Writ is boundless. So, I just drove the truck as best I could and did not worry about the name on the door panel. Joe Taylor had written to me that three years earlier he had seen Rufous-necked Sandpipers at Safety Lagoon, about thirty miles east of Nome on the Council Road. This bird is another Old World species that has extended its breeding range to western Alaska. As a matter of fact, it was first reported from Alaska about the time I was born, 1909. It resembles very much the common Semipalmated Sandpiper but in breeding plumage is russet on the neck. We spent the first two days at Nome, therefore, walking the tundra all along the south side of the lagoon. We saw many Semipalmated Sandpipers, a number of other species, including several Bar-tailed Godwits, but no Rufous-necked Sandpipers. Before we left Nome for St. Lawrence Island we had spent the equivalent of more than four days at or near Safety Lagoon looking for this Siberian wanderer but never saw it there or at any other place in Alaska. No, Safety Lagoon does not remind us of any particular sandpiper but, rather, a much larger bird of the same family—perhaps our most unexpected and exciting lifer to date. But before we add this latter bird to the list, let us observe the proprieties and journey north out of Nome instead of east in order that the proper temporal sequence of lifer acquisition be maintained.

Bill Foster, a school teacher at Nome and also an excellent birder, told us that Gyrfalcons were best seen along the Teller Road, starting at about mile 21. He also mentioned that White Wagtails had nested near Nome last year. If your memory is long and your patience exemplary, you will recall that you and I first met at Cold Bay, Alaska, scanning the sullen skies for the Gyrfalcon. That was August 9, 1967, and at Nome it was June 21, 1970; maybe during the interim the minor deity who controls the fate of listers had softened his capricious heart toward us. We could only hope—and so it proved. We did not see any Gyrfalcons on our way out to Teller but only a pair of Wheatears—you perceive how blasé we had become—feeding their young at mile 21. But when we drew close to this section of the road on the return trip, the impossible happened and we saw at a distance three falcon-like birds but with broader wings than any other falcons we had ever seen. One of these birds gradually drew nearer and granted us a positive identification. One Gyrfalcon for certain and perhaps two more! What more could one wish for after waiting thirteen years for a bird? And wouldn't you know it, the birder's old adage again, just eighteen months later Marybelle, I, and many others watched a Gyrfalcon hunting over the marshes of Brigantine Wildlife Refuge—our own back yard, so to speak. The day was a huge success, then, and when we reached mile 7 close to Nome, our cup ran over. Flying over the dwarf willows in a marshy area was a White Wagtail. We had seen this species on the lawns of green England and Ireland many a time, but it was here on the south side of the Seward Peninsula that we really welcomed this trim black and white bird. Yellow Wagtails are locally common in Alaska but the White is not. It was a day of good hunting, the best kind.

Something else of immense significance happened to us on that Sunday morning, driving the Teller Road out of Nome. It was a unique experience in our lives, and in all probability it will never happen to either of us again. Silence—complete, all-pervading, profound silence! There are many kinds of silence, usually intangible or negative, but this one was palpable, real, positive. Outside of ourselves and that battered truck, not one human-engendered sound did we hear from about 6:00 A.M. until 12:29 P.M.—I checked my watch when we first heard that plane. Not one shriek or whisper; not a clatter or a squeak; no distant muffled boom or fretful wail; no chink of boot on stone or bark of dog; no radio, no auto, no plane—just measureless silence. It was like those first early days of creation before the prophetic curtain of mist rose up from the face of the earth to veil God's handiwork. It was the cosmos, not chaos, we listened to that morning on our road to Damascus; for we too had been present at a miracle. For once, the world was very young again.

And now for the greatest birding event of the trip. Ever since we had departed from Bethel I had been feeling guilt pangs for not making some sort of arrangement with a bush pilot to land us on Curlew Lake and thus have a try at the Bristle-thighed Curlew. But more often than you might expect from the songs of the old bards, fortune does smile on the lesser man at times. It was our next to last day at Nome and we decided to make one more try for the Rufous-necked Sandpiper at Safety Lagoon. Once more we crossed the inlet into the lagoon on that ancient ferry, one of the few manmade contraptions that appeals to me. I hope it is still there when you drive to Council but, of course, there will be a shiny new bridge by then. It was a relatively hot day and we were discouraged and fretful. After four days or so, it becomes something of a bore to sedulously check every small shore bird that peeps off in front of you in a marshy tundra. We would have funked out in a few more minutes, but then a little to the east and overhead we heard it. Peeee-ur-it, Peeee-ur-it—a mellow, soft, slightly drawn out call. We had been watching the ground and had not observed the birds approaching. As we looked up, it sounded again and we saw three curlews circling close and almost overhead. They headed out toward the sound but soon swung around and flew back over us again, giving that mellow call Peeee-ur-it every few seconds. The last we saw of them they were flying straight for the hills to the north of Safety Lagoon. We had seen three Bristle-thighed Curlews! I felt we didn't deserve such a glorious lifer with no expenditure of effort on our part, but fate had decreed otherwise and we raised no objections. Perhaps it was compensation for all the blood (mosquitoes), sweat, and tears we had lavished to no avail on Bachman's Warbler, Ivory-billed Woodpecker, Rufous-necked Sandpiper, and others. Dan Gibson considered this sighting important enough to include in his compilation of summer bird records for Alaska (*AFN*, vol. 24, no. 5, 1970), otherwise I should now scarcely believe it.

For the sake of the few who may possibly, though inconceivably, know less about the Bristle-thighed Curlew than I do, let me append the following words of explanation. This bird is not especially a rarity insofar as numbers or recorded sight observations are concerned. It had been known for a long time that Bristle-thighed Curlews winter from Hawaii south through the Pacific Islands and migrate in summer to Alaska, but until Arthur A. Allen's party discovered the first nest in the high plateau region north of Mountain Village, it was always a mystery bird. It still is in some respects, for its breeding range in Alaska is still poorly understood. It was not, therefore, that we had made a great discovery. The mystery lies in the fact that the Bristle-thighed Curlew discovered us.

On the north wall of our breakfast nook at home hangs a large, framed map of Alaska. Because I face this map every morning I have the opportunity to study it, and usually do. Poor Marybelle, with her back to the map, must be content with watching our local birds at the back feeder or, occasionally in desperation, making a heroic attempt at conversation. But more often than not my replies degenerate into mere monosyllabic grunts. My fork travels more and more slowly to my mouth and my customarily wooden countenance gradually assumes an even more vacuous expression as I roam the Brooks Range, explore the shores of Bristol Bay, or circumnavigate St. Lawrence

Island. It is a world of latitudes and longitudes. So it is that I can tell you that Gambell, on the northwest point of St. Lawrence Island, Cape Chibukak, is approximately 4° longitude west of the U.S. side of Bering Strait, Cape Prince of Wales, and 2° farther west than the Siberian side, East Cape. It is about 6°, 30′ north of St. Paul Island in the Pribilofs and roughly half that distance north of tiny Hall and St. Matthew islands. Furthermore, Gambell is only about forty miles from Siberia and on very clear days—not often—the Asiatic mainland can be seen. If it is Sunday in Gambell and you travel about eighteen miles northwest, it will be Monday—you have crossed the International Date Line. Finally, St. Lawrence Island itself is approximately a hundred miles long from east to west and averages about fifteen miles in breadth. All told, it is quite a place and its remoteness lends it a certain air of mystery and adventure.

In the summer of 1970, Munz Northern Airlines made round-trip flights between Nome and Gambell twice a week. The small twin-engine plane in which we flew accommodated six people besides the pilot. On the outbound trip I was fortunate enough to be asked to occupy the empty copilot's seat, not for my navigational prowess but to help balance the plane. It was an exciting trip for Marybelle and me and the first time I had ever flown in a small plane. In jets and other large aircraft there is so little actual feeling of flight. You just hang in midair between heaven and earth. It is as though your bus or railway car suddenly took wings and very soon you are more conscious of the interior of your conveyance than the remote and often invisible earth. But in a small plane the altitude is so much less that mother earth is an omnipresent factor and demands your attention at all times.

From my vantage point in front I had a magnificent view of Norton Sound and then small Sledge Island just west of Nome, an island I had always wanted to see from the air. Then we were out over the cold, green Bering Sea, upon whose wave-tossed bosom floated innumerable drifts of the broken arctic ice pack. Like a child, I kept looking for polar bears on these ice floes although I really knew better and, besides, we were too high for that sort of picture-book stuff. It was not too long before the indistinct, cloud-shrouded island of St. Lawrence loomed up ahead. Once again I was reminded of Captain Bering's apparent dread of land. Vitus Bering "discovered" this island on August 10, 1728, on his first voyage. Because of the date, he named it St. Lawrence, after that faithful servant of Pope Sixtus II, but there exists no evidence that Bering or any of his crew ever went ashore. Long before we spotted the village of Gambell, population 385 and almost entirely Eskimo, we had gradually been losing altitude. As we approached Cape Chibukak, I could make out some large and many small flocks of sea birds flying swiftly over the water, and just before we banked for the final turn, I spotted a mixed flock of both Common and King Eiders. And then we headed straight for the runway and the ground raced to meet us. With a roar of engines and reversal of propeller blades, or whatever it is a pilot does to slow a plane, we came to a halt outside the small shack that serves as the Gambell airport.

Gambell, though infinitely less smelly than Hooper Bay and much neater than Barrow, is still a primitive Eskimo village and there is no hotel or public lodging facility. Several months earlier I had written to Darroll Hargraves, Principal of the BIA school, inquiring about food and lodging. Mr. Hargraves had written that he would be gone before our arrival and recommended Vernon Slwooko and his wife, Beda, as possible host and hostess during our brief stay. The Slwookos had agreed, and so we were to live with an Eskimo family while at Gambell, paying for our board and room, of course. Vernon is a registered Alaskan guide and lists himself officially as Walrus Hunter Guide. All the Slwookos, both old and young, did their best to make us feel at home. Most of our meals were eaten with the family and we had two cots in the loft upstairs which we shared—loft not cots—with the young fry. Sheets and blankets were not supplied so we used our sleeping bags. It was a novel experience for us living with an Eskimo family but hardly typical. Vernon's house, built by the army during the war with

Japan, was larger than most of the others in the village and the whole family had sufficient command of the King's English so that sign language was seldom necessary. With the exception of the food, mostly out of cans, Vernon's house was superior to Leen's Lodge in many respects.

Vernon and his eldest son were among the crowd of Eskimos that met the plane. They put our one duffle bag on a snowmobile and, taking turns, Marybelle and I were conveyed through the village astride this horrible contraption born of the Father of Lies. I was greatly surprised that snowmobiles were used at Gambell in the summer, when snow is mostly relegated to isolated patches in sheltered places. No doubt they are a great boon to people of the arctic but they are doing great damage to the tundra everywhere we've been in Alaska, especially around Barrow. The abominable snowman should be banished, restricted, or otherwise regulated where its use is not absolutely essential. At Gambell, fortunately, we did not see snowmobiles in use any place but in the vicinity of the village, where no real damage can be done except to the tympanic membrane. Of course, in winter the situation is different, I am sure. After a rollicking noonday meal of canned sardines and crackers, Marybelle and I spent the rest of the day birding the small cape upon which Eskimo villages of one sort or another have existed for at least fifteen hundred years.

The modern village of Gambell is built on a sand-gravel spit with only very sparse and meager vegetation in the immediate vicinity. The shoreline of the point is a shingle of large, smooth pebbles, and very laborious walking. Neither habitat is conducive to bird life. The chief attraction for birds is a sizable lake southwest of the village but even on June 23 it was still three quarters frozen and offered small inducement for waterfowl. The real tundra begins almost a mile south of Gambell, but a long, continuous hill of jagged rock bars access except far to the south and west, too far for an afternoon's round trip. The extreme tip of the point is excellent for sea birds but on that afternoon they were few and far between. Asiatic strays have been reported frequently from Gambell because of its proximity to Siberia but these are usually found during spring and fall dispersals.

We spent most of our time at the base of the long hill watching the Snow Buntings, Lapland Longspurs, and Dunlins. It is always a treat to see these birds in their colorful breeding plumage and the Snow Bunting's song is pleasant to hear. We were on the exact site where in the 1930's Henry B. Collins and Louis Giddings excavated for traces of the ancient Punuk and Old Bering Sea cultures of St. Lawrence Island. Beda was on hand at the diggings then and would have guided us about the site but, unfortunately for us, she had the mumps and did not feel up to it. All in all, it was not a rewarding afternoon out there on the cold, windswept point of Cape Chibukak. But it is never really dull birding new territory, especially when one is only forty miles from mainland Siberia. Anything could have happened that day—a Dotterel, a Mongolian Plover, an Oriental Cuckoo, or perhaps an overlooked fragment of carved fossil ivory—but it didn't. That evening when we were back with the Slwooko family, we decided that we must have indeed become very jaded during the last three weeks in Alaska to have regarded that afternoon as a fizzle. So I apologize most humbly to all decent members of the Brotherhood for not emoting more over Horned and Tufted Puffins, Arctic and Yellow-billed Loons, Emperor Geese and Long-tailed Jaegers, Murres and Guillemots, Arctic Terns and Glaucous Gulls, Crested and Least Auklets, and some others.

While we were musing over abandoned archeological sites and deploring the "lack of bird life" at Gambell, Vernon was busily engaged refitting his big walrus-skin boat for a trip down the coast of the island the next day. We had not yet seen Steller's Eider and St. Lawrence Island is one place where this species has been recorded as abundant during the breeding season. After a breakfast of oatmeal and hard-boiled Murre's eggs we found that Vernon was still at work putting finishing touches on the boat. We walked over to the other side of the village and gazed with some apprehension at the sea making up along the west coast. Birding is best along the west and south sides of the island and we were scheduled to travel this route as far as Southwest Cape if time and sea permitted. When we got back to the boat it was ready but Vernon with practiced eyes had also been noting the mounting swells and had decided that it would be too risky to round the point. Therefore we would have to be content with a trip east along the north shore to Niyrakpak Lagoon, and probably a few miles beyond. Vernon was eloquent in both word and gesture in making his point but he could well have saved his breath and effort. We had seen the cold green whitecaps, dotted here and there with big ice cakes, off the west shore and all my early ardor to round Southwest Cape had vanished. Our crew consisted of Vernon, his three sons, approximately twenty, twelve, and seven years, respectively, and his youngest daughter, about ten. Also, there appeared a formidable young fellow carrying two rifles and a shotgun whom Vernon greeted ecstatically as "our hunter." We were to discover before many more hours that instead of a birding expedition we had financed a slaughter crew that day.

The skin boat was about thirty-five feet long and wide in the beam. It didn't look heavy but it was. It was powered by an outboard sunk in a square well with high sides to prevent the inflow of water. Vernon's house was at least a quarter of a mile from the water and I had been speculating upon the device or method by which he intended to get his boat up and over the three or four high ridges of shingle that lay between us and the sea. I was not long in finding out. It was to be done in Old Bering Sea culture style, sans benefit of mechanical contrivances, namely, by well over an hour of backbreaking toil. Using two wooden rollers and a well-greased board, four of us—number two son was not of much help—tediously dragged that walrus hide up and over each of those twenty-foot ridges of loose gravel. The rollers were almost useless in this sort of stuff and more often than not we simply slid that hulk directly over the big pebbles by sheer strength and awkwardness. Even now, after almost two years, I feel my strength ebbing away and a mild shudder passes over me as I recall that wild, stentorian "aaaaaa-WUK" of our lead man, The Hunter. The "WUK" was never translated for me but I understood its import only too well—"Heave you bastards and wake the dead!" In my youthful days I did plenty of hard labor—railroad gang, shrimp boat, lumber company, shoveling dirt all day in a greenhouse at 120°F—but at sixty I felt somewhat out of training. "Aaaaaa-WUK!" And once again I felt the lash of the overseer and the head of my right humerus leaving the glenoid fossa. When we at long last reached the water's edge—an unparalleled triumph of brawn over brain—I bethought myself of Collins and his archeological discoveries back in 1930 at Gambell. As Collins had dug farther and farther inland from the contemporary village of Gambell, he found older and yet older villages. He concluded that as the spit of land was slowly extended out into the sea, during the passage of centuries, so did the ancient villagers advance in order to be nearer the water. I concluded on my own that day that it was high time Vernon and the other elders of the village once more move Gambell closer to the retreating sea.

That day was pure adventure for Marybelle and me. There were several memorable events, some of them not too pleasant. But from the birding standpoint, two things stand out; namely, we saw our first Steller's Eiders and before the boat trip was over we had seen all four eiders in one day—Common, King, Spectacled, and Steller's. I wonder how many other birders can make a like claim for the tribe Somateriini. The Steller's Eiders, and the only ones we saw at St. Lawrence Island, were eleven birds that overtook our boat from the rear and sped by on whistling wings with fantastic speed, within fifty feet of us. We did not need glasses and everything happened too fast anyway. Three of the birds were males and that small, black dot on the forward flank I had longed to see for so many years is now blazed on my mind forever. And then we sat in mute horror as three quick shots rang out and two of the females lay dead in the water. Both were tossed into the boat by The Hunter and we could only stare in glassy-eyed dismay. Later, I examined one of the birds closely, and in so doing got several blood smears on my pants. It was a sad memento of our last lifer on the 1970 trip, number 627 for North America and number 34 for Alaska.

We can never forgive Vernon and "our hunter" for the wanton slaughter that day. Neither can I understand myself for not raising hell about it at the time. Both The Hunter and eldest son poured volley after volley of rifle fire into flocks of flying birds that day, usually at a distance too far for accurate shooting—cormorants, loons, murres, auklets, ducks, and geese indiscriminately. A number of the less edible birds they left dead or dying in the water. It was a sickening spectacle—man the killer, not hunter. What a nightmare for a birder and conservationist! Later, I wrote to friends in the Alaska Fish and Game Department about our "birding" trip for which we had paid Vernon as a registered guide of the state of Alaska. It seems that Vernon and The Hunter had been reprimanded before for just this sort of butchery. Robert E. Pegau, Game Biologist for the Department at Nome, requested that I send him a notarized statement concerning the events of that day. Had I done so, Vernon's license would have been suspended and his unlawful actions fully aired. But at the last minute I backed down. We had, in a sense, been guests in Vernon's home and, secondly, I should have reprimanded him in no uncertain terms on the spot. I am convinced now that I made a mistake in not complying with Mr. Pegau's request. There can be no allegiance to either friend or foe who kills for the pure lust of the blood smell.

One more disagreeable episode and we'll head back toward Gambell, for even now the sea is running higher. I heard a sharp intake of breath from Vernon behind me and a single word of compressed excitement. That word in English would have been —walrus! Ahead of us some three or four hundred yards on the edge of a short, sandy beach was a walrus. Neither Marybelle nor I had ever seen a live walrus before and it was a never to be forgotten sight. But it was a good thing we had spotted him as soon as we did for even now The Hunter was exchanging his lighter rifle for one with telescopic sights. Shooting birds was clay pigeon stuff to these Eskimos but a walrus commanded great respect. Descended from a people that have inhabited St. Lawrence Island for centuries, where for a long time there have been neither trees nor caribou, the Eskimos consider walrus, whale, and seal an indispensable part of their heritage. Neither the Slwookos nor The Hunter made any pretense of concealing their excitement. You could feel it in their wordless quiet and the intense but orderly activity of their movements. This, I felt certain, was not killing for sport but instinctive and age-old self-preservation. And then the death-dealing thing cracked out. The great form stiffened for a second as though fighting the impact of the bullet and then slumped down upon the beach. When we were a little closer, we could see the terrific hole directly in the center of the head gushing buckets of blood. This scarlet suffusion of death covered the sands and stained the berylline waters of the shoreline. Nor was this all. The minute they had made certain the great beast was dead, The Hunter and two of the Slwookos rushed up the short bank to the tundra above and laid down a barrage that sounded like a major dawn attack. Vernon suggested that Marybelle and I go up on the tundra to look for birds while they were skinning the carcass. What birds? After that fusillade there wasn't a bird within miles except a few sandpipers and Dunlins. And, as it turned out, they took only the head for the tusks, and left the rest of that bloody wreck to rot on the shore. I was wrong in my earlier sanguine conjecture. It was just blood lust after all. If you ever go birding with Eskimos, don't—unless the guns are left behind. Do not misinterpret. It is the species, not the race, that is at fault. It's just easier for Eskimos, with no game wardens snooping about.

That return trip to Gambell took an eternity. The sea was kicking up and we were forced to hug the shore. The tide was low and many big rocks were close to the surface. We could not head directly into the oncoming waves; they were too big. It took all of Vernon's skill to keep that boat moving forward, hour after hour. It took us almost four hours to cover twenty-five miles. We were drenched with spray and despite thermal underwear and parka I have never been as cold. I know; I've said that before. But this time it's for keeps. Birding was out of the question. When we at last reached the end of the island, Vernon tried to round the point so we could make a safe prow-first landing on the west side, but this proved to be impossible. I am convinced that if he had persisted, you would not now be reading this. We did think of removing our heavy boots but with all the clothes we had on and the icy water, we would have sunk like stones. I'll let it rest here. Knowing I am a confessed tenderfoot, you will undoubtedly suppose that I exaggerate. We finally made a side crash landing on the beach and after this was repeated several times, all of us were out of the boat and managed somehow to pull it out of reach of the angry waves. Symbolically, the bloodstains from the dead Steller's Eider were almost washed from my pants. That lifer seemed to belong to another world and age.

The next afternoon we took the Munz plane back to Nome. It was almost another Hooper Bay fiasco, for the strong winds delayed the flight from Nome an hour or more. If we had not taken this plane, we should have had to wait five more days and our relations with the Slwookos were already becoming somewhat strained. Vernon knew we disapproved of his method of "bird watching" and we were not God-fearing enough to suit Beda. So that was that. While we were waiting for the mail and baggage to be loaded into the plane, the wind increased and all the passengers climbed on board to escape its fury. Because the back seat could not be put in place before the loading was completed, Otis, the pilot, told me to sit in his place. When the back seat was finally in place, Otis suggested, rather whimsically, that maybe it might be just as well if I exchanged seats with him for the takeoff. Never have I witnessed more whole-hearted unanimity of assent to a suggestion. Thus we said goodbye to the home of the eider ducks and the epigone of the Old Bering Sea culture.

Most, if not all, commercial flights to Barrow leave from

Fairbanks. And so it was with us on that thirtieth day of June. As we took off, Marybelle and I laughed over the rather startling little incident that had occurred to us and the rest of the Crowder group on a similar occasion in 1967. On that earlier trip we had been on our way for about twenty minutes when the plane slowly banked and kept on banking until we were headed directly south. Everybody looked at everybody else but then the captain announced over the speaker that a couple had mistakenly boarded this plane instead of their rightful plane to Nome. We were returning to Fairbanks just to put this couple on the right plane to Nome! They would get to their proper destination, I thought; but what about the rest of us? I glowered at their guilty backs ahead of me and hoped fervently that they would inadvertently catch the plane to Whitehorse. But it was really an amusing novelty. I could just imagine what would have happened in the lower forty-eight if Marybelle and I had been on a nonstop flight from Philadelphia to Los Angeles but had thought we were bound for Miami. I know the answer. We would have been looking at the Spotted Dove that evening, not the Spot-breasted Oriole. But today the plane sped steadily northward and before long the wondrous and beautiful Brooks Range began to pass beneath us. It was clear and for the third time in our lives we sat spellbound viewing this relatively undesecrated wilderness from the air. Someday, we vowed, we would see it on foot. But as we approached the arctic slope and soon after began to lose altitude for the descent into Barrow, streamers and wisps of fog began to drift by the window. We knew what that meant. Once again we would have low fog off the arctic ice pack enfolding us at Barrow. On that 1967 flight the pilot had missed the airstrip on the first trial but had landed us safely on the second. We hoped it would be no worse now.

Just before we had taken off from the Fairbanks airport and the stewardess was stationed in her position up front ready to give us her usual spiel, a noisy mob of young blades stormed through the rear entrance, sighted the anterior stewardess and rushed to greet her. "Chérie, my love. You again?" and they embraced and kissed the none too resisting and giggling girl. Naturally, this somewhat unconventional performance puzzled me a little. Marybelle and I were occupying the front seat and so had a ringside view of this bold infraction of airline rules concerning too-familiar fraternization with stewardesses. The explanation was soon forthcoming. This stewardess was the same girl who had been with this bunch on the morning flight to Barrow. That plane had made three attempts to find the runway at Barrow, given up, and returned to Fairbanks. The fog had been too low and dense for landing. Now they were trying again on the later flight. I shan't spin this one out because I have poor qualifications for suspense narration. Suffice it to say, those gay young adventurers sat through a total of eight attempts before landing at Barrow that day, and we, consequently, sat through five. The fog was so low and thick it seemed welded to the ground. As we circled for the fifth try, the captain announced that if this one was not successful, we would fly on to Dead Horse because the fuel was getting low. There was intense silence in that plane as we settled down to grope once more for that airstrip. When we finally felt the thump and saw the markers rushing by, the stewardess began automatically her recitation welcoming us to Barrow but her voice was noticeably tremulous and she stuttered a little. That broke the tension and the blades applauded vociferously and the rest of us began to take stock in the future again.

We were only two days and nights at Barrow. Tom Brower, in whose hotel we were staying, told us that Joseph Felder of Felder's Air Taxi was not available to fly us inland to the Meade River, one of the breeding locations of the Red-spotted Bluethroat. We had already learned by radio at Nome that our other possibility for a flight inland to see this colorful little Asiatic thrush was out. Harmon (Bud) Helmericks, pilot and guide, who makes his home to the east of Barrow at Colville Delta, was away on vacation. We were greatly disappointed. The Bluethroat was our chief reason for coming to the arctic coast this second time. This blighted hope was not the real reason, though, for remaining at Barrow such a short time. The basic reason lay deeper. Barrow three years later, and the end of our birding adventures, was to us an anticlimax. We did not suspect this at the time but blamed our apathy and lack of appetite upon some unknown virus. It was only after we reached home that the truth became apparent. The two of us together hardly made a whole. We had left too much of ourselves behind at Kodiak, Fairbanks, Eagle Summit, Hooper Bay, Nome, St. Lawrence— and even Bethel. We wandered along the shore of the Arctic Ocean and over the scarred tundra like lost souls, trying desperately to recapture the magic of former times. We had forsaken the present and were "between two worlds, the one dead, the other powerless to be born." One must delight in the present to enjoy birding or anything else, and here were we calling upon the past to bear witness that we were alive.

That first night at Brower Hotel was a dismal experience. Marybelle and I were the only people in the place and our footfalls echoed ghostlike in the empty rooms and hall. It was such a contrast to the incessant talk and noisy confusion of our first stay, when the Crowder gang had filled every room to overflowing. It was one of the few times I have longed to be part of the Lonely Crowd. And the next night was the exact reverse; the place was jammed with a clamorous mob of Wien Consolidated Airlines tourists. But it was not our own gang and we remained even lonelier in that loneliest of all crowds, the chartered supervised tour. The contrast was shattering and only seemed to accentuate our temporary isolation from the present. Also, Barrow itself had changed in the brief three years. Not so much the material town of muddy streets, not the contretemps of Eskimo shack versus new brick buildings, not the oil drum-littered tundra—the people themselves had altered. Before, we had "talked" with the Eskimo children and laughed with them over some stunt or other put on for our amusement and approbation. The few adults we had met were friendly and greeted us cordially whenever our paths crossed. This time the children were silent in our company and one small boy even spat at us. The taxi driver who took us from airport to hotel was reticent to the point of surliness. I do not blame them. In their situation I should behave likewise or worse. The white man is turning every Eskimo village into a wilderness slum. At Gambell, where contact with the white man is minimal, the village is clean and the folk still friendly, fun-loving, and courteous as only Eskimos can be. At Hooper Bay, where white interference with village life is probably more than at Gambell but certainly much less than Barrow, we experienced an intermediate situation. Barrow, on the other hand, is rapidly becoming disoriented by the influx of regular tourists, the Naval Arctic Research Station, and the oil travesty at Prudhoe Bay to the east. The situation at Barrow in 1970 was real, not an out-of-focus offshoot of our own sorry mood. But it did serve to exacerbate our gloomy reflections.

The Eskimo in Alaska is being exposed to many of the worst disruptive forces of the white man's civilization without benefit of meaningful participation in the latter's dubious experiment. I recall the difference between our guides at Hooper Bay, old and young Kopanuk. The old man, knowing only the customs and mores of his forbears, was far happier and content than his grandson, who had spent the last two years at school in Anchorage. Old Kopanuk knew and loved the birds and beasts of his native sea and prairie. Young Kopanuk, insofar as we could discern, neither knew nor cared. He, also, was between two worlds, neither his own. I do not advocate in simple words the doctrine of the "noble savage." But the younger breed of Eskimo must have his own, self-engendered axiology if he is to relinquish his past way of life. This applies, of course, to all other so-called minority groups caught in the age-old worship of the heathen god of progress. None of these remarks, to be sure, is very original. Which is just another way of saying that the problem has been with us for a long time, unsolved.

Birding was poor in the vicinity of Barrow. It may have been the earlier season but surely not altogether so. We saw no Yellow-billed Loons or Snowy Owls, both quite common at Barrow in 1967. I recall on that former trip four of the latter quite close to the village, all in view at one time. Telltale tracks of snowmobiles crisscrossed the tundra back of Barrow for miles and no doubt this was a partial explanation for the relative paucity of bird life. Where man invades the wildlife retreats. In a small waterhole, less than a mile out in the tundra, we did have an excellent view of a pair of Steller's Eiders. Now that we had already seen this bird on St. Lawrence Island, the unexpected find fit well into the irony of the situation. Marybelle and I had walked all over the tundra one entire day in 1967 hunting for this species without success. We had gone so far that the village of Barrow was only an indistinct blur on the horizon, but no Steller's Eider. This pair of eiders quickened our pulses for a brief space but did nothing to dispel the over-all spiritual malaise that held us prisoners. We walked and walked and walked, until the body was as weary as the mind. After all, there is no true night within the arctic circle at this season and one must perforce quit through sheer exhaustion. We hung a blanket over the window to keep out the light and did our best to get some sleep. The next morning we took the plane for Fairbanks, the first leg of our journey homeward. We were fugitives from ourselves but did not know it.

Before we close this travel-worn chapter, permit me to relate a small incident that did much to restore our flagellated spirits to their natural buoyancy. All planes on the return flight from Barrow to Fairbanks now stop at Dead Horse. Dead Horse is a synthetic name for a mushroom "town" that has become established overnight to accommodate work crews, oil experts, and others who for one sorry reason or another have become involved in Alaska's great petroleum disaster. It is in no sense a town but simply an outpost on the arctic tundra consisting of rows of shacks, mechanical monsters of every description, and an airstrip. I knew in a vague way that it lay to the east and south of Barrow but that was the limit of my knowledge. While we were on the ground at Dead Horse, I got out my map of Alaska and asked the stewardess to show me where we were. She didn't know exactly where it was but thought it was on the west

fork of some river or other. Not very helpful. Just then the
captain came out and the stewardess asked him. He took my
map and gazed at it for some time but finally shook his head as
he returned it. He didn't know either. He then proceeded to get
out his large flight maps and spread them on the floor in front of
us. The first three tiers of seats on each side had been removed to
make room for cargo, and since on this trip there was no cargo,
there was plenty of room for map inspection. The three of us,
captain, stewardess and myself, crawled on hands and knees all
over those maps trying to locate Dead Horse. We never found
it. In other words, the captain had unerringly set his plane down
on the airstrip at Dead Horse after half an hour or more of
navigating through fog without knowing in the least where he
actually was. For some reason I can't fully explain, this make-
believe world of the pilot of our craft reminded me of a news-
reel I once saw showing a man standing with his back to a
blazing building across the street while he watched intently the
same on a television screen in a dealer's window opposite the fire.
"A mad world, my masters." Or if you prefer the modern
version, "The media is the message." But this sterile geography
lesson hit the exact farcical note that effected our cure. By the
time we reached Anchorage that day it was complete.

I suppose a chapter this long and so fraught with vicissitudes
should have a proper, stylized ending. But I can think of none.
Perhaps the least I can do is to tell you that as I write these
words, Marybelle and I are planning a return trip to Alaska in
1972 with Bud Helmericks and his wife, Martha, as our guides
and hosts. It will be entirely by bush plane and will include
many places, and birds we hope, we have not yet seen. So you
see, Alaska 1970 was not an end, but only a beginning. I cannot
write an end to a beginning. This, at least, is my subterfuge.

X

... and After That the Dark!

Extinction of a species is a terrifying finality. Once gone, it is irrevocably lost. Forever and forever lost. An individual death can be replaced. The ethos of a work of art destroyed may be recaptured in some future age. A poem forgotten may be re-written many times in subtle form. But a new heaven and earth must be created before a vanished species can be refashioned. The young devotee of Molecular Biology will hint from time to time that ere too long the laboratory will replenish the beasts of the field and the birds of the air, but this is decidedly beside the point. As you will recall, the Homunculus of Wagner was devil's brew, not the work of the Creator. And like Faust, there is still only one cry down the centuries and under the cold, conceiving moon—"Ah, still delay—thou art so fair." Man may conjure and fumble with his test tubes but will there ever again be a Dodo? A Great Auk? A Labrador Duck? Since the last Dodo was slaughtered on the island of Mauritius in 1681, 78 species and 49 subspecies of bird have disappeared from the face of the earth. In the United States alone, 101 vertebrate animals, both species and subspecies, are nearing extinction or have already passed beyond the bourne of time and hope. Half of these endangered animals are birds, many Hawaiian. And, as everyone knows, one of these fifty birds is the Ivory-billed Woodpecker (IBW). The two other species of IBWs belonging to the same genus, Campephilus—the Cuban and Imperial of northwestern Mexico—are probably not much better off. Come, then, and join Marybelle and me in our quest of the IBW in one of the last of its supposed haunts, the Big Thicket of eastern Texas. But first permit me my moment in the sun, a retrospect of well over forty years.

As I look back upon my youthful days, it seems as though I was always dropping out of school. Usually it was to earn money for future schooling but there was one time, at least, when I just grew weary of conventional education and went off into the "wilderness" to fast. My wilderness was the north shore of Biloxi Bay, Mississippi, and the time was the winter of 1929–30, those lean years succeeding the puncture of the Wall Street bubble. Two of my boyhood pals, Abe Allen and Stew Springer, had left Indianapolis the preceding summer for Biloxi to start a biological supply business, euphemistically named the Caribbean Biological Laboratories. The wreck in which the two made this journey was optimistically christened "the ultimate good" by Stew. My inseparable buddy Jack Irwin and I joined Abe and Stew in the late fall. There is undoubtedly strength in numbers, but most practical of all I brought with me a small sum of hard cash which helped to keep us from starving that first winter. We rented a seven-room cottage with running, Artesian water and forty acres of land for ten dollars a month. It was the most carefree existence imaginable. Huck and Jim on their raft were no more vagabonds than we. We were a mystery to the folk of the surrounding countryside and there were many who, because of our seclusion, believed we were distillers of "spunk water," the local designation for illegal, raw corn whiskey colored with prune juice. I am sure that had we followed up this line of endeavor it would have proved far more lucrative than the CBL. Yes, perhaps we were the original hippy commune, except for the unfortunate unisexual situation that prevailed in our retreat. But we all fell in love with the young librarian of the Biloxi Public Library—Stew finally cut us out and married her—and so we had Platonic infatuation as a substitute. All in all, it was worth ten years of college, maybe even a whole university. Jack and I returned to Indianapolis in March of 1930 but Stew and Abe stuck it out for several more years, an impoverished but glorious existence. When that titanic financial structure, the Caribbean Biological Laboratories, did collapse, hardly an echo of this catastrophe was heard in the Street. But I ramble; let's get to my IBW, which I can never, never count.

One day the four of us set out in Jack's junker, a model-T Ford with a Frontenac head but no windshield, top, or fenders. It resembled nothing so much as a bathtub on wheels. Our direction, I think, was to the north and east of Biloxi. I can't recall that we had any specific destination in mind and I don't know where we ended up or how far it was from Biloxi. I would estimate roughly about thirty miles, probably the west side of the Pascagoula Swamp. The time was late December 1929. We were all "herpetologists" and snakes were our objective. But oh how I wish we had been ornithologically inclined instead! This big woodpecker was leaping up the bole of a yellow pine not more than seventy-five feet from us, in an extensive swampy area. We all watched it with what at the time seemed to us commendable tolerance, since it was distracting us from our snake hunt. Unbelievable, is it not? But so it was. We had heard, of course, of Pileated and Ivory-billed Woodpeckers, but Stew was the only one among us who knew anything about birds and he couldn't remember the distinguishing field marks of the IBW. As we disputed the issue, on no grounds whatsoever but our abysmal ignorance, the bird became restless, uttered a series of tin-horn, nasal yanking notes, and sailed off into the thick of the woods and was gone. Decades later, when birds first began to assume more than casual importance to me, I tried in vain to recall how much white, if any, that woodpecker had shown perched on that tree trunk. I just couldn't do it. The thing is just a despairingly ghastly blank. But that sound! And I remember the sound as though I had heard it yesterday. Probably, because I also remember well Abe's remark at the time: "That's a hell of a sound for a big bird like that to make." I do remember the red crest, so it was a male. Too bad I do not remember a black crest. Just eight years before this fiasco, Julian D. Corrington of Cornell saw one and possibly two IBWs in the Pascagoula Swamp: "The winter birds of the Biloxi, Mississippi, region" (*The Auk*, vol. 39, 1922). Have I seen an IBW? I think I have. But how can I prove it, even to myself? Besides, the entire adventure is so obscured with the patina of time that counting this bird now would be highly irregular. The Ivory-billed Woodpecker is not on my life list.

Late in 1967, the North American birding world was electrified by a report that an estimated five to ten pairs of IBWs were still extant in the Neches River drainage area of the Big Thicket of eastern Texas. John V. Dennis, an ornithologist from Virginia, had spent several months in this region and his account of this discovery appeared as an article in the November/December 1967 issue of *Audubon*, entitled: "The Ivory-bill Flies Still." Even in its heyday prior to the twentieth century, the IBW was probably not a common species. It was hunted ruthlessly by the red man, who traded the bird's large, white bill to his more northern brethren as ornaments, in exchange for deer skins. Presumably, large tracts of virgin forest are necessary for the bird's continued existence and these have disappeared rapidly with the advent of the white man, particularly during the early part of this century. Unlike our old friend the Common Crow, the IBW does not suffer fools gladly.

Unfortunately, when any species of bird, particularly a big

flamboyant one like the IBW, is nearing extinction, there are invariably numerous rumors, counter-rumors, and irresponsible reports that serve only to confuse the issue. In 1971, the American Birding Association announced that IBWs had been reliably reported from Florida. The next year the bird was supposedly photographed in Louisiana. But in neither case was the location stated and nobody but a handful of the inner circle really knows what is going on, and perhaps even this esoteric group doesn't either. The last authentic, published report of the IBW is the extensive and well-documented study of James T. Tanner in 1942. For a total of twenty-one months, covering the years 1937–9, Tanner investigated the small remnant of the IBW population inhabiting the Singer Tract in northeastern Louisiana. At the termination of Tanner's study in 1939, the IBWs in the area numbered only four males, one female, and one immature, and of this number two of the males were not actually seen by Tanner. In March of 1950, Whitney Eastman is reported by John Dennis—in the article alluded to above—as having seen both a male and female IBW in the Chipola Swamp of northwestern Florida. It is no wonder, then, that Dennis's article hit the birding world square in its solar plexus. All at once the little town of Silsbee, Texas, found itself the vortex of a whirlwind of unrest, confusion, charges, and counter-charges. Naturally Marybelle and I were sucked into this whirlwind along with many others and no doubt have played our small part in augmenting the controversy that ensued. But let's get on to the Big Thicket and see for ourselves.

At the suggestion of Whitney Eastman, unofficial guardian of the IBW, I wrote to John Dennis asking for information about the Big Thicket and the best means of covering the area. Mr. Dennis recommended three people, all of whom proved to be of inestimable help in our IBW hunt. The first of these was Mrs. Cleve Bachman, the second her brother B. D. Orgain, the third Ernest W. McDaniel. Allene Bachman is an ardent birder and an active conservationist but best of all from our standpoint she is a charming, intelligent, and warm-hearted woman who took us into her lovely home in Beaumont as though we had known one another for years. Her greatest regret while we were her guests was that her husband, ardent fisherman but not birder, could not be on hand at the time—he was off on a three-day fishing trip— to observe for himself that Marybelle and I, despite the stigma of being birders, were perfectly normal people after all. I think I even drank an extra martini that first evening at the Bachman's just to convince myself that Allene's tacit compliment was not unfounded. Mr. Orgain had written to me earlier that we would be most welcome to stay in his woodland cottage on the edge of the Thicket while we were there. John Dennis and Pete and Ruth Isleib had previously used this same cottage during their respective hunts of the preceding months. It was the coziest place imaginable and we blessed B.D. many times during those fifteen days for his kindness. Ernest McDaniel is a young school teacher and expert birder-woodsman who served faithfully as our guide and mentor through the entire period. He knows his woodpeckers from A to Z and at the time we were with him he was engaged in a joint study dealing with the nesting habits of the Red-cockaded Woodpecker. We found out also that it was he who had been guide to John Dennis on the latter's initial forays into the Thicket and, in addition, had accompanied Tanner and another man from the Bureau of Sport Fisheries and Wildlife Office of Endangered Species when these two men had investigated the area following Dennis' *Audubon* report. These three people and ourselves are the dramatis personae of the woodpecker hunt but you will have to be content with just Marybelle, Ernest, and me because the Bachmans soon left for Chiapas and Yucatán and Mr. Orgain was dragooned by his children into spending the Christmas holidays in New York City. We could only envy Allene and silently commiserate with B.D.

Ernest is a big, strapping fellow built along the lines of Al Capp's Lil' Abner. This comparison, meant as a sincere compliment by a rather runty old man, applies exclusively to Ernest's physique; nothing but contrast exists between the brains of the twain. Ernest met us that first morning at the cottage in the woods at the unholy hour of 5:30 A.M. It was not his fault but ours, for this was the time we had specified. He had his camper truck and metal boat in tow. We decided, largely at Ernest's suggestion, to leave the boat behind the first day and explore by roads some of the territory that Ernest had covered with both Dennis and, later, with Tanner. Marybelle and I were quite naturally buoyed up about the whole affair, for Allene had told us that Geraldine Watson, local botanist and chief protagonist for the IBW, had seen the IBW only three days before. Ernest took us over several roads that day and showed us the big hole in the black gum tree that Tanner had said was the most likely IBW residence he had seen in the Thicket. We saw several Pileateds, a Barred Owl or two, lots of Orange-crowned Warblers and other birds but, of course, no IBW. We were not in the least bit discouraged, for who but a rank novice would expect to see such a rarity on the first day. Dennis had written me that five women birders from Massachusetts had seen the bird after only two days in the field but Pennsylvania could never hope to compete with the Birding State in exploits of this sort. Ernest knew exactly where this feat had been performed and pointed it out to us one day. Later, our thirteenth day in the Thicket, Marybelle and I alone drove and walked to this spot and sat on the banks of the Neches River for hours watching, but not even a Red-headed Woodpecker deigned to fly across that silted stream.

The second morning we again watched the headlights of Ernest's truck thread their way down the rutted, uneven road to our cottage. This time we took the boat along and launched it at the public landing site on the Angelina River, a tributary of the Neches to the west. We were painfully expectant all that day and Ernest did his best to enter into the anticipatory excitement we must have radiated. He showed us another place where Dennis had seen an IBW but stated that although he had been close by, the only bird he had seen was a Pileated. We tramped for miles that day. When we exhausted one place we took the boat farther downstream and investigated another. And so it went all day. We were looking not only for the bird itself but for any bit of evidence that might point to IBW activity. The feeding procedure of the IBW is somewhat different from that of the Pileated. The IBW usually scales the bark of dead trees or limbs and feeds on the insect larvae it finds beneath the bark, while the Pileated uses a hole-drilling, chunk-tearing technique. Also, the IBW is reputed to chisel roost and nest holes that are more square than those of its slightly smaller relative. We found a number of small trees and branches with the bark scaled away but there was no way to ascertain for sure that it had been the work of an IBW. We spied a large woodpecker hole in a big gum tree that looked not entirely circular. The tree was partially hollow and Ernest and I sifted the debris of rotten wood and accumulated sawdust that covered the floor of the trunk cavity. The tips of the inner primaries of the IBW are white and we kept this in mind as we extracted the few bedraggled feathers from the rotting debris. None that we found was white-tipped. It was another day of intensely interesting birding, accompanied always with the omnipresent excitement of hoping for a miracle. But B. D.'s cottage felt awfully good that night.

We tried Bee Tree Slough on the third day and Marybelle and I succumbed immediately to its spell. I think it is Ernest's favorite place in the Thicket and I know it is mine. It is a mysterious and beautiful slow-running tributary of the Angelina River that one can penetrate for several miles, first with outboard and then with paddle. Old cypress trees festooned with Spanish moss and the still, brown water of the slough combine to make this part of the Thicket a veritable archetype of southern swamps. Ernest stopped the boat often and we explored much of the terrain on foot. Rattlesnakes, cottonmouths, and alligators inhabit the Thicket but it was much too cold for reptiles and we saw none. One time Marybelle livened things up for us by spotting a Red-headed Woodpecker at some distance and asked Ernest to backtrack the boat for a closer view. The Red-headed Woodpecker perched has a folded wing pattern somewhat resembling that of the IBW and this particular speci-men did seem unusually large. But Ernest without glasses and I with them soon set the matter right. I have never seen so many Red-headed Woodpeckers as we did in those fifteen days we spent in the Big Thicket. Literally, almost every fourth tree bore one of these handsome, noisy birds.

We lingered so long that day in Bee Tree Slough and its environs that it was almost dark when Ernest finally headed the boat into the Angelina River and upstream for our run back to the launching ramp. There was a dense fog on the river by this time and it was a good thing Ernest was handling our navigation and not me. It was nine o'clock or so and long after dark when Ernest left us at the cottage. It must have been ten or more by the time he reached his own home in Kountze. We met Mrs. McDaniel toward the end of our stay and she was still somewhat exercised over this little episode. I'm sure she had experienced no real alarm over our actual physical safety; she must have known too well her husband's competence in these matters, but she thought we were all slightly cracked. I can still hear her telling us her reactions. "I just said to myself when it got to be ten and Ernest wasn't back yet, those three people are crazy! That's what they are, just plain crazy! I just said those three people are crazy!" I cannot blame Mrs. McDaniel for her rather neat summary of the case and her vehemence of expression. She was more nearly correct than even she knew. For my own part, I was relieved that Ernest too had been indicted. It some way made our own insanity easier to bear.

Ernest did a magnificent job and took us every possible place that the IBW might have been found and every spot where it had been reported. He was with us for eleven of those fifteen days and did not spare us. Marybelle and I would have been lost ten times over if we had been by ourselves but Ernest possessed a directional sense that was phenomenal. He was never at fault and unerringly returned to the boat without so much as a single misstep in any direction. The only time Ernest ever hollered " 'nough" before we did was on one of the last days we spent on the Angelina River. It was still early in the day but I was so numb with cold and soggy from the intermittent rain that as we approached the spot where our boat was tied up, I felt I just couldn't endure that next leg of our journey down the river. Suddenly and with no prior indication of his intentions Ernest almost shouted, "I'm going to build a fire!" He began to grapple with logs and big branches lying on the ground in a manner that would have put Paul Bunyan to shame. He made a huge pile of this stuff and then strode to the boat for the gasoline can. He doused the pile with the contents of the can and asked me to toss in a match. My share in this frenzy was instantaneous and effective. In three seconds we had a raging inferno and I had singed eyebrows and no hair on the back of my hand. The three of us luxuriated around that fire for two hours or more, replenishing it from time to time with the inexhaustible supply at hand. When we had finished our lunch, we put out the fire and once more took to the boat. But this time we did not continue downstream but returned to the ramp and spent the rest of the day by truck on some of the outlying roads. It was our last day in the heart of the Big Thicket.

No, we didn't see or hear an Ivory-billed Woodpecker. No one whom I know personally has ever seen one either in the Big Thicket area since Vernon Bailey collected two specimens on the Trinity River back in 1904. Then why has almost everyone whom I don't know seen this bird in the Thicket? I'll leave you to wrestle with this one. I don't want to prejudice your answer but I think you have guessed mine. It is an exceedingly complex situation but an honest computer, having been fed all the data, would find the solution a simple one. Just one thing I wish to make crystal clear—if that phrase does not nauseate you: my belief that there are no IBWs today in the Big Thicket is *not* based on our failure to see or hear one in fifteen short days; it is *not* based upon the fact that Pete and Ruth Isleib did not see one either after a hundred days in the Thicket; it is *not* based on the fact that Ernest McDaniel, a native of the region and an expert birder, has never seen one. It is, rather, based on my knowledge of the human entanglements and frailties behind the scene. You and I have watched the play on the stage but it is in the dressing rooms backstage where the grease paint is removed that the solution will be found. And if you go to the Big Thicket tomorrow and see a real, live Ivory-billed Woodpecker, I shall be the first to congratulate you and swallow the biggest platter of cold crow you can prepare for my abasement.

XI

Finale

We are approaching the last milestone in this homely little epic
of a lister's triumphs and failures. Speaking more precisely, it is
the year 1971, the fifteenth year of our birding life and the last
that I shall be able to chronicle in this book. All else lies in the
future and I am neither seer nor soothsayer. Also, I do not relish
the role of the Sorcerer's Apprentice; enough is enough. After
all, 1971 was a good year for the list and Marybelle and I are
content that the tale should end here. It is a long way from Miss
Hanna's wood lot to bleak Gambell on St. Lawrence Island and
it seems ever so much longer in the reverse direction—from
Steller's Eider to the Rufous-sided Towhee. It is like looking
through the wrong end of a telescope into the past; form and
lines are blurred and one sees only remoteness. It is even farther

from Gambell to the Dry Tortugas but at least we shall be looking through the correct end of the scope; the events of 1971 are almost the present. So let us complete the terminal *Wanderjahr* while the water still flows over the dam and under the bridge at Furness's.

We saw no new birds during the last six months of 1970 but between January 2 and July 25, 1971, we recorded twenty-four lifers in North America to bring our total to 651 species north of the border. Twenty-four lifers are more than we have seen in any single year since 1964, when we recorded twenty-eight new species. It must be borne in mind, too, that it is much less of a feat to add twenty-eight birds to a list of 519 than to increase a list of 627 by twenty-four. But, I must confess, birding in 1971 was not quite as carefree and joyous an enterprise as it had been in former years. The reason for this lies in the nature of the situation, not in waning enthusiasm on our part. With the exception of Greenland, Bermuda, or Baja California, none of which we have yet visited, it is no longer possible for us to bird any region in North America, qua region, in the expectation of lifers. Naturally, we still have many birds to see and no doubt if we went to southern Arizona at the right season we should add the Five-striped Sparrow or Rufous-backed Robin, but we would be making the journey specifically for these particular birds. The motivation would not be a birding trip as such but a direct search at specific localities for certain birds. Birding new territory that harbors a number of indigenous lifers and taking them as they come is far more exciting than marking down one species and going after it. I realize that in making this point I have ignored previous instances of tracking down certain isolated species, such as the Colima Warbler or California Condor in earlier trips. Nevertheless, there is a subtle but real difference between birding a region and instigating a trip for the sole purpose of seeing one or two species. If someone were to call me next spring and offer to show me Bachman's Warbler, I should be on the spot with palpitating heart even if I had to crawl all the way. But I should much prefer to find my own gate and do the climbing myself. Discovery is the potent elixir that every lister craves. On the surface, there is no difference between going all the way to the Everglades to see a Short-tailed Hawk and going to Michigan to see Kirtland's Warbler. But when the hawk is number 631 and the warbler is number 330, there is a fundamental difference that must be sensed, not reasoned. This viewpoint, whether it be my own mental aberration or shared by the rest of the Brotherhood, transmutes in some obscure way the indefinable charisma of birding into a pastime more akin to philately. But we listers have fallen into a pit of our own contriving and no one is to blame but ourselves. So let us have done with this mawkish introspection lest our resolutions be sicklied o'er and our lists gather dust. When the wind is from the south, I shall still know a hawk from a handsaw. There is still balm in Gilead.

Our first trip in 1971 was by car, approximately seventy-three hundred miles during the month of January. We traveled the entire east coast to the Everglades, then through west Florida to the gulf coast of Texas, and so on into the Rio Grande Valley region. Despite my lamentations and carpings above, we had great fun, saw thirteen new birds, and suffered only two major disappointments—we failed to find the Masked Duck at either Anahuac National Wildlife Refuge or the Welder Wildlife Foundation, and the Blue-gray Tanager of Miami was apparently on furlough. I shall say nothing about Scarlet Ibis, Red-whiskered Bulbul, Java Sparrow, Budgerigar, and Short-tailed Hawk. All but the last of these are introduced species that have established themselves in Florida and all five were mopping-up campaigns we had shirked on former trips to Florida. The Budgies gave us a nasty scare, though. We found none the first day in St. Petersburg and only a very small flock the morning of our departure. Let's begin the trip with Myakka State Park in west-central Florida.

We should never have thought of stopping at Myakka Park except that two people had independently reported seeing an Ivory-billed Woodpecker there the previous year. Both sightings were reported from the same area within the Park, one on March 1, the other on May 10. Several prominent birders checked these two reports but none, so far as I know, could find the bird or birds. We did not expect to find it either but hope springs eternal in the most skeptical of breasts when that breast belongs to a birder. We spent two days in the Park and recorded fifty-eight birds but the IBW was not one of them. We knew the exact location where the IBW was supposedly seen but it yielded nothing more to us than three Pileated Woodpeckers—nineteen had been reported for Myakka Park on the recent Christmas Bird Count. We thought of Ernest McDaniel and wished he were with us. I am sure he would have agreed with us and the Park Naturalist that the Myakka River area might have harbored IBWs seventy years ago but not in populous west Florida of today. It seems inconceivable to me that such a bird could be overlooked by so many people for so many years. The place where the bird was seen is just off a dirt road and accessible to all Park visitors. I am no judge of these matters but I saw no extensive stands of virgin forest within the Park suitable for the IBW. If there is one IBW at Myakka State Park, there should be at least a pair at Turkey Run State Park in Indiana. But my advice is to go to neither of these places if you want to see an Ivory-billed Woodpecker.

The Pauraque is a close relative of the Whip-poor-will and Nighthawk, belonging to the goatsucker and oil-bird family. In the United States it is found only in the Rio Grande Valley and southeastern gulf coast area of Texas. Like the Whip-poor-will, it is a bird of the night and because federal wildlife refuges and most sanctuaries close at sundown we had missed this bird so far on our many trips to Texas. We had looked for them at night on fence posts bordering roads but never had any luck. This time I meant to see a Pauraque if I had to leave my bleached bones under the pitiless sun of the Lone Star State. We chose the Rob and Bessie Welder Wildlife Foundation as a likely place for this bird, twelve reported on the Christmas Bird Count, but also because the Masked Duck is found there too. Dr. Clarence

Cottam, Director of the Foundation, had written me that two years ago at Christmas thirteen of these wanderers from the West Indies and Mexico had been seen at Welder. We had not found the Masked Duck at Anahuac Refuge and hoped to see both it and the Pauraque at the Welder Refuge.

Unfortunately, when we arrived at the Welder Refuge, Dr. Cottam was away but the biologist, Gene Blacklock, was most helpful; through Mr. Glazener, the Assistant Director, he made arrangements for us to stay at the Foundation overnight. We had a comfortable and well-appointed room with private bath and could prepare our supper and breakfast in the big community kitchen. Welder is a private institution and the public is admitted only at stated times and in official caravans. That afternoon we had the whole place to ourselves except for the research personnel. It is a marvelous birding spot, but that afternoon we concentrated on looking for the Masked Duck, which explains the relatively small number of birds we recorded, just sixty-eight. We did not see the Masked Duck and Mrs. Cottam told us that her husband had not found even one for the recent Christmas Count. But that evening in the dusky calm between day and night we heard our first Pauraques. There were two of them calling and, although we knew the sound only from books, there was no mistaking the source. That night one of the visiting research ornithologists, David Smith, took us out in his jeep over the sandy back roads and we spotted two more Pauraques with all field marks well illuminated by the headlights. On one occasion, David gave me his powerful flashlight and by shining the beam directly on the sitting bird I was almost but not quite able to touch it. When my hand was within a few inches of the bird, it whisked off into the thick brush. That night was a singular triumph for Marybelle and me, for at long last we were on speaking terms with the elusive Pauraque. Of course, we should have seen it ten years earlier on our first trip to Texas, but it's just as well that a lister fumbles about now and then. It keeps his ego trimmed down to size.

We finally tracked down the Mexican Crow on the city dump

south of Brownsville, Texas. This bird is now considered by most ornithologists to be a separate species from our eastern Fish Crow. It took us considerable time to sort out the few crows from the numerous White-necked Ravens and a city dump is not the most Arcadian setting for such a task. It was not the sort of experience that one fondly returns to in dreams, but the lister cannot always wander through flower-strewn meadows and forest glades. On our way back to the car we spied a lean, mongrel dog that had contrived to get his nose stuck in a can. He wouldn't let us close enough to assist him in getting the thing off but the incident reminded me of my Gradyville woodchuck. Some years ago as we were standing on the bridge over Ridley Creek at Gradyville, we saw a most peculiar animal running back and forth across the road about three hundred feet up the hill from us. It had a big, blunt head not at all in keeping with the proportions of its body. Every now and then it would stop, sit up on its haunches, and twist its head from side to side. At last we realized what this strange little monster was. A woodchuck had gotten his head firmly wedged in a number two tomato can. I went to the rescue expecting any second that he would run off into the thicket of wild roses that bordered the road embankment. He didn't, and for some reason known only to himself, he stopped every time he reached the edge of the pavement. When I was within a few feet of him, he suddenly sat bolt upright and very still with that accursed can pointing skyward. His every taut muscle seemed to be saying, "Take this damned thing off my head!" As I reached toward him, he shot his head up still farther and I snatched the tormenting blinder away. The woodchuck gave one momentary glance all about him and plunged off the road into the tangle. I'll swear I heard him give a small sigh of relief just before he did so. I don't know why I have tricked both you and myself into this old reminiscence. It has nothing to do with Mexican Crows, White-necked Ravens or White-tailed Kites. It must be that on that bare, smoldering dump I longed for the sequestered odors of woods and stream.

Somewhere far back on the trail I promised to describe the

bird life of Laguna Atascosa and Santa Ana more thoroughly. I'm going to renege on that promise. You don't want an annotated list of birds and I don't want to prepare one. For eight cents you can request a list from either refuge and save yourself a lot of dull reading and me even duller writing. Suffice it to say, we did pick up an unexpected lifer at each place, a Barnacle Goose at Laguna and the Olive-backed Warbler at Santa Ana. We heard rumors that the latter bird had been seen on the Christmas Count, and Wayne Shifflett, Refuge Manager at Santa Ana, confirmed it when we reached this oasis of old Texas. It took us two entire days to ferret out this tiny bird, but we doggedly followed every small flock of Black-crested Titmice until we finally, after several split-second views, got a satisfactory look at the fidgety little wretch. We had seen this bird near Lenares, Mexico, six years earlier, but never north of the border and, of course, this meant a toast, along with the Barnacle Goose of Laguna. We should have liked to extend this token of respect to the Black-headed Orioles that came frequently to Wayne's feeders because they were so beautiful, but we had performed this ceremony for this species on the same spot in 1962. It is the worst kind of bad luck to toast the same bird twice. Almost as disastrous as not toasting at all.

We looked in vain for the Buff-bellied Hummingbird at Santa Ana. Wayne said he had not seen one since last summer. He produced a gorgeous colored snapshot he had taken of this green-headed jewel but had to snatch it back from me almost at once because my droolings were endangering the luster of the print. We had also watched many a clump of Red Turk's Cap for this hummer in the parks and lawns of Brownsville with no better luck. We resigned ourselves to the inevitable and sought instead information on the precise whereabouts of the Ringed Kingfisher. We had missed this bird some years ago at Rockport and were determined now to see it at Falcon Dam. This species, like its small kinsman the Green Kingfisher, is a Mexican-Central American-South American bird but has been reported of late to occur regularly along the Rio Grande below the dam. Wayne drew a map for me with explicit side remarks and cheered us with his assurance that we couldn't miss. This time the prophecy was fulfilled. We had been on Wayne's number one spot exactly twenty minutes when this big kingfisher flew past us upstream. We had hardly time to exult before a Green Kingfisher winged by us not ten feet from shore. Then in a moment or two another Ringed flew by on its way downstream. It was a different individual because the first had been a female and this one was a male. Just as we were turning our backs to the river for the short ascent back to the car, we heard a familiar rattle and, turning, we beheld our old friend of Gradyville and points east, the Belted Kingfisher. Three species of kingfisher in less than an hour! It was the best morning of the trip. I am not really a credulous man, at least no more than my neighbors, but I think I know the reason for our phenomenal success. It was that mesmerized Great Horned Owl that sat above us the entire time gazing steadfastly down with those great, talisman-like eyes. I could see that he was weaving spells and muttering incantations for our benefit. And who knows, perhaps later for his own.

And now if this has put you in the proper mood for spellcraft and other black arts, it may be that at long last I can relate how we broke the Inca curse. From Falcon Dam we drove back to the south toe of Texas and on over to Port Isabel and Padre Island. Wayne Shifflett had suggested that we contact Ned Hudson in a last try for the Buff-bellied Hummingbird. Ned has a fruit ranch south of San Benito, is an authority on Mexican birds as well as those of the Rio Grande Valley, and hummingbirds are more or less of a specialty with him. Wayne told us that Ned had often shown people the Buff-bellied Hummer right in his own yard. I called the Hudson residence several times that afternoon but no one was home. I tried twice more later with no better success. We concluded that Ned was on one of the Mexican bird jaunts. The Ringed Kingfisher had been our 639th North American lifer and we resigned ourselves to the melancholy supposition that number 640, the Buff-bellied Hummer, was not in the cards that trip. On a sudden impulse just as I was getting into bed, I phoned the Hudsons once more. It was late but not too late and, besides, no one would be home anyway. But Ned was home and not in Mexico as I had imagined. He told me we were welcome to try our luck in the morning, suggesting that we get there not later than eight o'clock because his wife, a school teacher, would be gone after that and we might not be able to locate him on his ranch without her help. He also mentioned that their huge, fierce coach dog had a decided aversion to unannounced visitors. And, finally, he made absolutely no guarantees concerning the hummer. As likely as not we wouldn't see it, especially if the violent wind continued. Hummingbirds have no fondness for strong winds, I knew. It was almost midnight, and if we were to reach the Hudson ranch by eight o'clock the next morning we would have to be up by six at the latest. All in all the prospects were not auspicious. I grumbled a little as I got into bed and decided in my own heart that we might as well relinquish our last glimmering hopes for the Buff-bellied and get an early start toward home instead. The wind was still shrieking around the corner of the motel.

I woke up about four o'clock and listened for the wind. It was still blowing but not so maniacally as before. The next thing I knew I was staring at our small bedside clock and the remorseless hands had advanced to ten after six. For some reason I am at loss to explain even today, I lurched out of bed, yelling to Marybelle to get up immediately or we would never get to the Hudson place by eight. I rushed about like a madman getting in my own way as well as Marybelle's. When she timidly suggested some sort of breakfast before leaving, I scoffed at this preposterous intrusion. Breakfast indeed! It was now almost six thirty. Well, we did get to the Hudson's just as Mrs. Hudson was crossing the yard to get her car. If we hadn't turned right once instead of left, we would have been there at exactly eight. The dog was roaming around and prevented our getting out of our car until Mrs. Hudson locked him in the garage, where he still moaned and roared. Later, we found out that, as Ned put it, he was largely a paper tiger. But no flesh and blood tiger could have put on a better act. He fooled us.

Ned got out two lawn chairs for us to use while we settled ourselves to watch the various flowering shrubs for hummers. The wind was still blowing violently but not as continuously as yesterday. And then I heard it: "No hope—No hope—No hope." A flock of Inca Doves had alighted in the yard and were beginning their dolorous prognostication. Ned had returned to his ranch duties by this time and we were on our own. We had to watch carefully, for Rufous Hummingbirds were also to be expected and, of course, it was necessary to distinguish between them and a possible Buff-bellied. An easy enough task if one got a good look, but would we? Color in hummingbirds is a function of the incidence of the light and rather tricky at times. We sat or prowled about for two hours or more and all the time that infernal, melancholy cooing: "No hope—No hope—No hope." Marybelle and I kept exchanging apprehensive glances, recalling only too well how the Inca curse had blighted our chances of seeing the Becard at Bentsen State Park ten years before. We saw a few Rufous Hummingbirds but because of the wind they never remained more than a few seconds in the exposed places where, unfortunately, most of the flowers were. "No hope—No hope—No hope." Despite the wind, which was abating somewhat, the sound seemed to swell and fill the whole valley with its mournful premonition. Why didn't the damned things stop! Or the wind stop, or something! This curse was getting me down.

At about ten thirty, Ned returned and I gave him my chair. I just couldn't sit still any longer. "Inca Dove," was Ned's laconic remark as he jerked his thumb in the direction of the awful sound. "Yes," said I, just as cryptically. I was afraid if I said more I would blurt out my own puerile fantasies concerning the Inca curse. "Don't seem to enjoy it much, though," he continued, apparently alluding to the constant cooing. "Don't they ever quit?" I asked nervously. "Sometimes," was the not too encouraging reply. We sat and waited and talked for another half hour. Just as I was on the verge of giving Marybelle the high sign for leaving, a small flock of Inca Doves whirled into the yard—and right behind them a hummingbird. The wind-blown sprite hovered in the air for fully five seconds just to our left and not thirty feet away. His front half was a brilliant green, his belly rufous and the tip of his red bill looked as though he had just sampled an open ink stand. The "No hope—No hope—No hope" rose to a tumultuous chorus but I was scarcely conscious of the sound. We had at last seen the Buff-bellied Hummingbird and Ned Hudson had been on hand to verify our identification! The Inca curse was unmasked at last. It, too, had been a paper tiger after all. Our score was now a good round figure, 640. And would you believe it? When we pulled out of the yard, not one single "No hope" did we hear. Doves and curse were gone with the dying wind.

In February we made a plane trip to the west coast and added two more birds, Xantus's Murrelet and Manx Shearwater. In May we saw a Curlew Sandpiper at Brigantine Refuge. These three additions to the list have been recounted in other chapters. In June we saw a Black-tailed Godwit, which remained at Brigantine most of the summer. There are four species of God-wit in the world and we had already seen three of them. The Black-tailed is a Eurasian bird recorded in the 1957 AOU Check-list as accidental in Greenland and Newfoundland. It was quite a rarity in summer as far south as New Jersey and hundreds of birders must have added this species to their life lists. The day we saw this bird it took exactly nine hours to appear; from nine to six. We had made the circuit of the dikes a number of times and at five forty-five in the afternoon we again stopped at Refuge Headquarters. We reluctantly voted to have just one more try and drove once more to the particular place where the bird had been most often seen. It was not five minutes before Marybelle spotted the bird. Others were there also, among them Ben King and Tom Davis, two sharp birders, so I was especially proud of Marybelle for her acumen. The bird had the pearly underwings bordered with narrow, dark lines so everybody was convinced of its identity. The Inca curse, it seems, had left for good.

Taxonomically speaking, there is no division of the Fringillidae, seed eaters, which embraces sparrows alone. At present, there are thirty-four species of birds that we commonly refer to as sparrows in North America, but towhees, juncos, longspurs, and buntings are also classified in the same subfamily that includes the sparrows. The Olive Sparrow, for instance, is more closely related to towhees than to Song and Chipping Sparrows, and juncos are sandwiched in between other genera we call sparrows. By the year 1971, we had finally managed to see all the appellative sparrows but two, the Dusky Seaside and Cape Sable. The former species is found in small numbers only in Orange and Brevard Counties, Florida, in the vicinity of Titusville and Merritt Island. The latter, the last species of bird to be described in North America, inhabits the Everglades region of southeastern Florida in very small, local colonies. Neither species migrates, although the small flocks are more dispersed in winter. Both are included in the list of endangered birds of the United States. On our trip south in January we had spent several days along the St. Johns River and on Merritt Island looking for the Dusky Seaside Sparrow without success. We had also stopped for a few hours at Ochopee, Florida, on the Tamiami Trail in a token inspection of the most northern breeding territory of the Cape Sable Sparrow. Louis Stimson, an authority on the Cape Sable, especially the Ochopee site, had so discouraged me by both letter and telephone from seriously looking for this bird in winter that I readily succumbed to his dissuasive arguments. Hence, the token search. But the first days of June saw us in Dusky Seaside and Cape Sable territories once more. We had decided it was now or never. If we waited much longer, it might be an Ivory-billed Woodpecker hunt all over again.

We experienced no difficulty in seeing both species of sparrow, so there is no real adventure to relate in either case. Our way had been made secure by the expertise of Allen D. Cruickshank, the personnel of Merritt Island Wildlife Refuge, Louis

Stimson, and others. We flew first to Orlando and then to Miami, renting a car at each place to take us to the respective breeding areas of the two sparrows. We saw eight singing males of the Dusky Seaside Sparrow in a sedge grass area some seven or eight miles west of Titusville and at Ochopee four singing males of the Cape Sable Sparrow. We were by ourselves when we saw the Dusky Seaside but in the case of the Cape Sable we had the rare good fortune to be accompanied by Louis Stimson.

Mr. Stimson discovered the Ochopee colony in 1953 and has, quite naturally, kept a close watch over the area ever since. In addition, he is the author of the life history of this species in the last volume of the Bent series. He drove out from Miami and met us in the field at seven twenty the first morning at Ochopee. We should probably have seen the Cape Sable without his assistance but he knew exactly where to look for this bird and saved us many hours of searching I am sure. Besides, he was there to verify the identification of both sparrow and song. With Louis Stimson in the field, we felt certain that no doubting Thomas would dare look with jaundiced eye at our 645th acquisition. It is a bit ironic that a species as rare and restricted as the Cape Sable Sparrow should have given us so little difficulty once we seriously set out to see it. For instance, the motel where we stayed is not over several hundred yards from the breeding locality in which we saw the four singing males. We could have walked to the spot, and did the next day. But, in retrospect, perhaps it was not so simple after all. I recall with a wry grimace my pathetic attempt to see this bird along the Tamiami Trail one afternoon in late June 1961 without knowing in the least where any specific colony was located off that burning strip of pavement.

The Dry Tortugas are a group of seven small islands in the Gulf of Mexico lying seventy miles west of Key West. It has the only breeding colonies of Sooty and Noddy Terns in North America. Also, Black Noddy Terns and Brown, Blue-faced, and Red-footed Boobies frequently visit these outermost keys, but their occurrence is irregular, especially the latter species. In addition, White-tailed Tropicbirds, Cuban Martins, and Thick-billed Vireos have been reported at Dry Tortugas. Finally, Audubon's, Cory's, and Greater Shearwaters, Wilson's Petrel, and Bridled Tern may be expected in summer on the boat trip to and from these islands. The Dry Tortugas are an eventual must for the North American lister and there are probably very few members of the 600 Club who have not made the trip. Marybelle and I finally did so July 23–5, 1971.

Our boat left the pier at Key West about midnight. This unorthodox departure eliminated our chances of seeing any oceanic birds except on the return trip but it did afford us the maximum daylight hours for birding the islands. We got aboard in the sultry subtropical heat of the July night with about forty other somnambulant birders, several of whom we knew. Most of us stretched out sleeping bags on the decks and sought to woo that minor deity, Morpheus. Like most gods whose authority derives from the caprice of a higher dignitary, Morpheus's performance that night was decidedly spotty. Each person had a maximum deck area of about one and a half by five feet and the snores of my neighbors were scarcely two inches from my ears. Needless to say, my own snores must have been just as menacing. Someone was always stepping on your ankles, stumbling over your head, or spilling coffee on face or hands. I gave up at last, tucked my feet out of harm's way, and gazed up at the stars. Not since camping on the desert floor of Sonora, Mexico, some forty years ago have I ever seen the heavens more spangled. The Milky Way stretched like an irregular girdle of opalescence across the deep black of the night sky. The Pleiades were all there. I even fancied I saw the Lost Pleiad. I was swept away and up into an infinitude of cosmic dust and for the first time in many years felt the immensity of space and the irrelevance of time. Boys sometimes experience · these things but men soon forget. So it was with me. Again, I was back on the summit of Crown Hill, comprehending because I did not try to understand.

Dawn overtook us just as the first of the islands began to slip by. I stowed our gear in the duffel bag and joined the sleepy crowd lining the side of the boat. Birds were flying everywhere but it took several more minutes before we could see them well enough to separate Sooty from Noddy and attempt to pick out Black Noddies from among the latter. None of us accomplished this feat, and although we all kept trying the rest of the day, no Black Noddy Tern was seen. After we had disembarked and deposited our belongings in the chimerical shade of a group of small trees, we trudged over with the others to search for other lifers on nearby Bush Key. No sea birds nest on Garden Key, where we were set ashore. After much argument we all agreed that we had seen a Brown Booby and not a cormorant— the two birds took turns interposing themselves between the telescopes and each other. The Brown Booby was number 649 for Marybelle and me and, to the best of my knowledge, no other bona fide lifers were present that day, either on Bush Key or the other islands we viewed from the boat later that afternoon.

It was terrifically humid, hot, and sunny all day and, after the first thrill of discovery and excitement wore off, mostly an endurance contest for all but the younger members of the weary group. Marybelle and I dragged our sleeping bags all over the island looking for an oasis of genuine shade but found none. There was the fort, of course, but in fair weather park regulations prohibited visitors from camping within its shelter. At one point early in the afternoon I found myself standing between two skimpy, shifting bits of shade trying desperately with fagged brain to choose between them. I was the human counterpart of Buridan's Ass, only in this instance it was not a matter of free will but lack of incentive. That allegorical creation of the fourteenth-century nominalist was no more stumped than I. It was about this time, as I recall, that a fevered gang swept by hot on the trail of a Cuban Martin suspect and I was saved the ignominy and fate of the ass—I joined the gang. But the "Cuban Martin" escaped us and once more we took up our peripatetic existence seeking shade, that ignis fatuus of the Dry Tortugas.

Later in the afternoon there was a small flurry of excitement on the upper ramparts of Fort Jefferson, for someone thought he had seen a Red-footed Booby on Bush Key. Marybelle and I joined this small group and contributed our share of confusion in an attempt to substantiate this myth. I had the only field guide that showed a picture of the Red-footed Booby, so for the brief duration of this frenzy I found myself in great demand. The bird was probably an immature Brown Booby; it certainly wasn't a Red-footed. Later there was another report of a Red-footed Booby but I was not involved and can only hope zeal did not exceed discretion.

About five o'clock a Coast Guard cutter with a large water hoy in tow cruised up to the pier of Garden Key. Twice a year the water tanks supplying the resident personnel of this National Monument are filled and this was the purpose of the Coast Guard visit. At first this interruption was a pleasant diversion but before long it became tiresome and later, when we tried to snatch a little sleep after dark, it became a downright nuisance. The sound of the pumps and the fumes blowing inshore kept us awake and the searchlights of the cutter eclipsed all but the brightest stars. Two days out of each year for this business, and the Coast Guard had to choose the day we were on the island. The captain of our own boat had spent some of his time fishing the teeming waters of these keys and we had a sumptuous fish dinner that evening. At three A.M. our birding crowd broke camp and we began the six-hour trip back to Key West. Never have I beheld a more weary, bleary-eyed group of birders. Most of us had had practically no sleep for over forty-eight hours. On the return voyage we garnered two more lifers—three Bridled Terns and one Audubon's Shearwater—numbers 650 and 651, respectively. The whole thing had been a glorious adventure but we were hardly in a position to appreciate this at the time. But as Tom Davis remarked as we bade each other goodbye at Key West, "It's something you just have to do." And he was right.

Valediction

Leave-taking is traditionally considered to be a sad affair but perhaps in the case of this particular book orthodox sentiment may be waived. Now that the charm is wound up, meaning that our birding junkets have been brought up to date, I have very little to add and nothing trenchant to say. Nevertheless, most of God's creatures have tails of one sort or another, even if these caudal appendages are sometimes more ornamental than functional. With this rather oblique Aesopian precept in mind, let us, then, pin a tail on this particular donkey of mine. If the tail ends up in the wrong place and therefore serves no useful purpose, be consoled by the fact that it is a very short tail and cannot embarrass the beast unduly.

The 600 Club has been the underlying theme of the story—

our efforts to see six hundred or more species of bird in North America. But I do not wish to leave the reader with the impression that North American birders necessarily limit their activity to this continent or consider the 600 Club as the last court of appeal, so to speak. With the exception of a brief sojourn in Ireland, England, and an almost nonstop trip through northern Mexico, Marybelle and I have concentrated entirely upon the birds of North America. But this has not been the case with many other listers, some of them prominent birders, and the American Birding Association periodically publishes life lists of other than the AOU Check-list area. There are birders who keep world, country, state, province, etc. lists. There are also "big day" lists, marathon lists, warbler lists, and the like. Almost anything you can name. When I look at Dean Fisher's 3,800+, Stuart Keith's 3,424, or Arnold Small's 3,226 world lists, my 600 Club list seems very small indeed. And there are many others with over two thousand lifers on their world lists. I have not troubled, as yet, to count up my world list because I know it would scarcely exceed seven hundred birds. Marybelle and I shall soon have to look for new worlds to conquer if we are not to be totally eclipsed by these stars of the first magnitude.

Like Alice and the Red Queen, I now feel as though I must run twice as fast just to remain in the same place. But it takes both money and free time to keep pace. Few people have both and I have neither, at least not what it takes after one reaches 650 birds. You may remember that in some chapter or other I made a few disparaging comments about the birder who eschews the list. I accused him of willfully neglecting broader horizons. This was not wholly fair. To compile a large North American list takes more time and money than the average salaried worker possesses. To compile a large world list requires either professional status—one's job takes one to foreign lands to study birds—or a bank account that permits leisure time and the other perquisites that money affords. Of course, there is always a third option—one can start one's own tour business, as Orville Crowder has done. The state list offers an alternative to expensive travel but it is a highly artificial and tedious sort of thing and one soon longs for distant hills and exotic birds. All I have said here is old hat to the Brotherhood but I emphasize the obvious because it may not have occurred to those outside the birding clan. Birding is one of the least expensive and most rewarding avocations, but the world list or 600 Club aspirations can be expensive. In all probability, Marybelle and I shall spend our declining years in some home for the indigent. But I face this eventuality with a calm and resolute heart knowing the Phoenix awaits me in that immortal realm beyond.

It has been suggested to me—I forbear from naming the miscreant—that I should give some advice to beginning birders. This I cannot do, but I can tell you why I won't. In the first place, belonging to the 600 Club does not ipso facto endow one with special knowledge or acumen. As I have said, when the wind is from the south I can usually tell a hawk from a handsaw, but often the wind is north-north-west. Also, I detest the show-off who vocally identifies every bird sound the second he hears it; he might have the good grace to assume that you, too, had cut your eyeteeth. Besides, only yesterday I mistook the loud, persistent spring song of the White-breasted Nuthatch for that of a flicker. Who am I to tell the novice that he must pay attention to sound! In the second place, birding is an intensely individualistic endeavor. What I might suggest could not only be wrong but, worst of all, inappropriate for the person in question. Soon after I began birding, I was continually nagged by old hands to keep exhaustive notes of all I saw and conscientiously write them up every night. Nothing could have killed my incipient enthusiasm for birding so quickly had I followed this most laudable and sound advice. On the local scene, I still never list Starlings or House Sparrows, except for "official" purposes. Furthermore, I take it for granted, perhaps erroneously, that almost anything I have noted during a birding day has been gathering dust on library shelves throughout the world for years. I do not flaunt my insouciance as the supreme good; I only state that in this respect I am not a serious birder. More power to others if they prefer to tread "the steep and thorny way to heaven." But leave me to my primrose path of dalliance. In the third place, it is much more fun and infinitely more stimulating to begin birding on one's own. Make your own ludicrous mistakes and false generalizations without tongue clucking and advice from more experienced hands. What would it have profited me in the long run had I known two months sooner that my "Spotted Sandpiper" at Furness's was really a waterthrush? Nothing, I feel sure, and this misidentification has been one of the most instructive highlights of my birding years. Very likely I betray my own avowed intention to give no advice by giving advice in reverse. So be it. An old school teacher learns many subtle and devious ways of inculcating precepts while looking out the window. Finally, when I consider how small a stock of knowledge I really possess, both of birds and birding, I am appalled at offering advice to anyone. I have written glibly about a few birds and much about birding but the truth of the matter is that I couldn't step up to the podium right now and give an informative, coherent five-minute talk on the life history of the Cardinal. I have been a teacher far too long not to realize that ignorance is no deterrence to homilies but I hate to dissemble when my livelihood does not depend upon it. Unlike the preposterous world of chess, the best birders are usually the most modest. While I cannot invert this relationship and thereby gain acclaim as a stellar birder, I certainly can hold my tongue and still learn from my betters. No, I have no advice to offer to the beginning birder.

And now a small task from which I shrink with an energy that amazes me. Just what is this thing called birding and wherein lies its appeal? What are the visible and invisible signs of the sacrament? My reluctance to approach this topic is understandable; to say anything meaningful one must walk a tightrope of platitudes over an abyss of the imponderable. One must hold to the obvious while consorting with "such stuff as dreams are made on." It is a task too difficult for all but the simple or the savant. I know beforehand that I shall fail and, consequently, it is a prospect that does not please. Let us begin with the commonplaces. Birding takes one out of doors; it satisfies the craving of every decent person to brush the morning dew from the grass and inhale what is left of our pure air. It is an engrossing pastime and one never wearies of it but only from it. It affords endless hours of armchair debate and exchange of bird lore with like-minded friends. It is exercise, of a sort. It offers an inexhaustible treasure store of knowledge to be assimilated; one never learns the millionth part of all. It helps one meet other people and make friends—if you like that sort of thing. It interrupts your work, which, in almost all cases, is a very good thing both for you and for the work. But more than all this, it is adventure. And here is where we come to the parting of the ways, the tangible and the intangible. It is pure physical adventure to climb a mountain, camp on the desert floor, or take a walrus-skin boat out to sea with Eskimos. But in so doing, one hears the ethereal song of the high mountain bird, and it becomes a religious experience, an ecstasy that brings tears unashamedly to the surface. It is a starlit night, and the rustle and skittering of creatures on the desert floor blend with the infinite vastness above until all are one and the same. It was St. Francis of Assisi, wasn't it, who preached to both animate and inanimate and recognized no difference betwixt? In the walrus-skin boat one learns a little of hardship, cold, and fear; it tempers one's arrogance and one sees oneself and others in true perspective. But adventure need not be associated with strange, unusual, or outré events. Adventure wears many garbs. And the truly great adventures are within ourselves. Birding is an introduction to this truth. Yes, you have guessed it. Birding is the adventure of one's self.

A Note About the Author

JEAN PIATT, born in Ohio, was educated in the public schools of Indianapolis, and at Butler University (B.S.), Haverford College (M.A.), and Yale University (Ph.D.). He is Professor of Anatomy in the School of Medicine of the University of Pennsylvania. His research is in the field of experimental embryology; his hobby, however, shared with his wife, Marybelle, is birding. Their travels in pursuit of this shared interest have taken them from the Arctic coast to the tropics, and their North American "life list" of species identified (also shared) now stands at 666. In the recent official summary of the 600 Club (April 15, 1973) they were in a three-way tie with Roger Tory Peterson for 14th place among those 88 gently competing birders who at present belong to this Club.

A Note on the Type

The text of this book was set on the Linotype in Janson, a recutting made direct from type cast from matrices long thought to have been made by the Dutchman Anton Janson, who was a practicing type founder in Leipzig during the years 1668–87. However, it has been conclusively demonstrated that these types are actually the work of Nicholas Kis (1650–1702), a Hungarian, who most probably learned his trade from the master Dutch type founder Dirk Voskens. The type is an excellent example of the influential and sturdy Dutch types that prevailed in England up to the time William Caslon developed his own incomparable designs from them.

The book was composed and bound by American Book–Stratford Press, Inc., Saddlebrook, New Jersey, and printed by Halliday Lithograph Corporation, West Hanover, Massachusetts.

Typography and binding design by Anthea Lingemann.
Illustrations by Matthew Kalmenoff